Experiencing Material Culture in the Western World

Contemporary Issues in Museum Culture
Series Editors: Susan M. Pearce and Elaine Heumann Gurian

Other volumes in the series:

The American Art Museum: Elitism and Democracy
Nancy Einreinhofer

Cultural Diversity: Developing Museum Audiences in Britain
Edited by Eilean Hooper-Greenhill

Material Obsessions: Postmodernity and the New Collecting
Steve Chibnall

Museums and Popular Culture
Kevin Moore

Experiencing Material Culture in the Western World

Edited by
SUSAN M. PEARCE

Leicester University Press
London and Washington

Leicester University Press
A Cassell imprint
Wellington House, 125 Strand, London WC2R 0BB
PO Box 605, Herndon, VA 20172

First published in 1997

British Library Cataloguing-in-Publication Data
A catalogue record for this book is available from the British Library.

ISBN 0-7185-0021-0 (hardback)
    0-7185-0022-9 (paperback)

Library of Congress Cataloging-in-Publication Data
Experiencing material culture in the western world / edited by Susan
    M. Pearce.
        p.   cm.—(Contemporary issues in museum culture)
    Includes bibliographical references and index.
    ISBN 0-7185-0021-0 (hardcover). – ISBN 0-7185-0022-9 (pbk.)
    1. Material culture.   2. Commercial products—Social aspects.
    3. Collectors and collecting.   4. Museums—Acquisitions.
    I. Pearce, Susan M.   II. Series.
    GN406.E96   1997
    306—dc20   96-26727
                                                              CIP

Typeset by BookEns Limited, Royston, Herts.
Printed and bound in Great Britain by
Creative Print and Design Wales, Ebbw Vale, Gwent.

Contents

List of contributors

Søren Askegaard is Associate Professor in the Department of Marketing at Odense University, Denmark.

Colin Campbell is a Senior Lecturer and Head of the Department of Sociology at the University of York.

Katharine Edgar read Classics at St John's College, Oxford, followed by an MA in Museum Studies at the University of Leicester.

A. Fuat Fırat is Professor of Marketing at Arizona State University West.

Sean Hides is a Senior Lecturer in Cultural Studies at Leeds Metropolitan University.

Christian J. Kay is Professor in the Department of English at the University of Glasgow.

Janine Romina Lovatt studied History of Art, Design and Film at Sheffield Polytechnic before completing a Diploma in Museum Studies at the University of Leicester.

Susan M. Pearce is Professor of Museum Studies at the University of Leicester.

Nigel Sadler is Keeper of Vestry House Museum in London.

Milena Veenis studied Cultural Anthropology at the University of Amsterdam, where she also completed an MA.

Julian Walker is an artist working in the field of collecting and museums.

Andrew Wernick teaches Cultural Studies at Trent University, Canada.

Helen Wilkinson is a research assistant at the National Museum of Photography, Film and Television in Bradford.

Mary McGee Wood is a member of the Department of Computer Science at the University of Manchester.

List of figures

List of tables

Preface

The study of material culture now involves many different strands of varying colours and origins (to choose a metaphor suitable to the subject). It can be approached from the angles of: consumption and commodity; social and political symbolism; personal experience; the museum as its expression as professional institution; text in its semiotic relationship to linguistics; narrative; and constructions of the self and the other – and this list does not exhaust its capacities or its interest. This book is intended to bring together some thought and work which are in progress. It is not intended, either by the editor or by the contributors, to represent final statements, or to address all the intricacies of objects, in terms of the approaches outlined above or any others; rather, as its title suggests, it tries to express the ways in which material things are being experienced in contemporary society, and by those engaged in their study.

Accordingly, the Foreword endeavours to set the scene by suggesting that objects are both our *alter egos*, and embedded in a system of reference in which the things which touch us most nearly – objects, food and body/sex – are all used to describe each other. This creates a reflexive circle which embraces fiction as well as 'real life', creating both collective culture and individual mind-sets. Hides's chapter positions this excursion into cultural material symbolism, and the other chapters in the volume, in their relationship to the broad history of ideas. He shows how the perceived link between material culture and identity has undergone a series of transformations in concert with the broadest shifts in European understanding. The point is picked up by Campbell, who restates the connection between modern hedonism, the repeated desire for new things and the Romantic Movement, itself an artefact of the Protestant Reformation. He shows how, as this kind of hedonism became 'good', so goods became 'good' also.

This brings us to consumption as a positive force. Veenis treats it as specifically political, showing how material symbols played in the relationship between the two parts of Germany and the collapse of the communist state in the east. Askegaard and Fırat foreground the consumer, seeing the material allegory as a way of enabling the consumer to speak within the market as medium. Consumption becomes the site of theatre, to which all can come (back) as players, in distinction to other sites in contemporary society in which most of us are spectators. Wernick approaches the themes of commodity and cultural symbol through a piece of 'high art', Rubens's *Adoration of the Magi*, now in the chapel of King's College, Cambridge. He shows, among other things, how the capacities inherent in one piece become immanent as it is engaged in the creation of a complex narrative with its social contexts.

Language and narrative are the topics in the group of chapters by Wood, Kay, Edgar and Wilkinson. Wood, writing from the standpoint of computerized linguistics, sees a fundamental distinction between language grounded in the material world and 'language beyond material'. Kay, writing from studies in earlier English and the history of vocabulary, explores issues of language, classification and taxonomy. Both Edgar and Wilkinson take up the theme of the way the object world is used in the construction of fictional narrative, an important and fascinating, but hitherto neglected, subject. Wilkinson discusses how things are used in contemporary 'respectable' novels, and suggests that the creating and remembering of narratives enacted by things, and especially collections of things, are positive materials for good at the heart of human experience. Edgar takes 'popular' fiction and the views of the collector found therein; here arise questions of stereotyping and the relationship of this kind of fiction to the fidelity of experience.

Collecting as social practice is explored further by Lovatt, who gives an analysis of the 1994 People's Show project, an enterprise which brought collectors across the country into some forty museums, there to display their own collections within the public institution. The light thrown on contemporary collecting practice is important, and the three-cornered relationship between material, people and museum equally illuminating. Sadler brings to our attention another aspect of life, material things and the collector/museum, and that a grossly neglected one: the material culture of left-handedness and its implications. This has a particular resonance for the writer who, like Sadler, is left-handed, and recognizes the fact that 13 August 1996 was Left-Handed Day (although by some oversight, this was not a Friday 13th).

Finally, the Afterword is written by Julian Walker. As a freelance artist interested in the nexus of objects and culture, and representation in art, and as one who has created a number of artistic installations in museums which are intended to reveal the nature of material and collected relationships, he is a particularly apt contributor to bring this volume to a close.

The operation of objects among us and within us is, and will be, a continuing debate. My grateful thanks are due to those people, too numerous to single out by name, who have helped to bring this volume to the press, and whose thoughts, works and practices are giving the debate its character and significance.

Susan M. Pearce
Department of Museum Studies
University of Leicester
May Day, 1996

*Crazy Quilt, by Maggie Warren, 1991. Polythene bags and masking tape,
196 cm × 256 cm*

1

Foreword: words and things

SUSAN M. PEARCE

Introduction: on being pink

Pink champagne, pink frou-frou, pink marble, especially when it is made of plastic: all these are objects whose thingyness is composed partly of shape and partly of colour, but partly also of another quality, that of the poor taste or moral dubiousness which surrounds essentially luxury things when they are coloured pink. We produce the same ambiguity when we talk contemptuously of 'parlour pinks', people who endeavour to live through both working-class values and genteel manners and end up as ineffectual misfits, or of the 'pink pound' as the buying power of the gay community. We understand the moment of inspiration which brought Rodney Ackland, in his play *Absolute Hell*, to call the grubby little World War II London drinking club in which the play is set 'The Pink Room'. Here the pink draperies fit the ethically queasy but bleakly sad clientele of weak, corrupt, selfish and self-deceiving individuals, carelessly exploited by invading Americans with archetypal names like 'Hank' and 'Butch', who come and move on. At the end of the play, we see how the whole pink structure, with its irresponsible homosexuality, its confused politics and its bomb-damaged house, will be swept away as newspaper stands announce the 1945 Labour landslide election results.

Much effort has been spent over recent decades (to go no further back) to elucidate the relationship between words and things, language and the material world. This has taken biological and social evolutionists to the study of primates and early hominids, where, historically speaking, the abilities both to speak and to create artefacts seem to lock together as the crucial development which distinguishes our human kind. It has taken psychologists, especially child psychologists, to consider how infants perceive, understand and express the world, and it has inspired neurologists to examine the biochemical basis of human understanding and action. In parallel with all this, assorted semioticians have endeavoured to illuminate the nature of communication in terms of the capacity of words and things to act as signified and signifiers in the production of meaning.

Meanwhile, economists and economic historians have been showing us how social development and goods interrelate and how the patterns of consumption and production are rooted in specific contexts, while political philosophers from Marx (1971) to Derrida (1992) have shown us how the social nature of the material world creates all-pervading patterns of power and dependence. Material culture theorists have picked up on most of these notions in their endeavour to start from the things and to show how these are of positive significance in their own right: people less *make things* than *are made by things*.

All of this has added enormously to our understanding of what words and things are, and how at the level of ideas they probably meet, since our thoughts are expressed in material images while our material images require abstract conception. Essential though this work has been, it sometimes leaves the material culture student with a sense of frustration and of conceptual poverty, because it does not seem to offer scope for understanding material culture as it is lived, or how the mental unity of words and things creates our lives day by day. To put the point in another way, it does not tell us why pink things have the ethical and aesthetic resonances which they have.

A starting-point is the undoubted fact that material culture is capable of touching a raw nerve of passionate interest; as humans we are able to feel strongly and bitterly about the objects around us and the symbolic meanings which they are capable of carrying. To appreciate this, we need look no further than the bile aroused by some women's fashions, or the banners of an opposing football team, or the objects of an 'alien' culture. Linked with this is our constant need to create and re-create our world, constantly reworking, reinterpreting and remaking through the only medium available to us, our physical surroundings organized by internal narrative; and in this process neither surroundings nor narrative is primary, but each perpetually feeds off the other. 'Feed' is a useful word because it leads to two thoughts which will be fundamental in this chapter. First, the physical world around us is composed not only of objects in the limited sense but also of two other kinds of material being (together with landscape, which is outside this discussion): edible things or food, and our own bodies viewed as things. Second, our appreciation of each of these things is bound up with our appreciation of all the others. In order to make language meaningful we have to use metaphors from food flavours ('sour', 'sugary'); food and bodies, especially sexual·bodies, are addressed in the same terms of consumption; and the notion of 'objective' object and of possession is bound in with all of these.

We live, it seems, in a self-referencing world in which the organizing narrative is always expressed in words proper to one physical experience but used to describe, and give meaning to, another. The sum of our activity at any given moment is what we describe as 'life', and it is one in which the object world, in all its guises, is the other self of each of us, the *alter ego* without which we cannot be ourselves. It is these notions of the interdependence of narrative, things, food and bodies which the rest of this chapter sets out to explore. We will start with things as stories.

Spinning yarns

The relationship between a narrative, acted or written, and a piece of woven cloth – between text and textile – spells out their identity. Yarns are spun out of inchoate, chaotic raw material. They are brought together into a complex narrative by the cross-weaving of vertical or chronological warp and horizontal or spatial weft. The resulting plot has substance and tensile strength created, as it were, out of nothing. It also has a beginning and an end, a finite shape suspended in space; its ends are carefully cut away and fastened off. The pattern in the weave may be a simple under-and-over, or it may be a complicated positioning and juxtaposing of threads, but in either case it will have elements of balance and symmetry. Texts, whether written, woven or knitted, are essentially binary in that textures in both substance and detail, and so the whole meaning, are created by the choice between under or over, this way or that way. A characteristic line in a knitting pattern might be 'k2 p2 [k2tog] p1 k1 p1 [k2tog] p2 k2'; this is also a structuralist binary analysis of classic form, and the kind of plot analysis fundamental to standard 'classic' fiction. Texts, of both kinds, can be worked on the bias, to create uneven moments of give and tension; and, we might add, both can be embroidered upon to the heart's content.

Weaving has been with us in central and northern Europe since perhaps the beginning of the Bronze Age, some four thousand or more years ago, so it is not surprising that the equivalence of material texts and the creation of self-constructing narratives has bitten deep into our cohesive consciousness. Fate is seen, both in the North and in Greece, as a woman who spins and cuts the thread of life. As King Alfred the Great's will, written about 890, shows us, while the father's line was spoken of as 'the spear side', the mother's line was called 'the spindle side' (Whitelock, 1955: 492–5, No. 96). We still talk in the same terms of 'the distaff side', although increasingly few of us realize what the phrase means. Similarly, although the process of weaving has in English generated a number of surnames – Weaver, Webster, Fuller, Dyer and so on – all of which probably began about 1300–50, 'spinster' is not a surname but a generic term for a whole class of women: those who are not yet married or never will be. It is still the legally accepted term for an unmarried woman, as millions of marriage certificates proclaim. The equivalent term 'bachelor' is rather obscure, but in practice was used to describe the stage of craft training between apprentice and master (and hence, of course, its continuing use as the name for the first degree). But bachelors do have pricks, and the sexual imagery of spindles, needles and the shuttle at work runs through European fairy stories like 'Sleeping Beauty' and the bawdy work songs of popular culture (all of which, incidentally, tend to show women in ambivalent but by no means powerless positions: Sleeping Beauty was, after all, to inherit the throne, and it was the prince who had to seek his fortune and find it in marriage).

Across our society, even though most of us have never touched either a spindle or a shuttle, the practice of weaving has come to give us an imaginative understanding of how the texture (*sic*) of our lives is composed, and how we stand in some fundamental relationships to each other. Such imaginative understanding would have to be different in a society, like that of the native Pacific, which created its cloth not from the interlacing of threads but from the beating out of bark. We shall pick up the same notion of rhetorical imagination, constructive but culturally limited, when we turn to food.

Food: chickens come home to roost

Figures published recently show that, contrary to general belief, we in Britain now eat considerably more meat per head than we did forty years ago, and that, more predictably, much of this increase, and much of the meat eaten overall, is chicken and turkey (Girling, 1996: figs 1 and 2). Clearly, our relationship to that area of material culture we call meat food, both physically and imaginatively, is as strong as it ever was.

The run of metaphors involving fowls is very large: women are 'birds'; men play 'chicken' or refer to white feathers; those recovering from addictions eat 'cold turkey'; and we all form part of a pecking order. At the heart of these elaborated notions of chicken lies the ability of domestic fowls to produce two kinds of food: eggs and a dressed bird. These goods have opposing status. Eggs mean children, invalids, breakfast, or a light informal supper perhaps for one, while a chicken cooked whole still means 'a good dinner', adult fare with 'all the trimmings', and a certain air of communal pleasant anticipation. There is reason in this, because a roast bird needs several hours in the oven, and cannot easily be left while cooking and preparing its accompaniments, and serving the lot requires a good hour of frenetic activity, as every cook knows; so the investment of time and effort is considerable. The exact opposite is true of cooking eggs, where speed and simplicity are what count.

But this is only where the metaphorical cooking begins. When fowls are stuffed for the oven the ingredients traditionally include their own liver, and perhaps other bits of giblets, chopped up, and the whole mixture is lightened and softened with beaten egg: what we enjoy are the detached innards and the potential young chick returned into the body from which it came, and reheated again to living warmth. Fairly recently we have learned, rather to our horror, that commercially reared chickens receive chicken flesh in their feed, so they make up their meat with their own kind. A chicken, and even more so a turkey, is seldom all eaten at a sitting, and so the carcass is put in the fridge until brought forth again. I once experienced a Christmas in which the turkey lingered in the fridge while a newly dead member of the family awaited burial in the morgue. Unspoken, but in all our minds, was the horrible correspondence between the two corpses, a 'cold turkey' withdrawal indeed. Cold meat is a status drop from hot roast. The carcass stewed down for stock and then made into soup becomes a hot food with a status, perhaps, between roast and cold.

The complex material imagery is extended in the serving style of fowls, for which there are often special dishes, and these invariably represent the bird as it was in life. The Fitzwilliam Museum, Cambridge, possesses a covered tureen and dish of English Chelsea ware, made about 1755. The tureen is in the shape of a chicken, and her neck and head form its handle. The feathers are carefully rendered in purple and brown, and the charming modelling is completed by chicks which shelter under one warm wing. Similarly, enclosed terracotta baking dishes in the form of a chicken have been fashionable for a long time, and recently the supermarkets have been selling cheap serving dishes which feature a life-sized cock in full plumage.

Habitually, therefore, we find it very satisfying to eat birds stuffed with their own dismembered innards, served in vessels which make a connection between warm, soft, dead, cooked meat and warm, soft living animal, and do so by mimicking the living bird in dead, hard, chicken-shaped ceramic. It is a material image of consuming death-in-life and life-in-death which stands at the heart of our culture.

'Habitually' is a significant word. For most people the main meal of the day is in the evening, after school and work. This meal is often going to be meat-based, and may well include chicken or turkey, although probably casseroled or grilled rather than roast. Roast chicken comes into its own for Sunday lunch, still frequently the best meal of the week, and the one likely to be served and eaten with most ceremony. Roast turkey and its trimmings are, of course, the principal eating event of Christmas Day, itself the chief family and gift-exchanging festival of the year, the main marker of time, and principal orgy of material consumption.

Stuffing birds

As the vulgarism at the head of this part suggests, our capacity to create explanatory images about our bodies, sex and its consequences is intimately linked with our imaginative appreciation of food and objects. The relationship created between birds and women is both ancient and widespread in human culture (and worthy of detailed consideration), but here let us simply recall that fowls kept domestically for their eggs are hens and so give rise to phrases describing women's groups as 'hen houses' or 'hen parties', and individual women of a certain age as 'old boilers'. Birds stuffed and roasted, however, are usually cockerels, so as a phrase indicating male sexual satisfaction, 'stuffing a bird' leaves some clarification to be desired. Presumably the image has arisen partly because of its obvious metaphorical power, and partly as a result of steadily decreasing knowledge about domestic livestock.

What appears to be true is that sex, food and objects are the three ways of engaging with the material world outside our specific individual system, with our own bodies forming, perhaps, a halfway house between sex and object (and sometimes, of course, human bodies serve as a rather special kind of food). Each of these, therefore, supplies a range of words and phrases to the others, which both illuminates how we feel about the interrelationship in question, and weaves the whole into a network of interconnecting thoughts, feelings and images. The list given in Figure 1.1 is not exhaustive, and in any case only covers those terms known to me, but it is, I think, sufficient to underline the point made here. A similar set of metaphors cover bodily sex and hunting, originally, of course, a food-gaining activity as well as a pleasure. Here we find phrases like 'chasing' and 'running after' doing double service. The language of hunting and war is much the same, and martial metaphors, like 'besieging' and 'overcoming', are similarly used; and these bring us back to the range of *double entendre* material phrases, like those relating to firing and guns.

The role of the body in relation to materiality is, of course, capable of much deeper elucidation (Falk, 1994). It is used as a metaphor for the choosing and organizing of objects which we call collecting, so that a collector speaks of the 'backbone' or the 'heart' of the collection, and the complete 'corpus' of his or her holdings. From another angle, we speak of childbirth as 'labour', equating it with all other forms of bodily effort aimed at a result, and regard the birth of the child as a piece of production – all metaphors drawn from material reproduction.

Sex described in terms of food

Dish, beefcake, cheesecake, tart, tasty, crumpet, buns, bun in the oven, slice off a cut loaf, cupboard love, good enough to eat, sugar/honey (as terms of endearment)

Objects described in terms of sex

Fetishes, possession, hot stuff, bit of stuff, blue (jokes, films, etc.), potent/sexy/dreamy (as of desirable objects)

Sex described in terms of objects

Object of desire/affection/love, out of the closet, get up steam, cocking a gun (and virtually all gun language), everything to do with shuttles and pistons, tools and to be tooled up, old bag, screw

Objects described in terms of food

Goodies (especially used by archaeologists), biting off more than one can chew, making a meal of something, having a lot on one's plate

Figure 1.1 *Objects, sex and food described in terms of each other*

Fiction parallels life, and we would expect the writing of fictional narrative to bear a relationship to this life of the metaphor.

Novel matters

Sustained prose fictional narrative, which itself bears a relationship to the lengthy poetic narrative which preceded it, is one of the characteristics of modernist Western society. But within this tradition, the older criticism (at least) would distinguish two elements of unequal size and greatly unequal value, expressed as 'classic literature' (much the smaller and more important) and 'popular fiction' (the larger and less significant). The analysis of narrative fiction is a thorny area, but as a rough guide it might be said that the (or a) distinction between the two revolves around the view they take of living. Popular fiction parallels life in that it offers its readers what they would wish to have or to be, and hence its character as fantasy, which ranges from crude erotic or commercial orgies to more subtle consolations. Serious fiction, on the other hand, considers life as it is. It tells us more about living and about ourselves, while popular literature leaves us knowing more, which is not the same thing.

In the light of this distinction it is interesting that popular writing features the object world to a much greater extent, and in a more fundamental way, than do most serious works (although not, of course, all; in a subject such as this there is often as much grey as black and white). For the purposes of this discussion we might hazard the notion that popular fiction divides (raggedly) into five main groupings: contemporary and historical romance of the kind published by Mills and Boon, and its brunette friend, the erotic fiction aimed at women and published under imprints like Black Lace; sword and sorcery narratives, which outrun the Victorian three-deckers, and related science fiction; the classic detective story, written (apart from Simenon's) almost wholly in English, and its cousin, the spy thriller; and, a smaller group, ghost stories of the kind written by most of the Victorians and continued by writers like Susan Hill. There is also a large and amorphous 'action' class, which ranges from C.S. Forester to a series about SS units.

Objects tend to be at the heart of all this writing. In most detective writing the plot is moved forward as much by discoveries of material evidence and its parameters of time and place as it is by personal relationships or voices from the past. The same is true of spy thrillers, which also tend, as do many whodunits, to have at their heart the recovery of some special object – the cryptograph machine, say, instead of the Shakespeare manuscript or the compromising letter. Ghost stories rely largely on the material world for their creation of atmosphere and on freakish material manifestations for their substance. Sword and sorcery, in the very nature of its genre, makes this relationship clear, because the essence of sorcery is to conjure the material world to behave in ways which are not normal. Erotic fiction has, perforce, to spin out the action with a range of material contrivances, and even popular love stories rely heavily on the material details of the *mise en scène* – the emergency ward or the design studio, say – to give structure to the story.

In much contemporary and post-war popular fiction (and indeed in much of it this century), then, objects are not simply the necessary furniture of the story; they provide goals and ends, they animate the relationships between the actors, and they give structure to the narrative and mechanisms to the plot. Equally, they give their own colour and tone to what is going forward. Serious fiction, by contrast, tends to take the material world as given, allowing its circumstances to intrude only when they might do so 'naturally', and creating its movement through the complex interaction of character and social circumstance.

This contrast may in part be accounted for by the different legacies which the two broadly contrasting forms drew from their genealogy. It is probable that significant objects, invested with numinous power, stand at the head of much social development that can be characterized as European (Pearce, 1995), and consequently the quest for such objects is an integral element in the earliest European fiction, whether from the East (Greece), the West (Ireland) or the Germanic North. But these early epics and lays also pose questions of honour, personal integrity and moral choice within their material contexts. The Western body, transformed into Arthurian romance, became the mainstream of medieval fiction, and here magical objects and strange gaps in material normality loom far larger than the ethics of character, mingling as they do with romantic love and a softer piety. During the same centuries, it seems, stories of ghouls and ghosts were also told, stemming from the same broad tradition, but drawing on its darker, Northern side.

By the later eighteenth century, the various contemporary genres are beginning to sort themselves out. Gothic novels (Miles, 1993), epitomized by *Vathek*, written in 1786 by William Beckford (who was also a major connoisseur and collector), descend from a mixture of ghoulishness and medieval fantasy. They, in turn, father modern ghost stories and modern detective fiction, with a line which runs through Poe, M.R. James, Sheridan Le Fanu and Wilkie Collins (and it is no accident that what is generally regarded as the first detective story, *The Moonstone*, takes the name of a special object as its title). Modern sword and sorcery narrative comes from the same milieu. Popular love stories descend from the early novels of sentiment (which is why the adaptation of Richardson's *Clarissa* was such a major television hit), and erotica from much the same, with a dash of gothic thrown in. The significant point is that, while serious fiction from the eighteenth century onwards concerned itself with social relationships (and still does, in its own inimitable postmodernist style), and did so by drawing on these elements in its inheritance, popular fiction, by contrast, shaped itself by drawing on the materially centred elements in the same inheritance. Approaching the contrast from a different angle suggests that the complementary role given to objects in the two fictional traditions has to do with the parallel nature of the popular and the overarching view taken by the serious. We argued in the first part of this chapter that objects are our other selves. The parallelism is probably closer than this; each set of symbols, material and human, is constructed in terms of the other, and each is the other's *alter ego*. Consequently, we would expect an essentially fantasy fiction to work within the symbol system and cross-identify humans and things, while a fiction intended to lay bare the nature of the symbolic, as all serious fiction does, might reject an object-oriented discourse.

Conclusions: drawing some threads together

This chapter has tried to suggest how our imaginative construction of the world depends upon a perpetually interlinking sequence of

Susan M. Pearce

transferable metaphors drawn from the physical nature of our surroundings, particularly objects, food and bodily activity. These metaphors are expressed and communicated in language, especially slang, and together the words and things create our alternative selves.

All meaning, therefore, becomes symbolic of something else, whose meaning is also symbolic. Thought processes, especially ethical ones, begin to appear not as independent intellectual assessment, but as part of the product of metaphor, as pink relates to the rosy rush of blood through fleshy skin and fleshly love. The symbolic narrative of living is matched by the correspondingly symbolic narrative of fiction, and the two are attached by an infinity of cross-filaments which influence both. Objects, like words and bodies, are not 'themselves', but symbols of themselves, and through them we are continuously at the game of resymbolizing ourselves.

Bibliography

Derrida, J. (1992) *Given Time*, trans. P. Kamuf, Chicago: University of Chicago Press.

Falk, P. (1994) *The Consuming Body*, London: Sage.

Girling, R. (1996) 'Carnal desires', *Time*, 20 January, pp. 31–4.

Marx, K. (1971) *Capital: A Critique of the Political Economy*, trans. S. Moore and E. Aveling, Moscow: Progress Publishers (first published 1867).

Miles, R. (1993) *Gothic Writing 1750–1820: A Genealogy*, London: Routledge.

Pearce, S.M. (1995) *On Collecting: An Investigation into Collecting in the European Tradition*, London: Routledge.

Whitelock, D. (1955) (ed.) *English Historical Documents*, vol. 1,· London: Macmillan.

2

The genealogy of material culture and cultural identity

SEAN HIDES

Introduction

> The concrete is concrete because it is the concentration of many
> determinations, hence a unity of diverse elements. In our thought it
> therefore appears as a process of synthesis, as a result, and not as a point
> of departure.
>
> (Marx, *Grundrisse* in McLellan, 1980: 34)

The relationship between objects and identity has always been
important for archaeology and its cognate disciplines, in particular
anthropology. For Mauss objects were the most reliable evidence, being
'authentic, autonomous objects ... that thus characterise types of
civilizations better than anything else' (Mauss, 1931: 6–7). Whilst for
other disciplines objects are interpreted in their social context,
archaeologists must re-create that context from the objects themselves.
This has important consequences for the way in which objects and
identity are linked and understood. Early antiquarians, such as Camden
and Aubrey, sought to differentiate the Saxon and Celtic influences on
English history (Piggott, 1967). An interest in similar themes has
continued through numerous transformations of the study of the past,
but difficulties in defining cultural/ethnic groups and theorizing their
relationship to material culture have persisted.

This chapter will argue that archaeological theorists and historians
have seen the link between artefacts and identity as an intrinsic
property of social existence, upon which universal theoretical abstractions can be based. Yet the nature of this relationship is itself the
product of socio-historical transformations and should, therefore, be
subjected to critical scrutiny in those terms. Through an analysis of the
epistemological contexts of interpretations of archaeological material, I
show that the relationship between materiality and identity has

undergone a series of transformations in concert with the broadest shifts of European culture.

Problems

Conventionally, it has been taken as self-evident that objects were produced and used by specific social or cultural groups, peoples or tribes, and therefore reflect that group in some manner. Yet attempts to define these groups and their relationship to material culture patterning have proved difficult. This difficulty has not called into question the assumption of an intrinsic link between artefacts and groups. Rather, it has been attributed to the complexity and incompleteness of the artefactual record, or to the problems of deriving an appropriate interpretative method. This problem is evident in numerous twentieth-century instances (Abercrombie, 1912; Piggott, 1938, 1954; Shennan, 1978; Harrison, 1980; Renfrew, 1984). The ideas of one of the earliest theorists of archaeological cultures, Gordon Childe, and one of the most recent, Ian Hodder, conveniently encapsulate and periodize the characteristic features of modern archaeological theory.

Gordon Childe's concept of an archaeological culture was an abstraction identified by 'certain types of remains ... pots, implements, ornaments, burial rites, house forms ... constantly recurring together' (Childe, 1929: v–vi), and recognizable in a series of interacting diffusions and evolutions (Childe, 1929: 418–19). This abstraction was based on the concept of *Kultur-Gruppe*, a coextensive artefactual distribution and ethnic unit, devised by Gustaf Kossinna in his 'settlement archaeology'.

In his early writings (Childe, 1925, 1926, 1929), Childe's character-ization of the ethnic equivalent of an archaeological culture[1] was largely linguistic, perhaps reflecting his limited awareness of anthro-pology. Although Childe questioned whether archaeological evidence could reveal ethnicity (Childe, 1930), he saw the value of relating ethnographic and archaeological 'cultures', advocating a societal classification which was 'perceptible to archaeologists, but also meaningful to ethnographers and historians' (Trigger, 1980: 148). However, such a scheme was never achieved, and Childe came increasingly to recognize the difficulty of theorizing the link between archaeological cultures and specific social groups (Trigger, 1980: 149). Moreover, whilst Childe rightly eschewed the racist, ideological linkage between archaeological cultures and *Volk* asserted by Kossinna (1911), he was unable to develop a sustainable theoretical linkage of his own.

A second, more recent consideration of the relationship between material culture and identity is Ian Hodder's (1982) ethnographic analysis of material culture in the Baringo district in Kenya. He observed artefacts not merely used as tools, possessions or simple badges of rank or belonging, but being actively manipulated in the negotiation of identities based on age, gender and ethnicity. With recourse to a complex theory of interpretation and social determination, Hodder (1982: 185; 1986) argued that all objects, including prehistoric artefacts, were meaningful in this way, and further, that the archaeologist is able to 'read', i.e. interpret, that meaning.

Through an idealist historical perspective, derived from Collingwood (1946), he suggested that once an artefact's archaeological context is identified, the artefact can be 'read' within this (Hodder, 1982, 1986, 1987). The contemporary context of excavation, conservation and interpretation enables the past context (the culture) to be reconstructed from artefacts and their distribution. A problematic circularity exists here: the artefact's meaning is derived from its context, and its context is defined by those associated artefacts which give it meaning. For example, cultural/ethnic identity is always recoverable from artefacts, and/or is a contextual presence shaping all aspects of the object's meaning. Circularity also undermines the necessary separation of past and present contexts. If ideology and social organization determined the significance of an artefact in the past, surely the same determinations operate on it in the present. This implies that artefacts do not reveal past (in the strict sense) social contexts, but are only 'meaningfully constituted' by the specific context of the ideologies and codes of contemporary archaeology.

These examples reveal two difficulties which have beset most archaeological theories of cultural identity (Kossinna, 1911; Childe, 1929; Clarke, 1968; Hodder, 1986; Renfrew, 1987). First, they attempt to place their conceptual definition beyond historical determination; the relationship between artefacts and identity must be an intrinsic property of the artefacts themselves. Childe conceptualized artefacts through functionalism and a normative concept of culture; Hodder asserts that all objects are meaningfully constituted. These propositions make 'culture-historical' and 'contextual' archaeology possible. Second, with both Childe's culture-historical and Hodder's contextual archaeology, there is an apparent acknowledgement of the contemporary context of the discipline, which is in fact an exercise in circumscribing and negating its relevance.

History

Michel Foucault's characterization of the culture of modern Europe is distinct from that of conventional histories of knowledge or science on two accounts. First, he emphasizes the importance of major discontinuities in the description of the material and social world through formal knowledge, and second, he describes these discourses without direct recourse to moral or philosophical judgements based on contemporary criteria. In conventional histories of archaeology (e.g. Daniel, 1981; Piggott, 1976; Trigger, 1989) the activities of antiquarians are described accurately, but evaluated according to their manifestation of elements of contemporary theory and practice. Examples include the first recognition of stone tools as artefacts (Trigger, 1989: 53, 88), the first theory of appropriate ethnic divisions in prehistoric Britain (Piggott, 1967: 11) and the pioneers of scientific excavation techniques.

Foucault's (1970) description of the 'epistemes' (modes of knowledge) which operated in the late Renaissance (*c*.1550–1650), the classical age (*c*.1650–1790) and the modern age (*c*.1790–1900) offers a persuasive framework through which to re-examine the development of archaeological theories of cultural identity.

The late Renaissance: collecting the world

Archaeological historians (e.g. Daniel, 1967, 1981; Trigger, 1989) have identified the aspects of Renaissance culture which prompted an interest in antiquity. From this perspective, the 'quasi-historical' activities of antiquarians like John Leland (1503–52) and William Camden (1551–1623) are important because they reject medieval, mythological frameworks like that of Geoffrey of Monmouth (Kendrick, 1950: 4–5). They are, however, presented as lacking a coherent methodology with respect to evidence, and limited by their irrationality and reliance on literary sources: 'they did little deliberate digging and had no sense of chronology apart from what was known from written records' (Trigger, 1989: 48). Antiquarians produced itineraries – literary collections – assembling, without priority, genealogical material, heraldic imagery, monastic literature, local folk tales, myth and anecdote, together with the occasional description of a curio or artefacts (Piggott, 1976: 6–8). However, these apparently haphazard activities take on a different significance when examined in relation to the form of knowledge and the conceptions of identity current in the late Renaissance. These formulations can be summarized in terms of three concepts: resemblance, the microcosm (as collection or book) and the exotic.

In *The Order of Things*, Michel Foucault (1970: 17–45) describes the way in which the world could be known during the late Renaissance. He suggests that scholars attempted to read signs visible in all things which revealed their resemblances to others. Resemblance, in the form of four specific kinds of similitude – Convenientia, Aemulatio,

Analogy, Sympathy (and its opposite, Antipathy) – united and structured the Renaissance universe, articulating every object, word and being.

Foucault argues that the process of acquiring knowledge consisted of recognizing and reading the visible signs, 'signatures' which revealed other, deeper or invisible resemblances:

> 'It is the same with the affinity of the walnut and the human head: what cures "wounds of the pericranium" is the thick green rind covering the bones – the shell – of the fruit; but internal head ailments may be prevented by use of the nut itself "which is exactly like the brain in appearance" (Crollius, *Traité des signatures*, 4).
>
> (Foucault, 1970: 27)

However, this mode of understanding only produced the same knowledge of each object, i.e. what resemblances it held. This in turn implied that certainty, with respect to even one analogy, could only be attained through the infinite collation of resemblances across the entire world; each resemblance pointed immediately to the next before confirming the first.

This potentially endless project of accumulation was, Foucault argues, limited by the concept of microcosm, wherein the visible, concrete world constituted a finite instance of the greater, divine macrocosm. For example, Man acted as the focal point of the operation of analogy, 'his face is to his body what the face of heaven is to the ether' (Foucault, 1970: 22). Two particular forms of the microcosm, the book and the collection, are important for this discussion.

The enormous social and cultural impact of the development and expansion of printing during the fifteenth and sixteenth centuries is now widely accepted (Einstein, 1979; Mandrou, 1978; Mukerji, 1983). Printing induced the broad dissemination of texts, wresting their control from clerics and transforming their content. The emergence of editor-printers, the reprinting of classical (secular and pagan) texts, and the expansion of a Latin-literate, international academic community are inextricably bound up together. However, the book was also important as a configuration of knowledge. During the late sixteenth and early seventeenth centuries language was implicitly enmeshed in the similitudes and signatures which ordered objects:

> The great metaphor of the book that one opens and pores over and reads in order to know nature, is merely the reverse and visible side of another transference, and a much deeper one, which forces language to reside in the world, among the plants, the herbs, the stones, and the animals.
>
> (Foucault, 1970: 35)

Indeed, there was not the clear distinction we draw between words and

things. Words were seen to be ordered through the same principles of
resemblance which linked other signs; letters were drawn together by
their sympathies.

The book both authorized the writing, the signs, that are manifest in
nature with the word of God (Foucault, 1970: 38), and offered a figure
of containment, a microcosm, in which knowledge could be fixed. It is
unsurprising, then, that the activities of Renaissance antiquarians were
focused on and expressed through literature, as Evans (1956: 3) notes of
John Leland, and Hunter (1971: 118–19) of William Camden and Ole
Worm (1588–1654). The priority of the written word and the reliance
on literary sources are also evident in the interpretation of historical
identity at this time.

Generally, identity was traced through resemblance. Foucault (1970:
39) cites Aldrovandi's *Historia serpentium et draconum*, which
characterized the serpent through these features, amongst others: the
etymology and synonyms of the word, its form, its anatomy, habits,
antipathy, sympathy, modes of capture, wounds caused by, remedies,
epithets, allegories, emblems and symbols, historical facts, dreams,
miscellaneous uses.

This is the kind of 'mass of miscellaneous notes' (Piggott, 1976: 12)
in which Leland collected accounts of antiquities, topographical
features and genealogies, etc. Camden's *Remains Concerning Brittaine*
(1607) includes a history of costume, place-names, 'an essay on British
coins, ... and another on Anglo-Saxon, with examples; a very full list
of proverbs current in his day, [and] two selections of medieval Latin
verse' (Piggott, 1976: 37). No priority was attached to different types of
historical, genealogical or mythological evidence, because it was, as
Foucault (1970: 39) puts it, 'all *legenda* – things to be read'.

Clearly, Renaissance antiquarianism was also implicitly bound up in
the political interests of the day. Scholars, churchmen and statesmen
were concerned to establish the ancient precedents and genealogical
derivation of contemporary institutions, particularly with reference to
their Celtic or English origins (Evans, 1956: 11; Piggott, 1976: 6). The
identity of the nation was interpreted through genealogical studies of
quasi-historical documents and etymological comparisons of 'named'
tribes, such as *Galatae, Celtae, Galli*. Aylett Sammes's *Britannia
Antiqua Illustrata* (something of an anachronism when published in
1676) links Britons with the '*Cimbri*' of the continent because of 'the
similitude of Name between these *Cymri* of Britain and the Ancient
people, the *Cimbri*' (Piggott, 1967: 9).

Whilst antiquarians were not often explicitly concerned with
artefacts, the collection of objects was a crucial feature of late
Renaissance culture. Collection emerged from medieval clerical stores
of relics, the hoarding of wealth, and early Renaissance 'princely'

collections (Hooper-Greenhill, 1992: 47–52; Piggott, 1976: 102). Several socio-cultural changes of this time (Mandrou, 1978; Burke, 1974) are relevant to the proliferation of collecting. These include the emergence of formal discourses concerned with the secular; aesthetic valuation of objects;[2] the partial dissipation of clerical authority in the face of expanding mercantile power; and the burgeoning class of editor-scholars. Each marks the growing distinction made between the natural world and the artificial one which reproduces (mirrors) nature (Baudrillard, 1994: 50–2).[3]

The collection of objects in 'cabinets of curiosity' (*Wunderkammer*) and 'cabinets of art' (*Kunstkammer*) has been characterized as the acquisition of a disorganized mass of rarities (Malina and Vasicek, 1990: 26). However, the radical diversity of objects found in collections such as those of Francesco Calceolari and Ulisse Aldrovandi in Italy, Ole Worm in Denmark and the Tradescants in England is in fact closely ordered according to the forms of similitude, visible or innate, which linked them, and the mirroring of nature in art. Collections were often organized into natural and artificial objects (Hogden, 1964: 123; Hooper-Greenhill, 1992: 13, 125; Piggott, 1976: 107). What appears to be incongruous juxtaposition of natural curiosities – mineral and animal rarities – with exotic artefacts and antiquities is in fact an attempt to represent the whole world, an encyclopedia. Antiquities were not separated from other exotic objects by their age, but united with them through resemblance. The web of resemblances between the diverse objects could be read in this microcosm in much the same way as in the literary collections or the signatures inherent in nature.

One feature uniting all such collections was the emphasis on rarity, curiosity and the exotic (Murray, 1904: 186–7). Collections manifested this interest in a number of ways.[4] In part, rarity itself conferred value on these objects; they were collected less avidly when more common-place (Impey and MacGregor, 1985: 3). However, the taste for exotic objects was widespread enough to generate both an academic (Findlen, 1991) and a commercial exchange (Piggott, 1976: 107). This interest can be directly linked with the rapid expansion of knowledge of the world beyond Europe. Not only did the limits of the known world recede dramatically after the discovery of America in 1492, but the number and diversity of 'voyages of discovery' increased exponentially (Hogden, 1964: 112).[5]

The exotic, in the form of customs, practices and objects, was incorporated into both forms of microcosm: the book and the cabinet. The narratives (histories) in which the ship's captain or doctor chronicled these voyages were assemblages of information, interweaving navigational observation, accounts of customs, mythological and biblical quotations, etc. Occasionally, these were separated into an inventory and a chronology (Defert, 1982: 12–14), but similitude still united the interpretation of observations (Boon, 1982: 38; Defert, 1982: 12). Johann Boemus in 1520 produced one of the first collections of this proto-ethnographic material, published in England in 1555 as *The fardle of facions*, with the aim of assembling information on exotic cultures in print, 'as others had employed the *"cabinet de curiositiés"* ' (Hogden, 1964: 131).

The relationship between the identities of these cultures (Patagonians, Feugians, etc.) and Europeans was also interpreted through resemblance. Medieval conceptions of monstrous races were amalgamated with Old Testament antediluvianism and direct observations (Mason, 1990; Boon, 1982). Moreover, the effort to assimilate 'other' cultures into Renaissance understanding operated in concert with the interpretation of ancient peoples through the observation of similitudes. For example, circumcision identified the resemblance between Indian tribes and Old Testament Jews (Boon, 1982: 162); and for Samuel Purchas, in *Purchas His Pilgrims* (1625), sodomy was a similitude of devil-worship (Boon, 1982: 165). The interpretation of such similitudes also integrated exotic peoples into the realm of European political identities, Protestant–Catholic conflicts, and disputes between sovereigns. Thus, for Samuel Purchas and Theodori de Bry (a Huguenot), natives in South America and the East Indies were corrupted by the Spanish and Dutch emissaries of the pope (Antichrist) into such fallen practices. The analogy between exotic and ancient cultures became explicit in John White's illustrations (1580s) of ancient Britons, which combined his observations of Virginian Indians made in North America with elements of the Britons of Lucas de Heere, based on classical sources (Piggott, 1976: 9). Images of exotic peoples had been available in England from the 1560s (e.g. Edmund Harman's monument, 1569) (Piggott, 1976: 10), and 'Indians' became the constant point of reference for ancient cultures.

During the late Renaissance, objects and identity were both interpreted through the philosophy of resemblance. The microcosm provided the concrete dimensions which limited encyclopedic collection, either in the book or in the cabinet of curiosities. Ancient peoples and their artefacts were principally understood through their curiosity or strangeness. They, like the exotic cultures being discovered at the time, constituted, in different ways, the limits of the world, and this explains the emphasis which Renaissance culture placed on the strange or curious (Mullaney, 1983). The 'cabinet of the world' had to manifest the similitudes which crossed the entire known world. This could best be achieved by assimilating, and therefore controlling, the most diverse and strange objects: the extremities of the world. Viewed in this context, Renaissance antiquarians were neither confused nor lacking rigour in their interpretations of ancient peoples. Rather, their mode of ordering the world was radically different from our own.

The seventeenth and eighteenth centuries: the well-laid table

By the mid-seventeenth century, 'scientific antiquarianism', characterized by Baconian empiricism, is taken to have gradually rationalized the study of antiquity to some degree (Trigger, 1989: 61). However, Foucault suggests that at this moment a seismic shift occurred from an episteme based on interpretation to a 'classical' episteme based on representation.

Foucault perhaps overemphasizes the discontinuity between the Renaissance and classical epistemes; certain practices, such as collecting, continue into the eighteenth century and later. However, it is clear that in the mid-seventeenth century the way in which knowledge was accumulated changed dramatically. Language was removed from the world of similitude to become the transparent medium of representation. 'The essential problem of classical thought lay in the relations between *name* and *order*: how to discover a *nomenclature* that would be a *taxonomy*, or again, how to establish a system of signs that would be transparent to the continuity of being' (Foucault, 1970: 208). For Foucault this episteme is typified by: attempts to define a general grammar, or ideal language, e.g. Condilliac and Adam Smith (Foucault, 1970: 124); the development of classificatory systems in natural history based on observing differential morphology, e.g. Linnaeus, Buffon (Foucault, 1970: 162); and the analysis of economic exchange in terms of wealth, e.g. Hobbes, Locke, Condilliac (Foucault, 1970: 167–8). The attempts to derive a universal grammar implied that language should reflect objects in as direct a way as possible; understanding consisted of ordered representation. Foucault argues that it was neither Cartesian rationality nor Baconian empiricism that made natural history possible (Foucault, 1970: 125–6), but rather the restriction of the gaze to the observation of a species's morphology. The *Systems* of Linnaeus, Ray and Grew (1681: 150) provided a language through which each species was represented in the grid of identities. Each acquired its place (name) through observable features, and was simultaneously differentiated from others approximating to it.

Similarly, the understanding of commerce was transformed, from an interpretation based on money as a sign of all intrinsic values to one in which money was valued because it was the means to conduct exchange. All wealth was seen to be convertible into coinage: 'For Classical thought in its formative phase, money is that which permits

wealth to be represented' (Foucault, 1970: 177). The analysis of goods
in circulation, on the basis of the exchange of monetary values, follows
the same pattern as the differentiation of species in natural history, and
of words in grammar. In this case the table or grid of values (identities)
is established by the monetary values with which all goods are
commensurate.[6] Locke (1960) extended the analysis of wealth in this
way in the labour theory of value, viewing a man's body as his
inalienable property. For Locke, man can, through labour, incorporate
material parts of the state into his own property, as extensions of
himself. This definition construes the individual as prior to society,
which is itself founded on the needs of these 'social atoms' and the
exchanges of their property. However, the individual is defined by his
possessions, and, moreover, his identity is linked, through labour, to
the analysis of wealth. Thus in the philosophy of 'possessive
individualism' (Macpherson, 1962) there is a conflation of the relations
between things and between people. Market relations are taken to be
the same as (and the sum total of) social relations.

The analysis of other cultures similarly proceeded through the
measurement of their customs as deviations from the natural norm.
Buffon (1971) defines a series of human kinds and examines
'traditionally sensational cross-cultural topics – eunuchs, harems,
human sacrifice – by charting them as innocuous, physiological
correlations between sexual forces and vocal range' (Boon, 1982: 34).
Helvetius analyses human diversity 'from Hottentots and Caribs to
Fakirs and Brahmins' in terms of gradable divergences from natural
moral laws (Boon, 1982: 34). These proto-ethnographies also display a
clear concern to identify (name) groups, and attempt to differentiate
(order) them in terms of the material conditions which each displayed.

In England, the institutional centre for such projects was the Royal
Society, founded in 1660. One of the aims of the Society was to replace
the collection of curiosities, in 'cabinets of the world', with the
systematic acquisition and cataloguing of objects representing the
whole natural order. The establishment of this collection, the
'Repository', was articulated through the 'scientific' schemes of natural
history and general grammar. The initial ordering of the collection was
based on the universal language schemes with which several of the
Society's fellows, including John Wilkins and the curator Robert
Hooke, were involved (Hunter, 1985: 164). Hooke made explicit the
link between the collection of objects, the universal languages and
taxonomic tables in his *General Scheme or Idea of the present state of
Natural Philosophy* (Hooper-Greenhill, 1992: 154).

However, the classical character of the Royal Society Repository
came entirely from the *post hoc* attempts to order and catalogue the
collection. It remained an eclectic assemblage of objects, founded, and

later added to, from private collections of curiosities. Following the Society's ideas on rational language and classificatory schemes, Nehemiah Grew catalogued the Repository's artefacts in 1681. Whilst Grew hoped 'That not only things strange and rare, but the most known and common amongst us, were thus describ'd' (Grew, 1681: preface), the Repository contained little that was commonplace. Only the parochial questionnaires, sent out in the 1670s by Ogilby, Machell and Lhywd (Piggott, 1967), offered a possible model for such a collection.

Collection continued, both as a private concern related to the aesthetics of mercantilism (Bunn, 1980), and also institutionally. However, it was no longer central to the understanding of the material world. This was the age of the catalogue, the written expression of the classical table of ordered knowledge. The Tradescants' collection was also catalogued in the late seventeenth century (MacGregor, 1983). Ole Worm's Museum was catalogued and rehoused by King Frederik III (Klindt-Jensen, 1975), and antiquarians were now, in effect, writing annotated catalogues of field monuments.

Several figures of the Royal Society, such as John Aubrey (1626–97), Edward Lhwyd (1660–1709) and Robert Plot (1640–96), were interested in antiquities. Antiquarianism underwent a radical transformation in the mid-seventeenth century, typified by the work of John Aubrey. Aubrey himself was highly specific about this change in the nature of scholarship, dating it to 1649 (Piggott, 1976: 102). Antiquarianism in the Royal Society's mode, from the 1680s onwards (Hunter, 1971: 114), was characterized by the observation, classification and visual recording of field monuments, coins, inscriptions and architectural features. An excellent example of this approach is Aubrey's plan of Avebury from *Monumenta Britannica* (*c*.1687) (Trigger, 1989: 48). Many antiquarians at the time, like Aubrey and Anstis, believed that recording field antiquities visually and collating them was essential to their interpretation. Lhywd's classification of fossils even offered a model typology for artefacts (Piggott, 1976: 20–1).[7] Perhaps most notable of all was William Stukeley (1687–1765), who systematically produced illustrations of field monuments, classified into types, according to their form (Trigger, 1989: 62).

The interpretation of antiquities, and their identification with tribes or peoples, was not obviously helped by the application of classificatory schemes to ancient objects. However, language classification came to bear directly on the question of ancient Britons in the form of Lhwyd's hypothesis of C- and P-Britons (Piggott, 1976: 20). The established Renaissance analogy of exotic and ancient cultures was retained, but in the transformed mode of classical comparison and differentiation. Whilst the Society's collection included ethnographic specimens, under 'humane rarities', it was rarely concerned with the study of other cultures *per se*. John Locke compiled an annotated 'ethnographic' bibliography, and Robert Hooke collected a series of programmes of enquiry for travellers in 1692 as *General heads for the natural history of a country, great or small; drawn out for the use of travellers and navigators*. But the discussion of other cultures was usually raised only in relation to other topics, including antiquity.

Hobbes, a friend of Aubrey, presents a model of the state of nature, an ancient time in which pre-social men lived. This state is defined, like exotic cultures, in terms of those aspects of rational society which it lacked:

> In such condition, there is no place for industry; ... no culture of the earth; no navigation; ... no knowledge of the face of the earth; no account of time; no arts; no letters; no society; and which is worst of all, continual fear, and danger of violent death; and the life of man, solitary, poor, nasty, brutish and short ... The savage people in many places of America ... live at this day in that brutish manner.
>
> (Hobbes, 1969: 97–9)

Aubrey turned Hobbes's abstract model into an explicit comparison in his *Essay Towards the Description of the North Division of Wiltshire* (1659). He described the topography and flora of the area, the language, transport (curricles), social units (*Reguli*), defences and religion, concluding: 'They knew the use of Iron. They were 2 or 3 degrees, I suppose, less savage than the Americans' (Aubrey, 1659, quoted in Piggott, 1976: 9).

Aubrey's description shares Hobbes's low estimation of ancient Britons' lives, and assesses their circumstances in the same terms: their difference from the Native Americans (the state of nature), and its representation in material conditions. Unlike the Renaissance form, which integrated antiquities, with other exotic objects, into the microcosm through similitude, classical antiquarianism classified and represented objects according to the concrete criteria of the natural sciences, and identified them through their graduated divergence from a natural–moral order. Stukeley, often praised for his field work, is criticized for his continual association of monuments with druidic practices – the beginning of antiquarianism's decline into Romanticist fancy (Trigger, 1989: 63–5). But this interpretation is not categorically different from his contemporaries' identifications of ancient Britons. Stukeley too utilizes the notion of a scaled decline from the natural–moral order, but produces a contrary estimation of ancient cultures. To him Druids are highest in that order, closer to primordial monotheism than contemporary religions.

Analysing antiquities through the table of identities itself inhibited the development of antiquarianism. Unlike natural objects of study, which provided an almost endless series of instances and forms, antiquities were intrinsically rare and unusual. Hence, as Grew notes of the Repository, a systematic taxonomy was impossible 'because as yet the collection itself is not perfect' (Grew, 1681: 124). Grew devised a complex system for classifying shells, but only a crude categorization for antiquities. Moreover, whilst the ordering of exotic cultures was possible (their culture and material circumstances being observable), the classification of antiquities itself offered few insights into ancient cultures. The context of the natural sciences enabled the identification and ordering of antiquities, but circumscribed their historical interpretation. As Trigger (1989: 65–7) points out, by the mid-eighteenth century, Romanticism and nationalism offered new narratives through which artefacts could be interpreted. But their influence was a measure much more of the limits of the classical episteme than of the foolishness of eighteenth-century antiquarians. Romanticism and, particularly, nationalism were implicit in the development of the institutional interpretations of the past that was characteristic of the nineteenth century.

Nineteenth century: modernity, man, language, life, labour and nation

Rationalist philosophy and systematic field practices are usually seen to have transformed nineteenth-century archaeology into a recognizably modern, scientific form (Trigger, 1989; Daniel, 1981). Yet there were other dimensions to archaeological thought at the time. For example, it has become the accepted view that nineteenth-century archaeology was characterized by theories of racial superiority, and was used to legitimize imperialism (Trigger, 1984; 1989). However, neither conventional models of the progressive influence of rationality nor simple ideological critiques of colonialism can explain the emergence of new archaeological discourses relating objects to collective identities, or the development of the competing evolutionary and culture-historical models of human prehistory and social development.[8] It is clear, though, that new modes of interpretation, new forms of discourse and new practices characteristic of the modern discipline *did* emerge in archaeology.

In the late eighteenth century, 'the Age of Revolution', socio-political and economic transformations were so numerous and far-reaching that the constitution of knowledge could hardly be expected to remain constant. However, Foucault does not directly link the emergence of a modern episteme to such social shifts. Rather, he explains it as the exhaustion of the classical episteme's reliance on the representation of the natural order, and the development of the 'new empiricities' of 'Labour', 'Life' and 'Language' (Foucault, 1970: 250). In Ricardo, and later Marx, labour ceases to be an abstract equivalence, but as a productive process 'is the source of all value' (Foucault, 1970: 254). After Cuvier, biology is constituted around the investigation of the processes of life, organic structure and functions, rather than the form of organisms (Foucault, 1970: 263). Language, for Grimm, Schegel, Rasp and Bopp, is an object of study in its own right, examined in its operation. It is no longer a transparent medium of expression.

Uniting these new discourses is the figure of 'Man'. In what Foucault terms the 'analytic of finitude' (1970: 313), Man is both the source of all intelligibility and the subject of all enquiry. He is 'a living being (the subject of Biology), an instrument of production (a labouring subject), a vehicle for words which exist before him (subject to the language)' (Foucault, 1970: 313). Man, recognizing his finite nature, approaches the world through those empirical fields he himself defines; he is thus separated from God's creation, becomes sovereign in place of God, and therefore makes nature intelligible for himself.

'History' – the emergence of the empirical – came to occupy a similar place in the modern episteme to that which order had occupied for the classical mode of thought. The task within the new empirical fields was to examine the point of origin of its features, and to analyse their processes of operation and their analogous relations to other structures. Given the foundation of history as the fundamental mode of being, together with the recognition of the historicity of thought itself (Foucault, 1970: 219–20), new academic disciplines – the human sciences of philology, economics and biology, but also anthropology, psychoanalysis and others – emerged to articulate Man's relation to the material world (Foucault, 1970: 344).

As a human science, archaeology was principally concerned with the origins and development of humanity – its history. The question of the relation between human beings and nature had been resolved in the classical episteme through the revelation of the natural order. However, in the nineteenth century the notion of history – i.e. the depth of time and the coming to being of the knowable, empirical world – implied that the human past could only be articulated through an abstract or objective measure of the time of the past.

Such a chronology, the 'Three Age System', enabled Thomsen (1788–1865) and then Worsaae (1821–85) to analyse the (pre)history of Denmark. The chronology offered a framework through which the successive phases of the transformation of material by labour could identify distinct epochs, and the societies which produced these technologies. At the same time, the scholars' nationalism was expressed in the exploration of the origins and history of Denmark, shaped by the ideals of the Enlightenment as manifested in revolutionary France (Trigger, 1989: 74). Archaeologists' explanations of materiality and identity were also shaped by the practices linking the two in other institutional contexts.

The discourses of the human sciences found practical expression in a series of new institutions: asylums, hospitals, prisons and schools (Foucault, 1965, 1970, 1973, 1977). Each of these institutions, whilst expressing a specific social function, simultaneously promulgated new modes of existence, actively determining the lives it sought to improve. The early nineteenth century saw the emergence of the concept of society as a totality: 'the people', or nation. Foucault argues that this social body is an effect 'not of a consensus [shared bourgeois values, democratic participation, etc.] but of the materiality of power operating on the very bodies of individuals' (Foucault, 1980: 55). These institutions operated practices of subjectification: the production of complicit citizens – 'docile bodies' (Foucault, 1977). Foucault's exemplary instance of such practices is represented by Bentham's Panopticon, an ideal prison in which docility is achieved by continuous surveillance and routinization. The subjects ultimately become the instrument of their own subjectification by the inducement of self-surveillance (Foucault, 1977: 201).

Revolutionary France was a primary site of emergence for such institutions.[9] The establishment of the Musée Français in the Louvre in 1793 instituted the explicit integration of artefacts within a disciplinary framework (Hooper-Greenhill, 1992: 171). Conflict and military-bureaucratic organization enabled the post-revolutionary commissions to acquire new collections of artefacts and to establish a hierarchical system of central and regional museums (Bazin, 1967). Moreover, a new administrative apparatus was established to extend the principle of surveillance to the acquisition, distribution, conservation and exhibition of artefacts within the museum (Hooper-Greenhill, 1992: 179–85).

Artefacts within such collections were reordered and exhibited according to the artist's country of origin, and so as to represent the historical development of that country's art (Bazin, 1967: 159). Thus philosophical discourse linked artefacts with disciplinary practices. The educative function of such displays was an explicit discursive mode of the constitution of the social body. The history of France was identified with history *per se*; as Hudson (1987: 42) points out, the Musée Central des Arts recognized no 'English School' of painting, because England was not part of the empire.

Whilst Hooper-Greenhill's characterization of the disciplinary museum is located within the practices of the institution itself, Bennett (1994) examines the ordering of artefacts from positions outside the cabinet. He argues that the viewpoint of power implicit in institutional surveillance has its counterpart in the gaze invited by the 'exhibitionary complex'. The large-scale and public exhibition of artefacts, either as an instructional device in museums or as a spectacular mode of consumption in the exhibitions and arcades, which emerged in the mid-nineteenth century was exemplified by the Great Exhibition at the Crystal Palace in 1851, and the Paris Exhibition in 1855 (Bennett, 1994: 128, 132). In these and later exhibitions the visitor consumes the artefacts only by looking at them: through the spectacular (Richards, 1991). The visitor to museums and exhibitions was not subjectified by the surveillance of the museum officials; rather the viewing of objects on display caused an elision of the viewer's gaze with the gaze of power. The power of the exhibitionary complex is not a reversal of the principles of surveillance; its effect 'lies in its incorporation of aspects of these principles together with those of the panorama, forming a technology of vision which served not to atomise and disperse the crowd but to regulate it, and to do so by rendering it visible to itself, by making the crowd itself the ultimate spectacle' (Bennett, 1994: 131–2).

In such spectacles the social body[10] is constituted from individual human beings through three domains (Dean, 1994): the discursive practices which articulate objects within the domain of knowledge (the exhibition narratives); governmental practices problematizing objects in relation to power (the administrative and professional roles which produce and control the space of the exhibition); and the ethical practices or 'techniques of the self' which order the formation of the self as a desiring but self-referencing subject (the constrained but 'free' choices offered by commodity consumption v. the decorum of the crowds) (Bennett, 1994: 134). The arcades and department stores, like the great exhibitions, with their spectacle offered 'the spatial and visual means for a self-education from the point of view of capital' (Tafuri, 1976: 83).

Exhibition was a pivotal form, through which the dramatic expansion in the number and diversity of commodities available to large urban populations changed the way in which people constructed their lives. Mass-produced goods became integrated into practices through which middle- and working-class identities were articulated (Briggs, 1988; Richards, 1991; Bennett, 1994). The discourses which ordered objects within these contexts were crucial to the definition of those identities, and to related notions of identity produced by academic discourses. Labour, for Ricardo (Foucault, 1970: 253–63) and later in Marx's analysis of capitalism, constituted the activity which transformed inert matter into value. This value was both economic and cultural. The Great Exhibition represented national identities, and the hierarchy of those identities, through displays of the artefacts produced in each country (Richards, 1991: 25). Moreover, exhibition, together with its street counterpart the advertisement, offered instances through which cultural development could be analysed. 'The Language of the Walls presents us with an *epitome* of this history of civilization – the progress of commerce – a chronicle of passing events – and a *multum in parvo* of all things' (James Dawson Burn, quoted in Richards, 1991: 47). The view that labour, in transforming nature (the production of artefacts), constituted the fundamental activity in the rise of civilization was widely held, and was certainly central to the modern mode of archaeological interpretation.

Narratives in both exhibitions and archaeological discourses on the past, addressing history in terms of progress, were significantly bolstered at this time. *On the Origin of Species* (1859), Darwin's account of the origin and development of Man in biological terms (in terms of life), quickly influenced thinking on social development.[11] The work of Herbert Spencer and Thomas Huxley (Trigger, 1989: 113),[12] amongst others, established theories of social evolution based on racial differences.

John Lubbock (1834–1913) argued in *Prehistoric Times* that modern Europeans were biologically and culturally more advanced than their 'primitive' counterparts in Africa and elsewhere, and that parallels existed between contemporary primitives and ancient cultures because they occupied similarly low evolutionary positions. He also emphasized the 'degenerate' nature of primitive cultures as a justification for Britain's imperial rule (Trigger, 1989: 116–18). Imperialism of course also allowed access to antiquities and enabled excavation. Lubbock's work was extremely influential, particularly in America, and similar colonial ideologies shaped archaeological studies of Africa and other English colonies (Trigger, 1989: 119–47).

Such views were common in the late nineteenth century. Many museums and exhibitions characterized the history of humanity in racial terms and evidenced differential social evolution through the display of artefacts. Thus the subjected peoples of Africa and the Americas, represented by 'primitive' handicrafts, occupied the lowest levels of civilization (technological, social and physical evolution). Naturally, European metropolitan cultures were the most spectacularly shown (Bennett, 1994: 146). The Paris Exposition of 1889 included a colonial city where the whole ambit of social evolution was displayed, the primitive 'other' present in simulated villages populated by Africans and Asians (Bennett, 1994: 148). In the displays of the Pitt-Rivers Museum the biological analogue of history – evolution – was most closely linked with the production of culture, in the genetic or typological series into which Pitt-Rivers arranged Australian Aboriginal artefacts.

> Human ideas, as represented by the various products of human industry,
> are capable of classification into genera, species and varieties in the same
> manner as the products of the vegetable and animal kingdoms, and in
> their development from homogeneous to the heterogeneous they obey
> the same laws.
>
>   (Lane Fox [Pitt-Rivers], 1874: **xx**)

Probably the most notorious archaeological attempt to link material
culture and identity was made by Gustaf Kossinna (1858–1931)
(Trigger, 1989: 163–70). The 'settlement archaeological method',
through which Kossinna identified distributions of artefact types, was
important to his work and influence. However, Kossinna sustained his
linkage of artefacts and ethnicity through a philosophically derived
nationalism, acquired in an intellectual context shaped by Herder and
Fichte (Dumont, 1986). Kossinna elided the themes of historical
development in language, and human progress (life) into the racial
concept of *volk*. The vigour – the productivity – of the *Germani* was a
consequence of their superior Aryan racial and linguistic characteristics. Kossinna's search for the origins and historical emergence of the
Germani was a quintessential expression of modern philosophy.[13] In
common with the progressivist and evolutionary discourses ordering
museum and exhibition displays, Kossinna's archaeological theory
utilized the empirical – language, labour and life – to produce a
hierarchical (racial) history of Man, which was typically nationalistic.

Whilst Gordon Childe rejected the excesses of Kossinna's nationalism, the two had more in common than the definition of an
archaeological culture.[14] Childe's culture-historical approach utilized
the same empirical domains of language, labour and life in explanation
of the human past. The difference lay in that culture-history did not
adopt the biological, unilinear model of social evolution. However,
Childe's definition of the ethnic groups which related to archaeological
cultures was almost entirely linguistically based. The history of
humanity – the development of social groups and the increasing
complexity of human culture in general – was a constant theme of his
work. The means by which social evolution took place and could be
discerned in the artefactual record were an amalgam of labour (*Man
Makes Himself*, 1936), a particular racial 'vigour and genius' (Childe,
1925: 151), and linguistic and therefore intellectual superiority (Childe,
1926: 3).

It seems clear, then, that from the early nineteenth century onwards
a distinctive mode of formal discourse on the past had emerged. Thus
modern archaeology sought evidence, conceptualized problems and
interpreted artefacts in similar ways to the other human sciences. But
the emergence of this mode of analysis marked a disjunction from the
ways in which materiality and identity had been related in classical

rationality. Philosophy defined the relationship between objects and identity historically, through the figure of Man, in the study of his languages, his racial origins and his industry.

Conclusions: late/postmodernity

In this chapter I have argued that the way in which the artefacts and identities of the past have been articulated has undergone a series of radical transformations since the late Renaissance. This implies that the conventional picture of the development of archaeology, in which there is a gradual revelation of more information about the past, and a steady improvement of our theories and interpretations of that data, cannot be sustained. The archaeologists of the twentieth century are not simply making better use of the same (though more abundant) objective evidence as was available to antiquarians in the seventeenth century. Furthermore, the importance of the cultural context in which the past is studied is not limited to its influence on interpretation (Trigger, 1989: 379). Contemporary concerns do focus the minds and activities of archaeologists, as others, but their 'subjectivity' is not the central issue, as is often argued:

> The importance of ethnic issues and conflicts of interest in the modern world at least partly explains and justifies our interest in them in the past. Unfortunately, in investigating these questions as with so many others, we have tended to create the past in our own image. The challenge for the future ... is to try to transcend this parochial subjectivism.
>
> (Shennan, 1989: 30)

The pre-conceptual frameworks (epistemes) through which our culture orders the material and social worlds have changed through time and are themselves specific to each time and culture. This affects not merely the interpretation of evidence, or the articulation of subjective influences with material data, but the very fabric of our understanding. The concepts and modes of analysis through which we interpret the past are not neutral, abstract tools; they are cultural products. As Binford has pointed out (1962, 1972), archaeology must be anthropological in that it must produce general theories. However, the historical and cultural derivation of concepts undermines the universalist assumptions which such theories have generally been founded upon. In essence, I would argue that the importance of both anthropology (ethnography) and history is that, when applied to the analysis of the construction of knowledge, they offer the possibility of deriving theories of materialism and identity which are more than parochially based generalizations.

It is likely, for example, that the concept of alienation will be useful in the analysis of the development of nineteenth- and twentieth-century mass consumption in industrialized societies; but it becomes problematic when extended to the investigation of the ritual use of objects by the Walbiri of the central Australian desert (cf. Miller, 1987: 53–63). Alienation, as a tool for analysing the material and social worlds, is as much an artefact of the modern world as is a cotton mill. It could constitute an element of a general theory of materialism if it were situated within an historical and cross-cultural context. This context would have to include its own historical derivation and the materialism and socio-cultural contexts of a diversity of other peoples. In contrast to previous and existing attempts to theorize materialism and identity in archaeology (examples would include Childe's cultural history, Binford's new archaeology and Hodder's contextual archaeology), it must eschew the temptation to claim a transcendental, immanent or objective origin in the artefacts themselves.

The thorough re-evaluation of the epistemic/cultural circumstances of European intellectual practice has already been addressed by anthropologists. They are beginning to see their discipline as just that: a cultural practice, rather than an objective scientific instrument (Clifford and Marcus, 1986; Clifford, 1989). Therefore the prospect of producing a similar archaeological theory of materialism and identity may not be so daunting. Such a theory would offer a useful perspective from which to analyse theoretical archaeology's contemporary concern for the distinctly 'postmodern' themes of textuality, critical theory, multiple identities, consumption, individualism, etc. It might also illuminate the current preoccupation, in heritage and museum presentation, with nineteenth-century industrial culture (Walsh, 1992). More specifically, the internal contradictions in archaeological conceptions of cultural identity can only be resolved with reference to their own historical emergence.

Notes

1 Childe's neo-Marxist notion of socio-historical evolution led to analyses based on generalized types or stages of social development, within which he framed a normative conception of anthropological cultures and a functionalist conception of material culture (Trigger, 1980).

2 An interesting example of these emerging discourses is to be found in the city-states of Italy in the Renaissance, where mathematical education, concerned with solid geometry and the estimation and valuation of objects as commodities, developed, as did contractual and aesthetic valuation of paintings (Baxandall, 1972).

3 An example is Robert Fludd's cosmography, *Integrae Naturae Speculum*

Artisque Imago (*The Mirror of the Whole of Nature and the Image of Art*) (Hooper-Greenhill, 1992: 111).

4 The letter from John Tradescant 'To the marchants of the Ginne Company & the Gouldcost Mr. Humphrie Slainy Captain Crispe & Mr. Clobery & Mr. John Wood Cape marchant' (1625) gives an excellent illustration of this theme. It requests that they find amongst other things:

on Ellophants head with the teeth In it very larg . . .
of All ther strang sorts of fowelles & Birds Skines and Beakes Leggs & phethers that be Rare or Not Knowne to us
of All sorts of strang fishes skines of those parts the Greatest sorts of shellfishes shells of Great flying fishes & sucking fishes withe what els strang
of the habits weapons & Instruments
of ther Ivory Long fluts . . .
of All sorts of Serpents and Snakes Skines & Espetially of that sort that hathe a Combe on his head lyke a Cock . . .
Of All sorts of Shining Stones or of Any Strang Shapes
Any thing that Is Strang.

(MacGregor, 1983: 20)

5 In 1532 William Hawkins presented a Brazilian king to the court of Henry VIII; in 1550 a whole Brazilian village was sent to France (Piggott, 1976: 30–1); and in 1600 the East India Company was granted a charter by Queen Elizabeth I, consolidating the commercial exploitation of these discoveries.

6 For Hobbes this grid corresponded to the natural order by virtue of the sovereign's power to legitimate its denominations (by minting the coinage) in the heart of the Leviathan (state) (Foucault, 1970: 179) and through the utility of the objects exchanged. Hobbes also invests authority over the meaning of words and the definition of identities in the sovereign of the absolutist state, identifying its configurations with the natural order (Ryan, 1982: 3).

7 Others, like Elias Ashmole (1617–92), William Dugdale (1605–86) and Robert Sibbald (1641–1722), operated with essentially the same frame of reference.

8 The idea that these differences are the result of the different academic biographies of authors or their divergent beliefs merely displaces the question to another level of enquiry.

9 The situation in late eighteenth- and early nineteenth-century France produced specific expressions of the new episteme and the disciplinary regimes, but it was not an isolated instance. In England, from the early nineteenth century onwards, numerous local philosophical societies were established. These often included museums, founded with donations from colonial administrators, which were also intended for 'public education' (Walsh, 1992). Indeed, similar institutions formalized cultural practices throughout Europe at this time.

10   The social body implied 'the people', or a nation as a whole, integrated by their common history, language, practices, institutions, etc. It was obviously the condition upon which sociology was founded.
11   The idea of social progress had been established since the Enlightenment and described in evolutionary terms by Lamarck.
12   Huxley suggested in 1863 that there was a similarity between Australian Aboriginal and Neanderthal skulls.
13   As Foucault characterizes it, 'In the nineteenth century, philosophy was to reside in the gap between history and History, between events and the Origin, between evolution and the first rending open of the source, between oblivion and Return' (1970: 219–20). This is more than evident in the titles of Kossinna's work: *The Origin of the Germani* (1911) and *German Prehistory, a Pre-eminently National Discipline* (1914).
14   See Trigger (1980, 1989) for a conventional account of the relationship.

Bibliography

Abercrombie, J. (1912) *A Study of the Bronze Age Pottery in Great Britain and Ireland and Its Associated Grave Goods*, Oxford: Oxford University Press.

Baudrillard, J. (1994) *Symbolic Exchange and Death*, London: Sage.

Baxandall, M. (1972) *Painting and Experience in Fifteenth Century Italy*, Oxford: Oxford University Press.

Bazin, G. (1967) *The Museum Age*, Brussels: Desoer.

Bennett, T. (1994) 'The exhibitionary complex' in N. Dirks, G. Eley and S. Ortner (eds), *Culture–Power–History*, Princeton, NJ: Princeton University Press.

Binford, L. (1962) 'Archaeology as anthropology', *American Antiquity*, 28(2), 217–25.

Binford, L. (1972) *An Archaeological Perspective*, London: Seminar Press.

Boon, J.A. (1982) *Other Tribes, Other Scribes*, Cambridge: Cambridge University Press.

Braudel, F. (1967) *Civilization and Capitalism*, New York: Harper Row.

Briggs, R. (1988) *Victorian Things*, Harmondsworth: Penguin.

Buffon, G.-L. de (1971) *Histoire naturelle de l'homme*, Paris: François Maspero (first published in 1749).

Bunn, J. H. (1980) 'The aesthetics of British mercantilism', *New Literary History*, 11, 303–21.

Burke, P. (1974) *Tradition and Innovation in Renaissance Italy*, London: Fontana.

Childe, V.G. (1925) *The Dawn of European Civilization*, London: Kegan Paul.

Childe, V.G. (1926) *The Aryans: A Study of Indo-European Origins*, London: Kegan Paul.

Childe, V.G. (1929) *The Danube in Prehistory*, Oxford: Oxford University Press.

Childe, V.G. (1930) *The Bronze Age*, Cambridge: Cambridge University Press.

Childe, V.G. (1936) *Man Makes Himself*, London: Watts.

Clarke, D.L. (1968) *Analytical Archaeology*, London: Methuen.

Clifford, J. (1989) *The Predicament of Culture*, Cambridge, MA: Harvard University Press.

Clifford, J. and Marcus, G. (1986) *Writing Culture*, Berkeley, CA: University of California Press.

Collingwood, R.G. (1946) *The Idea of History*, Oxford: Oxford University Press.

Daniel, G. (1967) *The Origins and Growth of Archaeology*, Harmondsworth: Penguin.

Daniel, G. (1981) *A Short History of Archaeology*, London: Thames and Hudson.

Dean, M. (1994) *Critical and Effective Histories: Foucault's Methods and Historical Sociology*, London: Routledge.

Defert, D. (1982) 'The collection of the world: accounts of voyages from the sixteenth to the eighteenth centuries', *Dialectical Anthropology*, 7, 11–20.

Dumont, L. (1986) *Essays on Individualism*, Chicago: University of Chicago Press.

Einstein, E.L. (1979) *The Printing Press as an Agent of Change*, Cambridge: Cambridge University Press.

Evans, J. (1956) *A History of the Society of Antiquaries*, Oxford: Society of Antiquaries.

Findlen, P. (1991) 'The economy of scientific exchange in early modern Italy', in B. Moran (ed.), *Patronage and Institutions*, Woodbridge: Boydell and Brewer.

Foucault, M. (1965) *Madness and Civilization: A History of Insanity in the Age of Reason*, London: Tavistock.

Foucault, M. (1970) *The Order of Things: An Archaeology of the Human Sciences*, London: Tavistock.

Foucault, M. (1972) *The Archaeology of Knowledge*, London: Tavistock.

Foucault, M. (1973) *The Birth of the Clinic*, London: Tavistock.

Foucault, M. (1977) *Discipline and Punish*, London: Allen Lane.

Foucault, M. (1980) 'Body/power', in *Power/Knowledge: Selected Interviews and Other Writings 1972–1977*, ed. C. Gordon, Brighton: Harvester.

Grew, N. (1681) *Musaeum Regalis Societatis*, London.

Harrison, R.J. (1980) *The Beaker Folk*, London: Thames and Hudson.

Hobbes, T. (1969) *Leviathan*, Menston: Scholar Press (first published 1651).

Hobsbawm, E. (1990) *Nations and Nationalism since 1780*, Cambridge, Cambridge University Press.

Hobsbawm, E. and Ranger, T. (1983) *The Invention of Tradition*, Cambridge: Cambridge University Press.

Hodder, I. (1982) *Symbols in Action*, Cambridge: Cambridge University Press.

Hodder, I. (1986) *Reading the Past*, Cambridge: Cambridge University Press.

Hodder, I. (1987) *The Archaeology of Contextual Meanings*, Cambridge: Cambridge University Press.

Hogden, M. (1964) *Early Anthropology in the Sixteenth and Seventeenth Centuries*, Philadelphia: University of Pennsylvania Press.

Hooper-Greenhill, E. (1992) *Museums and the Shaping of Knowledge*, London: Routledge.

Hudson, K. (1987) *Museums of Influence*, Cambridge: Cambridge University Press.

Hunter, M. (1971) 'The Royal Society and the origins of British archaeology', *Antiquity*, 65, 113–21, 187–92.

Hunter, M. (1985) 'The cabinet institutionalised: the Royal Society's "Repository" and its background', in O. Impey and A. MacGregor, *The Origins of Museums*, Oxford: Clarendon Press.

Impey, O. and MacGregor, A. (1985) *The Origins of Museums*, Oxford: Clarendon Press.

Kendrick, T.D. (1950) *British Antiquity*, London: Methuen.

Klindt-Jensen, O. (1975) *A History of Scandinavian Archaeology*, London: Thames and Hudson.

Kossinna, G. (1911) *Die Herkunft der Germanen*, Leipzig: Kabitzsch.

Lane Fox, A.H. (1874) *Catalogue of the Anthropological Collection Lent by Colonel Lane Fox ...* , London: British Museum.

Locke, J. (1960) *Two Treatises of Government*, edited by Peter Laslett. Cambridge: Cambridge University Press (first published 1690).

MacGregor, A. (1983) *Tradescant's Rarities*, Oxford: Clarendon Press.

Macpherson, C.B. (1962) *The Political Theory of Possessive Individualism*, Oxford: Oxford University Press.

Malina, J. and Vasicek, Z. (1990) *Archaeology Yesterday and Today*, Cambridge: Cambridge University Press.

Mandrou, R. (1978) *From Humanism to Science, 1480–1700*, Harmondsworth: Penguin.

Mason, P. (1990) *Deconstructing America*, London: Routledge.

Mauss, M. (1931) *Instructions sommaires pour les collecteurs d'objets ethnographiques*, Paris: Musée d'Ethnographie.

McLellan, D. (1980) *Marx's Grundrisse*, London: Macmillan.

Miller, D. (1987) *Material Culture and Mass Consumption*, Oxford: Blackwell.

Mukerji, C. (1983) *From Graven Images*, New York: Columbia University Press.

Mullaney, S. (1983) 'Strange things, gross terms, curious customs: the rehearsal of cultures in the late Renaissance', *Representations*, 3, 40–67.

Murray, D. (1904) *Museums: Their History and Their Use*, Glasgow: Glasgow University Press.

Piggott, S. (1938) 'The Early Bronze Age in Wessex', *Proceedings of the Prehistoric Society*, 4, 52–106.

Piggott, S. (1954) *The Neolithic Cultures of the British Isles*, London: Cambridge University Press.

Piggott, S. (1967) *Celts, Saxons and the Early Antiquarians*, Edinburgh: Edinburgh University Press.

Piggott, S. (1976) *Ruins in a Landscape*, Edinburgh: Edinburgh University Press.

Renfrew, C. (1984) *Approaches to Social Archaeology*, Edinburgh: Edinburgh University Press.

Renfrew, C. (1987) *Archaeology and Language*, London: Jonathan Cape.

Richards, T. (1991) *The Commodity Culture of Victorian England*, London: Verso.

Ryan, M. (1982) *Marxism and Deconstruction*, Baltimore: Johns Hopkins University Press.

Shennan, S. (1978) 'Archaeological cultures: an empirical investigation', in I. Hodder (ed.), *The Spatial Organisation of Culture*, London: Duckworth.

Shennan, S. (1989) *Archaeological Approaches to Cultural Identity*, London: Unwin Hyman.

Smith, A.D. (1986) *The Ethnic Origins of Nations*, Oxford: Blackwell.

Tafuri, M. (1976) *Architecture and Utopia: Design and Capitalist Development*, Cambridge, MA: MIT Press.

Trigger, B. (1980) *Gordon Childe: Revolutions in Archaeology*, London: Thames and Hudson.

Trigger, B. (1984) 'Alternative archaeologies: nationalist, colonialist, imperialist', *Man*, **19**, 355–70.

Trigger, B. (1989) *A History of Archaeological Thought*, Cambridge: Cambridge University Press.

Walsh, K. (1992) *The Representation of the Past*, London: Routledge.

3

The Romantic Ethic and the Spirit of Modern Consumerism: *reflections on the reception of a thesis concerning the origin of the continuing desire for goods*

COLIN CAMPBELL

Introduction

As it is almost a decade since *The Romantic Ethic and the Spirit of Modern Consumerism* was first published (Campbell, 1987), this seems an appropriate time to reflect upon its reception by the academic community. Gratifyingly, the argument presented in the book has generally been well received, and (especially pleasing for a sociologist) this has been particularly the case among academics in other disciplines. Social and cultural historians, especially in the United States (Brewer and Porter, 1993), have shown a special interest in the thesis, as too have many anthropologists, ethnologists and students of material culture. It has also been well received by historians of art and design (Banks and Vowles, 1989), by academics in marketing and consumer research (Arnould, 1989; Belk, 1989), and by psychologists interested in questions of ownership and human–object interaction (Rudmin 1991). Finally, even literary critics have been kinder in their comments on the discussions of eighteenth-century sentimentalism and Romanticism than I had feared would be the case (Christensen, 1993). As I anticipated, economists have either ignored the argument or dismissed it as quite implausible. Many of those who have either reviewed or commented on the book have raised pertinent and important questions, especially concerning the manner in which the argument could be extended or refined, something that I hope to have the opportunity to do before long. In this chapter, however, I should like to confine myself to clarifying the nature of the thesis as presented in the book and addressing some of the more common misconceptions that have arisen, before commenting briefly on the question of whether it could be said to imply any particular judgement on modern consumerism.

The thesis restated

The initial premise underlying the thesis is that what distinguishes the modern mode of consumption is the fact that consumers have the ability to generate new wants in an apparently endless series, one after the other, without any effort or difficulty; all that is necessary for this process to continue being that they are exposed to new goods. What is more, it is assumed that these wants are typically for novel products, ones that the consumer has not encountered before in precisely that form, the institution of fashion being the principal mechanism to ensure that these regularly appear on the market. These assumptions imply that, in effect, it is largely novelty itself that is being consumed, and since novelty is necessarily extinguished in the very process of its consumption, this serves to explain how it is that the generation of wants is endless. However, this insight merely causes the problem of explaining modern consumption to be restated so that what is now needed is an answer to the question of why novelty should be so highly valued and desired.

A hedonistic theory is proposed in order to provide an answer. It is suggested that the primary desire, from which all specific desires and wants spring, is that for pleasure itself (something that I distinguish sharply from the economists' utility or satisfaction). However, not only is pleasure-seeking a universal feature of human society, and one which hence cannot be regarded as distinctive of modernity, but there is no obvious reason why hedonism should lead to a high value being placed on novelty. The focus is therefore placed on a distinctively modern form of pleasure-seeking, one identified as autonomous, self-illusory hedonism. This distinction between traditional and modern hedonism is frequently overlooked by those who summarize the argument, so that the theory is commonly represented as merely hedonistic in character. However, modern hedonism is critically different from its traditional counterpart, centring as it does on emotionally generated sensations. In fact, modern hedonism centres on the covert rather than the overt consumption of sensations, with individuals enjoying the sensations that stem from an environment that they have provided for themselves.

That is to say, they conjure up scenes in their imagination that effectively cause them to experience a chosen emotion, and it is then this emotion which yields the stimulation that in turn provides the pleasure. This is self-illusory hedonism, or day-dreaming, an activity that enables the individual to experience pleasure at any time and place, and is thus quite independent of the nature of the real environment.

Day-dreams – as opposed to fantasies – involve versions of real, or an least possible, events and experiences, typically those that might be anticipated as occurring some time in the future. Being constructed purely for pleasure, however, these imagined versions yield an unblemished form of pleasure unknown in reality. Consequently day-dreamers tend to live in two worlds, the real one and a perfected version of it, and it is the tension between these two worlds that generates longing. It is the presence of this sense of longing– a longing to experience perfected pleasures, or at the least more nearly perfect pleasures, in the real world rather than simply in imagination – that is really the critical consequence of this form of hedonism. For it is this that leads to increased dissatisfaction with life as it is currently experienced, and consequently to an enthusiasm for all that is perceived to be novel. Since the pleasures associated with novel products and experiences are necessarily unknown, it is possible to believe that they might resemble those more perfect pleasures already experienced in imagination. However, since the gap between the real and the imagined can never actually be closed (no matter how good the reality one can always imagine a more nearly perfect version), consumption of the novel merely serves to create a need to consume yet more novelty. This then is the central dynamic of self-illusory hedonism, one in which dissatisfaction with reality leads to day-dreaming, which in turn leads to longing and a desire for the novel, only for consumption of the novel to lead to disillusionment, renewed longing and a desire for more novelty.

Now it is comparatively easy to relate hedonism of this kind to modern consumerism. The most obvious and important link is through fashion, which in its modern form is nothing more than an institution for the controlled and organized production of novelty. In addition, that other dominant institution, advertising, functions to draw the consumer's attention to the promise of new experiences which, it is suggested, novel products can offer. However, the crucial point is that such a theory provides an explanation for the modern consumers' apparently insatiable desire for novelty and hence for their ability to experience a continuous series of wants.

Day-dreams and desires

Probably the most common misunderstanding of the thesis is the assumption that consumers day-dream about particular goods, and that desire for these goods is born in the course of such day-dreaming. Now it is quite possible that some wants may be generated in this way. But such a process cannot explain the high valuation placed on novelty, or the process through which desire is perpetually being reborn, and hence was not in fact the thrust of the argument. What was suggested was that individuals day-dream about possible pleasurable experiences and scenarios, ones which are improved versions of the reality they know, these being improved in imagination to the point of near-perfection. It is the imaginative consumption of these self-created, illusory dreams which then generates dissatisfaction with the gratifications that life currently offers, and consequently longing; the latter being defined as a general desire to experience in reality the more nearly perfect experiences already enjoyed in imagination. It is longing which becomes the basis for the generation of the desire for particular novel goods and experiences, for this is essentially a non-specific desire that can become attached to particular goods in a fairly fortuitous fashion. Hence one does not have to day-dream about a specific item in order to desire it, and of course consumers do characteristically 'fall in love' with (i.e. desire) objects that they have never encountered before, and which therefore could not possibly have featured in their day-dreams.

This is not to suggest that the content of a consumer's day-dreams is irrelevant to the nature of the products that are subsequently desired. We know, for example, from research that women's day-dreams frequently involve scenarios in which they themselves figure as glamorous and fashionable objects of attention (Singer, 1966; Wagman, 1967). It is not surprising, therefore, that they should commonly desire new, that is to say more fashionable (i.e. novel), clothes. But the dress that is desired does not have to feature in the day-dream, merely to have 'something about it' (however vague) that triggers an association with the day-dream and hence taps into the longing. Indeed in the day-dream the details of the dress may only be vaguely imagined, for the focus is upon the general impression that wearing it has on others. It is important to note that the pleasure derives less from wearing the dress than from the admiring glances and compliments that it is anticipated will be forthcoming from those who witness it being worn. Thus, with the exception of the more instrumental consumer durables, products are desired less because of their character as material objects than because consumers anticipate their possession will bring pleasurable experiences.

The nature and scope of the theory

A second common misunderstanding concerns the nature and scope of
the thesis. On the one hand, there have been those who have assumed
that it was intended to be a general and universal theory of
consumption, on a par perhaps with neo-classical economics or
Veblen's theory of conspicuous consumption (Campbell, 1995a). On
the other hand, there have been those who have regarded it as no more
than a specific, historical account of the conduct of consumers in
eighteenth-century England, and hence of little relevance to an
understanding of consumerism in other societies at other times
(Howes, 1987). It is therefore important to state that the theory is
neither of these. For it was not my intention to propose a universal
theory of consumption, or indeed to suggest a framework that would
encompass all known features of consumer behaviour. On the other
hand, I do believe that the thesis applies to more than a select group of
eighteenth-century, English, middle-class young ladies.

What should also have been apparent, if only from the title of the
book, was that I was following Weber's example (Weber, 1964) in
making a clear analytic distinction between 'traditional' and 'modern'
economic practices. In *The Protestant Ethic and the Spirit of Capitalism*
(1992), what Weber sets out to explain is the origins of the spirit of
'modern, rational, bourgeois capitalism', and not simply the spirit of
capitalism. In a similar vein, I was attempting to identify the 'spirit' of
what could justifiably be described as 'modern, bourgeois consumerism'. It follows from this that not all features of contemporary
consumer behaviour are *ipso facto* deemed to be 'modern', merely that
the overall pattern constitutes a mixture in which the 'modern' is
considered to predominate. My endeavours were thus not directed at
explaining all aspects of contemporary consumption but at eliciting the
mechanisms which accounted for its distinctly 'modern' dynamic.
Indeed I observed that 'it is not consumption in general which poses
special problems of explanation, so much as that particular pattern
which is characteristic of modern industrial societies' (Campbell, 1987:
39). Significantly, however, the critical adjective 'modern' is missing
from many discussions of the thesis.

One reviewer upbraided me for apparently having little interest in
explaining 'contemporary' consumerism, commenting that I 'had little
to say about our own times' since I concentrated my attention on
cultural changes in England in the eighteenth century (Howes, 1987). In
fact, as I explained in the introduction, my original concern was to
explain cultural change in the 1960s, and it was only because I came to
the conclusion that this was not possible without a detailed understanding of those processes of change that accompanied industrializa-

tion and commercialization that I turned my attention to the eighteenth century. The naïve assumption that what happens in contemporary society cannot possibly be understood by turning to the past not only fails to recognize the nature of the theoretical problem to be resolved, but also embodies the popular conceit that our lives are fundamentally different from those of previous generations.[1]

The terms 'modern' and 'traditional' do not simply refer to a chronological difference in institutions or social and cultural practices. Their usage implies theoretically deduced, analytic concepts. As Weber (among others) observed, modern productive economic practices are marked by rational, calculating attitudes and beliefs, while the nature of this rationality can be deduced from certain fundamental first principles concerning the maximization of utility and the relationship of means to ends. In a similar fashion, modern consumption practices can be deduced from first principles – in this case those relating to the generation of desire and the creation of wants. In neither case, however, is this 'modern' quality of action directly equatable with entire substantive, or concrete, patterns of conduct. There cannot be such a person as a totally modern consumer (or producer) any more than there can be a person who always behaves in a completely rational manner. Such elements of modernity as can be discerned will always be found to coexist with traditional elements in both the productive and consumer sides of the economic equation. Hence it follows that traditional forms of consumer behaviour should not be considered to be entirely extinguished by the revolution that is modernity; rather, modern forms of consumer conduct are 'added to' the traditional ones to constitute the single overall pattern of consumer conduct that prevails in contemporary society.

Consequently, identifying the distinctly modern ingredient in consumer behaviour is quite different from simply describing contemporary consumerism, whatever that might be. It involves a conceptual and theoretical analysis of how consumerism 'works', of what exactly constitutes its dynamic. As outlined above, I attempt to show that this essential dynamic is in the modern consumer's ability to generate endless wants, especially for novel goods. Hence I identify the key problem for social science as the understanding of how desire is continually being created and exhausted. Now my attempted solution to this problem is to suggest that it can be understood in relation to a new form of hedonism, something that I refer to as modern, autonomous, self-illusory hedonism, and which, following Weber's style of argument, I call 'the spirit of modern consumerism'.

Hence there are two critical features of my argument that are frequently glossed over: first, that I address the sociological concept of *modern* consumerism and not the hybrid traditional-modern combination which is contemporary consumerism; and second, that I consider its *spirit* and not the whole economic and material system of which this is but a part. Both these points are specifically highlighted in the argument, and in both I am following Weber very closely; but then his argument has also been widely misunderstood in precisely the same manner.

In addition, of course, I devote a large part of the book to an attempt to explain the cultural developments which made the emergence of modern hedonism possible, developments which I identify largely with the Romantic Movement and which I trace back to Protestantism itself. Comparatively little attention has been paid to this aspect of the thesis, yet to my mind it is in fact the more important, as it presents a theory of cultural change (not, in the first instance, mine but Weber's). The significance of this discussion is that it attempts to explain how autonomous, self-illusory hedonism became an acceptable form of conduct; how it was that the very powerful cultural forces that supported asceticism and branded hedonism as both unethical and evil came to be overcome to such an extent that hedonism itself became equated with morally correct behaviour. An understanding of this process is critical to any adequate explanation of the emergence of modern consumerism.

The role of material factors

Finally I need to note that some commentators feel that such a theory is lacking because insufficient attention is paid to the material basis of consumption, either to 'things' themselves in the form of products offered for sale in the marketplace, or to the nature of the production and distribution processes, or to the material constraints that affect consumers' ability to purchase goods.

Like the previous point, this criticism also follows from a failure to grasp the nature and scope of the theory. Perhaps a general theory of consumption might need to attend to its 'material' basis by paying more attention to these features. Yet there is no good reason to assume that such a materialist perspective can help in explaining the origin of wants, even if it is pertinent to an understanding of the manner and extent to which people are in a position to satisfy them through purchasing goods. It is also true that the thesis really has little to say about the use made of consumer goods. But then what individuals actually do with products once they have purchased them is not germane to the thesis. The only assumption made is that whatever they do will be accompanied by a greater or lesser degree of disillusionment, and consequently that all consumption helps to prepare the ground for renewed desire.

The question of evidence

Discussions of the 'romantic ethic thesis' have often come, as have those concerning Weber's more famous original, to centre on questions of evidence. What evidence is there to support the contention that modern consumerism is based on autonomous, self-illusory hedonism? Is this claim to be regarded as merely speculation, or can it in some sense be considered as a valid interpretation of the behaviour of modern consumers?

There are two ways of approaching this issue. The first, and to my mind the more important, concerns questions of plausibility and theoretical coherence. As suggested above, the whole thrust of the romantic ethic thesis is predicated on the need to resolve the puzzle of modern consumer behaviour. This is the peculiar ability of the modern consumer to generate apparently endless wants for novel goods. The only extant explanations for this phenomenon available when the book was written were (1) traditional economic theory, (2) theories of consumer manipulation, and (3) Veblen's theory of status maintenance and enhancement. What seemed self-evident to me was that only a little reflection was needed to conclude that none of these alternatives offers a plausible account of this phenomenon (Campbell, 1987: 36–57, 1995b). Consequently I concentrated on trying to develop a more plausible and convincing theory to account for the phenomenon of modern consumerism. Therefore, although it is quite correct to insist that all theories should indeed be tested empirically by reference to evidence, in the first instance they should be judged against rival theories, the test being the simple one of deciding which offers the most comprehensive, parsimonious, yet plausible answer to the problem as posed. In this case I would contend that modern, autonomous, self-illusory hedonism meets these requirements, for the simple reason that none of the alternatives on offer provides any explanation for the ability of modern consumerism to generate endless wants for novel goods.

A satisfactory theory contains a statement of the relative significance that should be attached to each identified element, together with a precise specification of how they interact to produce the phenomenon to be explained. This was what I attempted to do in my account of the dynamic interaction between evolving religious teachings and ethical and aesthetic ideals, on the one hand, and people's hedonistic conduct on the other. As far as the former was concerned I was trying to follow Weber first in analysing the immanent processes of development which, in accord with the principle of rationalization, determine the evolution of cultural systems of meaning (Weber, 1964, 1965), and then in showing how this in turn affects the prevailing patterns of motivation and 'practical systems of action' of ordinary people. This meant trying

(1) to understand Puritanism and Romanticism in terms of their own inner logic, and (2) to specify the particular forms of practical ethical and aesthetic action which a commitment to their precepts might be considered to have engendered in those who embraced them. In particular, I was interested in the development of a distinctly romantic ideal of character and the effect that this would have on those actions in which individuals would need to engage in order to convince themselves that they lived up to it. My interest in consumerism is limited to the part played by autonomous hedonism, and it is only in relation to the 'spirit' of the latter that I regard Romanticism as entering into the picture. Indeed, since Romanticism is essentially a moral and ethical movement involving a commitment to a transcendent ideal, I believe that the Romantics were correct to perceive their philosophy as fundamentally opposed to those essentially mundane and utilitarian attitudes which characteristically accompany consumption. I was merely concerned to observe that those self-same Romantics actually aided the emergence of modern consumerism, since their advocacy of a romantic worldview unwittingly served to legitimize autonomous self-illusory hedonism.

However, to stress the importance of judging competing theories in terms of coherence and plausibility is not to suggest that there is no evidence that can be cited in support of the thesis. In the first place, the close association, both in time and place, between modern consumer- ism and Romanticism – especially in the form of Bohemianism – is strongly suggestive of a close association between the two. This, however, is not regarded as sufficient by some critics, and they ask for the evidence that Romantics and modern consumers are the same people. The problem here is that they forget that the link between Romanticism and consumerism is essentially indirect, one mediated by the 'spirit' of modern consumerism, or self-illusory hedonism. The actual thesis has two stages. First there is the connection between Romanticism (or the romantic ethic) and 'autonomous, self-illusory hedonism', and second there is the connection between self-illusory hedonism, or the 'spirit' of modern consumerism, and the practice of modern consumerism itself. Regarding the claims in this light, it is not difficult to find evidence to support both. What is more, the first of the two embraces other phenomena than modern consumerism, such as the rise of romantic love and novel-reading, with the consequence that data of this kind can be invoked in support of the primary contention that Romanticism can be regarded as promoting and legitimating modern, autonomous hedonism. Particularly significant in this respect, yet the subject of comparatively little attention, is the reading revolution that occurred in the eighteenth century. For this effectively marked the transition to a society in which autonomous, self-illusory hedonism became a significant part of the everyday life of a majority of the population.

Silent reading as self-illusory hedonism

As critical as any distinction between literate and non-literate societies or individuals is that between forms of literacy. Traditional literacy typically involved the literate person reading aloud, often to others and while standing. This oral, communal, literate tradition survives today in the public readings that are part of most church services. As in this example, the written material was often familiar both to the reader and to his or her audience, having been read many times before, and was generally instructional or improving in character. By the eighteenth century, however, a new form of reading was developing. This was silent reading, and the reader usually sat, alone, immobile and thoughtful, absorbed in the book. This was more likely to be a novel than anything educational or instructional, and was typically read only once before being replaced by another and similar work. Consequently this newer, individual and essentially silent, and hence covert, mode of reading was closely linked with reading for pleasure.

In fact such activity is necessarily creative. For as Tinker says of novel reading, 'what any reader derives from the printed page is not exactly what the author had in mind, but to a certain degree at least a personal recreation on the part of the reader' (Tinker, 1965: 5). Lubbock endorses this view by noting that the reader of a novel is himself (or more probably herself) a novelist (Lubbock, 1957: 41), while Escarpit observes that 'When we hold a book in our hands all we hold is paper, the book is elsewhere' (Escarpit, 1966: 17). These remarks make it clear that the rise of the novel and the reading revolution with which it was intimately associated heralded the arrival of autonomous, self-illusory hedonism, or the practice of using one's imagination to construct illusory scenarios for covert and pleasurable consumption. Whether this end is achieved by means of words printed on a page or not is unimportant; for such an ability, once developed, does not need such props in order to be employed.

The historical record reveals that the new practice of novel-reading was credited with causing revolutionary changes in the conduct of the middle-class young ladies who were the principal consumers. As one might expect, novels were held to affect the morals of such young ladies adversely. More interestingly, there was also a common complaint that it made them dissatisfied with life. As an eighteenth-century German writer complained:

> the reader fills his or her soul with a host of overheated, fanciful, romantic ideas that cannot be realized in this sublunary world, learns

about the world not from the world itself but from books, dreams of a world not as it is but as it should be, judges human beings not according to the actual history of humanity but according to fictional stories of the world of novels; such reading produces a creature who is always dissatisfied with the creator and his creation.

(Harbsmeier, 1989: 9)

Here we have an excellent description of that attitude of longing and consequent dissatisfaction with life that characterizes the self-illusory hedonist. So it is no surprise to learn that these young ladies, in addition to their addiction to novel-reading and romantic love, were also the first generation of truly modern consumers, eager for the novel and enthusiastic about fashion.

Hedonistic consumption and moral values

The last question to be posed is whether this hedonistic theory of consumerism carries with it any implied evaluation of the modern world. Does the suggestion that modern consumers tend to relate to goods via the critical mediating process of day-dreaming and longing contain an implicit valuation of this mode of consuming? Some commentators seem to believe it does, and have judged my account to reveal an essentially pessimistic outlook, one that sees modern consumerism as prefiguring the unrestrained subjectivism and relativism of a postmodern society (Taylor, 1988). This conclusion is reached on the assumption not merely that day-dreaming is unhealthy but that a lifetime of disillusioning consumption is hardly an attractive or worthwhile prospect. Other critics, however, have discerned a very different message in the book and have accused me of 'celebrating' contemporary consumerism; that is, of giving legitimacy to a lifetime spent in the pursuit of material goods.

A careful reading of the argument should reveal that I endorse neither position. It may be true that modern consumerism embodies an illusory hedonism, but I did not claim that this was true of modern society as a whole. On the contrary, I claimed that a very different principle was embodied in the fields of science, technology and the productive side of the economy. Here the values of rationality, efficiency and empiricism generally dominate. Indeed I suggested that the very dynamic of modern society rests on the dialectic between these two spheres, a dialectic experienced by the individual, to use Freud's terms, as a conflict between the pleasure and the reality principles.

As for the question of whether my portrayal of modern consumerism is essentially optimistic or pessimistic, there can be no simple answer. This is because hedonism, like most human activities, can serve either to diminish or to enhance human life. It certainly does not necessarily follow that, because pleasure-seeking plays such an important part in the consumption activity of individuals, this means there cannot be an idealistic or ethical dimension present. After all, although people's day-dreams differ, a common factor, apart from the quality of pleasure, is the representation of the dreamer as an idealized person. Thus the pleasure that people derive from these imaginings is not separate from their moral life – it is intimately associated with it. 'Doing good', or, more accurately perhaps, imagining oneself 'doing good' and 'being good', often constitutes an important part of the pleasures of day-dreaming. In this respect the pleasures associated with imagining 'perfected' scenarios relate directly to imagining oneself as a 'perfected' person, exemplifying certain ideals. It follows from this that I believe that it is deeply misleading to see contemporary society as 'materialistic' or 'acquisitive' in character, or to blame 'consumerism' – as some churchmen and politicians have done – for an apparent decline in spirituality. Whether there has indeed been such a decline (as opposed to a decline in overt religiosity) is a complex and debatable issue. But I am convinced that it is a mistake to see modern consumerism as in some way fundamentally opposed to spirituality. For, since it is essentially a dream that drives people to acquire and to prize material goods – the dream of having more perfect experiences – it is not separate from, but rather part of, the dream of a better world (Campbell, 1994).

Note

1   It is a mistake to treat the problem of understanding modernity as different from that of understanding the emergence of modernity. These are not essentially different problems. What is more, there are good grounds for believing that the characteristics of modernity are more clearly discernible when they first appear than they are subsequently. This is because the emergence of a new set of attitudes and behaviours naturally arouses much comment and debate – one could say that they are noticed and commented on – while once they have become a taken-for-granted part of a way of life they cease to be the subject of comment and debate. Hence the historical record may reveal the essential nature of modernity more clearly than does the contemporary record. This I believe to be true of modern consumerism.

Bibliography

Arnould, Eric J. (1989) 'Review', *Journal of Marketing*, 53, 131–3.
Banks, Glyn and Vowles, Hannah (1989) 'Romantic consumerism', *Building Design*, November, 17, 28–41.
Belk, Russell (1989) 'Review', *Journal of Consumer Research*, 16, 1–3.

Brewer, John and Porter, Roy (1993) (eds) *Consumption and the World of Goods*, London: Routledge.

Campbell, Colin (1987) *The Romantic Ethic and the Spirit of Modern Consumerism*, Oxford: Blackwell.

Campbell, Colin (1992) 'The desire for the new: its nature and social location as presented in theories of fashion and modern consumerism', in Roger Silverman and Eric Hirsch (eds), *Consuming Technologies: Media and Information in Domestic Spaces*, London: Routledge.

Campbell, Colin (1994) 'Consuming goods and the good of consumption', *Critical Review*, 8 (4), 503–20.

Campbell, Colin (1995a) 'Romanticism, introspection and consumption: some comments on Professor Holbrook's paper', in Russell W. Belk, Nikhilesh Dholakia and Alladi Venkatesh (eds), *Consumption and Marketing: Macro Dimensions*, Cincinnati: South-Western College Publishing.

Campbell, Colin (1995b) 'Conspicuous confusion? A critique of Veblen's theory of conspicuous consumption', *Sociological Theory*, 13 (1), 37–47.

Christensen, Jerome (1993) *Lord Byron's Strength: Romantic Writing and Commercial Society*, Baltimore: Johns Hopkins University Press.

Escarpit, Robert (1966) *The Book Revolution*, Oxford: Blackwell.

Harbsmeier, Michael (1989) 'Consumption and cosmologies: some notes on travel accounts and the reading revolution in late 18th century Germany', paper presented at the Fifth International Conference on Consumption, Copenhagen.

Howes, Graham (1987) 'Go out and buy', *Financial Times*, 5 September, p. 7.

Lubbock, Percy (1957) *The Craft of Fiction*, Oxford: Oxford University Press.

Rudmin, Floyd W. (1991) (ed.) *To Have Possessions: A Handbook on Ownership and Property*, Santa Barbara, CA: Select Press.

Singer, J.L. (1966) *Daydreaming*, New York: Random House.

Taylor, Keith (1988) 'Review', *Political Quarterly*, 59 (1): 120–2.

Tinker, M.A. (1965) *The Basis for Effective Reading*, Minneapolis: Minnesota University Press.

Wagman, Morton (1967) 'Sex differences in types of daydreams', *Journal of Personality and Social Psychology*, 7 (3), 329–32.

Weatherill, Lorna (1989) 'Review', *Journal of Historical Geography*, 15, 438–9.

Weber, Max (1964) *The Theory of Social and Economic Organization*, trans. A.M. Henderson and Talcott Parsons, ed. and intro. Talcott Parsons, New York: Free Press.

Weber, Max (1965) *The Sociology of Religion*, trans. Ephraim Fischoff, intro. Talcott Parsons, London: Methuen.

Weber, Max (1992) *The Protestant Ethic and the Spirit of Capitalism*, translated by Talcott Parsons, London: Routledge.

4

Historical semantics and material culture

CHRISTIAN J. KAY

Introduction

Scholars working in linguistics, including historical linguistics, have long been interested in ways in which the study of language can throw light on the development of culture. At the most obvious level, those words of a language which refer to the material environment of its speakers are part of the evidence for that environment. Thus the occurrence of words such as *biggin* (child's cap, night cap), *blue-cap*, *bonnet*, *cap*, *cockle hat* (as worn by pilgrims), *corner-cap* (square or triangular hat worn by clerics), *Monmouth cap* (worn by soldiers and sailors), and *porringer* (with jocular reference to the shape of the hat) in the plays of Shakespeare would be of interest to anyone studying the clothing, and particularly the headgear, of that period (Spevack, 1993: 46–7).

More subtly, linguistic evidence may be adduced to support general claims about the nature of a society. The classic approach here is that of the so-called Sapir–Whorf hypothesis, which holds that a link exists between the structures and vocabulary of a language and the worldview of those who speak it. In its strongest form, the claim is that the worldview is actually determined by language. Thus, the selection of *he* as a generic pronoun in English could, at least until recently, be said not only to reflect but to perpetuate the dominance of the male in English-speaking cultures. Writing on culture and archaeological analysis, Tilley seems to take just such a strong view when he says: 'The individual does not so much construct material culture or language, but is constructed through them' (Tilley, 1989: 189). A weaker and more generally accepted version of the hypothesis, in linguistics at least, claims that a language will reflect the interests and preoccupations of its speakers.[1]

This latter claim is particularly persuasive in the study of vocabulary. Areas of life which are important to a culture, or to subsections of it, will be highly lexicalized; that is, there will be words or phrases available to describe many aspects of those areas, and to make fine distinctions of meaning. Examples for recent English are to be found in the growth of terminologies for space travel, computing or the media; thus the words *software, bootstrap, toggle* (in the computing sense) and *email* are all recorded in the *Oxford English Dictionary* as first appearing in the written language after 1950. Tracing the origins of such words can throw further light on their cultural implications. They may be borrowed from a foreign language and used largely in reference to the source culture, as with *cosmonaut*, generally used of Russian space-travellers. More commonly in the fields mentioned, they may come into British English from American English, the dominant culture of the technology, as with *soap opera* or *game show*. They may be formed from elements already available in the language, whether native or borrowed, as with *spaceman, moonwalk* or *astronaut*, or they may be extensions of meaning of existing words, as in the computer's metaphorical *mouse, menus, bugs* and *housekeeping*. As the words are used by increasing numbers of speakers, some will pass from technical terminologies into general use, as *interface* or *going into orbit* or *to nuke* have done, often developing more abstract meanings in the process. Conversely, terminologies which are no longer of general concern will go into retreat, becoming known only to the involved or historically minded few, as has happened to the agricultural terminologies of a more rural British society.

The nature of the evidence

The relationship between words and things has long been a controversial one in theoretical semantics, even where words refer to objects and artefacts in the material universe.[2] Words are more than simply names or labels for objects; they are a cognitive phenomenon, the means by which we organize our perceptions into manageable types and categories. The criteria by which such categories are established have been of interest in anthropological linguistics and are a main concern of psycholinguistics and cognitive semantics.[3] Inevitably, given the nature of experience and the numerous occasions on which most words are used, the meanings of individual words and the boundaries between categories may be unclear. Everyone with normal perceptual apparatus can presumably distinguish the creatures referred to by words such as *cat, dog* and *elephant*, and hence agree on the meanings of these words, but we may well be less certain of the boundaries between *cup/mug, rain/drizzle, green/blue* or, more subjectively, *tall/ short* or *rich/poor*. Equally, the identification and definition of such apparently straightforward terms as *bun, cookie, roll, scone, crumpet* and *pancake* will vary widely among speakers of different varieties of English. In such cases, meanings will be constructed by interaction among subsets of speakers.

When problems of definition arise, the native speaker of a language has a reference point in his or her own usage, or can interrogate the usage of others. Informants will also be available to the linguist or anthropologist investigating a living foreign language. The historical semanticist is less privileged, and must instead depend on written texts to supply information about the meanings of words. Such texts, especially those for the early stages of a language with a relatively long written record, such as English, share many of the problems of more tangible objects descending to us by hazardous routes from the past. A manuscript may have been physically damaged or left incomplete by some accident of history. Meanings may be unclear because of obscure contexts or simple illegibility. A surviving text may be generations removed from its originator, copied by scribes who have misunderstood elements of its language or deliberately changed them in order to update or relocalize the text. Such alterations may well be interesting in themselves, but add extra layers of complexity to attempts to pinpoint the meaning of a word at a particular period of time. If a word is common, then cumulative evidence may allow a fair degree of certainty about its meaning; for less common words attribution of meaning may remain speculative.

Texts, then, like fabrics or pottery, are vulnerable objects, and our knowledge of the vocabulary of past periods is necessarily skewed and incomplete. In addition to texts that are damaged, there will be many that have disappeared entirely over the years, or survive only as references in other texts. Furthermore, for most of the history of English, the texts that survive focus on the concerns of powerful and literate groups, increasingly small in membership the further we go back into the past, rather than on the life of society as a whole. About 50,000 meanings (that is, senses as opposed to word forms, since many forms have more than one meaning) remain to us from the Old English of the pre-Conquest period, far fewer than in the average modern desk dictionary.[4] Although the vocabulary of Old English was undoubtedly much smaller than that of modern English, which has grown rapidly in response to socio-cultural changes and pressures from other languages, a good deal of Old English must have been lost. The record is further skewed by the fact that many of the surviving texts are poetic, describing feats of secular or religious heroism rather than the activities of everyday life.

To all this must be added the caveat that literary works do not necessarily refer to the contemporary scene but may be displaced texts describing societies distant in time or space. The browser in Marvin Spevack's *A Shakespeare Thesaurus*, for example, would find in addition to the 'headgear' terms mentioned above a section entitled 'mantle' and containing the words *toga* and *toged* (Spevack, 1993: 46), but only the most naïve would assume that the toga was an acceptable form of dress in Renaissance England.

The study of vocabulary

Despite these restrictions, vocabulary is still a rich resource for students of culture, and one which can both inform and be informed by related disciplines such as history, archaeology and sociology. Roberts writes:

> Archaeology reveals a silent past, and it is notoriously hard to match the words that remain to the artefacts removed from the earth. Yet, just as archaeologists build up from things an interpretation of the past, treating the things as a code or language, so too it is possible to look at a picture put together from the words of a thousand years ago.
>
> (Roberts, 1993: 185)

The lexicon of a language will reflect both external pressures on that language and the physical, social and intellectual concerns of its speakers. A classic example of the former is the influx of French words into English after the Norman Conquest of 1066, when English was temporarily overtaken by French as the language of power and government. In addition to the replacement of large numbers of words in fields such as law, social class and religion, French words such as *mutton, beef, veal* and *pork* were added to English to refer to meat on the table, while the native words *sheep, ox/cow, calf* and *swine* remained to describe the live animals (Baugh and Cable, 1978: 180). Such evidence reinforces what we know from other sources about the relative status of Normans and Anglo-Saxons at the time: the discussion of delicacies on the table belonged largely to the former, while the tending of livestock remained with the latter. As an example of intellectual concerns affecting vocabulary, it is interesting to note that crusading vegetarians are nowadays reversing this change, using *(dead) cow, sheep*, etc., for the meat of the animal in conversation with *carnivores* (itself a word transferred pejoratively in general use to human beings), and thus presumably drawing attention to the barbarity of eating these creatures.

An extended example of how dictionary evidence may be used in the study of material objects is provided by Alexander Fenton in a discussion of the structure of kilns in various parts of Scotland, both Scots and Gaelic speaking. He writes:

> Dictionaries must always be used critically, but if this is done, the

chronological and spatial dimensions of some aspect of the human social or cultural fabric will readily appear from dictionary entries, given that the sources have been adequate, and can be set in comparative relationship with data from the dictionaries of other areas and other countries. The historical skeleton thus obtained can be mounted and its joints provisionally strung together, and the flesh filled in through non-linguistic methods of investigation.

(Fenton, 1974: 257)

Thus, the investigator will start with the words of the language, preferably dated and localized, but will draw on whatever else is available, whether archaeological remains or objects in museums or pictorial evidence or reports in other languages, in order to establish meanings. Because the evidence is patchy, historical semantics must necessarily be interdisciplinary in its approach. Biggam makes this point when she attempts to reconstruct the information used by an Anglo-Saxon scholar to identify a plant called *Britannica* in his Latin original:

He must have made his identification of the plant from some or all of the following points of information in his source text: the cures which it is said to effect, the instructions on how to collect, store, and use it in these cures, a list of its names in several languages, and an illustration.

She goes on to use this knowledge, and modern botanical knowledge, in an effort to adjudicate between rival identifications (Biggam, 1994: 618).

The Oxford English Dictionary

Apart from texts themselves, the primary source of information about the development of the English lexicon is the monumental *Oxford English Dictionary on Historical Principles* (OED), compiled under the editorship of James Murray and published between 1884 and 1928. This dictionary was subsequently updated by supplementary volumes and is now available either in an integrated paper copy or on CD-ROM, which immensely increases its ease of use in extended research. In order to create the dictionary, volunteer readers worked their way through manuscripts and printed texts, providing the editors with slips containing examples of words in context, which in turn formed the basis of the definitions.[5] The resultant volumes offer the reader fascinating histories of individual words, arranged chronologically and illustrated by quotations, which themselves often give intriguing glimpses of distant lives. Thus, if one looks up the word *girl* in the OED, one finds that its first meaning, recorded between around 1290 and 1450, is:

1. A child or young person of either sex, a youth or maiden. Chiefly in *pl.*: Children, young people. **knave girl**: a boy. **gay girl**: applied to a young woman. *Obs.*

The second meaning, beginning in 1530, is more familiar to us:

2. a. A female child; commonly applied to all young unmarried women.

Further developments are indicative of the status of women in society, and follow common semantic pathways for words of this meaning, such as *mistress, hussy* (from *housewife*) and *woman* itself:

old girl: Applied *colloq.* to a woman at any time of life, either disrespectfully or (occas.) as an endearing term of address, spec. one's mother or wife; also, a former pupil of a girls' school or college; also attrib. similarly, to a mare, etc.
b. A maid-servant. Also in *girl-of-all-work*.

The illustrative quotation here from Pepys's *Diary* perhaps gives some idea of the status of such girls:

1668 Pepys *Diary* 24 Aug., My wife is upon hanging the long chamber, where the girl lies, with the sad stuff that was in the best chamber.

c. A sweetheart, lady-love. Also (*U.S. colloq.* or *slang*) **best girl**. Similarly, one's wife.
d. († More fully, *a girl about* or *of the town, a girl of ease*): a prostitute. † a kind girl: a mistress.
e. A black woman. *U.S. colloq. Obs.*
1835 J. H. Ingraham *South-West* II. 242 They always address them [*sc.* the slaves] as 'boy' and 'girl', to all under forty years of age.

There is thus considerable social as well as semantic information available in the OED. There is also an extra layer of meaning here because many of the definitions were written in the nineteenth or early twentieth centuries, and reflect the attitudes of that period, as perhaps with sense 3 of *hussy*:

In some rural districts a mere equivalent of Woman, lass; hence, A strong country woman, a female of the lower orders; a woman of low or improper behaviour, or of light or worthless character; an ill-behaved, pert, or mischievous girl; a jade, minx. Also jocularly or in raillery.
The bad sense was at first mostly with qualification (*light*, etc.), or contextual.

The OED can be equally informative about the histories of material objects. The words *bonnet* and *cap* were mentioned above as occurring in the writings of Shakespeare, but it would be foolish to assume that they occur there with the meanings which they would have had for Jane Austen two hundred years later, or would have for a working man today. Although the form of a word may remain relatively constant, its meaning may change in line with changes in the object it refers to. The relevant meanings of *bonnet* are:

BONNET
1. An article of apparel for the head; 'a covering for the head, a hat, a cap'. (Johnson.)
a. A head-dress of men and boys; usually soft, and distinguished from the *hat* by want of a brim. In England, superseded in common use (app. before 1700) by *cap*, but retained in Scotland; hence sometimes treated as = 'Scotch cap'.

. . .

d. A head-dress of women out of doors; distinguished from a *hat* (at present) mainly by the want of a brim, and by its covering no part of the forehead.

Both meanings were current in Shakespeare's time, but the first is more common and is the one attributed to him by the OED (though one would need a Shakespeare concordance and reference to the texts to be sure that he did not use the second as well). If one were seriously interested in headgear, one would, of course, also need to consult surviving caps and bonnets, pictures, etc., and look at the written references more fully. The OED's definition of the key features of a bonnet 'at present' (the fascicle containing the word was published in 1887) is contradicted by a roughly contemporary citation:

1881 Grant White *Eng. Without & W.* ii. 55 A bonnet has strings, I believe, and a hat has not.

There is scope for further research based on evidence of this kind.
The word *cap* has in fact a more complex history than *bonnet*, having followed a circular route from an item of headgear to something resembling a cape in Latin to a variety of English headgear meanings:

CAP
I. A covering for the head.
1. A hood, a covering for the head. (Precise sense not definable; in first quot. still in Latin form.)
2. A cloak with a hood; a cape or cope. (But prob. *cappa* here is really Latin, and not OE.)
3. A head-dress for women, varying according to fashion and taste. In later times a light covering of muslin, or the like, for the head, ordinarily worn indoors, or under a bonnet. Cf. mob-cap.
4. a. A head-dress of men and boys: commonly applied to every kind of ordinary male head-dress which is not called a 'hat', from which it is distinguished by not having a brim, and by being usually of some soft material; also to a number of official, professional, and special head-dresses.

There are quotations from Shakespeare under senses 3 and 4a which

readily distinguish the gender of the wearer. The caveats under senses 1
and 2 show the problems of dealing with early material, where it is not
clear whether the words are 'really English', or whether Anglo-Saxons
actually wore these objects. Owen-Crocker lists them in her glossary of
clothing terms, but remarks that they may be restricted to ecclesiastical
use (Owen-Crocker, 1986: 207). In the body of her text, she endeavours
to reconstruct what Anglo-Saxons may actually have worn, using the
evidence of grave goods, illustrations, etc., as well as linguistic evidence
(1986: 51–3, 81–2, 102–3). A similar range of types of evidence is used by
Hagen in her discussion of Anglo-Saxon food production (Hagen, 1992).

Problems of metalanguage

'Words, words. They're all we have to go on' laments Guildenstern in
Tom Stoppard's play *Rosencrantz and Guildenstern Are Dead*
(Stoppard, 1967: 30). As we have seen, for the historical semanticist
this is not the case: there are other sources of evidence to draw on,
albeit often equally problematic. However, whatever discipline we
follow, the problem remains that words are our only serious tool for
describing the results of our investigations. To quote Fenton again:

> Words and language occupy with right a main position in historical
> research, for by their means the accumulation and transmission of
> knowledge is made possible, and without them each generation would
> be faced with the new creation of a great part of its social fabric.
>
> (Fenton, 1974: 257)

Words are equally important in describing the social fabric of past
generations, but the fuzziness of meanings and categories mentioned
above is similarly an issue when we try to apply words to the
description of unfamiliar objects from the past. Pearce recognizes this
when she writes:

> Imagine trying to describe the difference between two shirts, similar in
> cut and each in two different shades of blue, or between the appearance
> of two different types of box files, or the design of a flower pattern on
> curtain material. We are all acutely aware how inadequate language is to
> encompass this kind of detailed materiality and how frustrating it is to
> try and make it serve the purpose. We also know that one glance at the
> actual object will solve the problem and create immediate under-
> standing, because we are capable of making fine perceptual differences
> between one object and another. This quality of material discrimination,
> presumably a combination of eye, sometimes hand, and culture stored in
> the memory, is immensely significant in the construction of the social
> world.
>
> (Pearce, 1992: 22)

It is only when objects are sufficiently valued in a society to be frequently discussed and referred to that detailed terminologies will emerge, although they may remain at the level of phrases rather than single words, as in Pearce's examples of museum terminology, ' "razor Type 3b" (for a Bronze Age piece of uncertain contemporary function) or "with urn-shaped baluster stem with gadrooning" (for silver ware)' (Pearce, 1992: 123).

Even with precise descriptors of this kind, problems of metalanguage remain unless such everyday words as 'stem' and 'razor' are rigorously defined within their museum context and agreed by all who apply them. The problem becomes even more acute when words are used to define words. Dictionaries are notorious for the circularity of their metalanguage of definition, and it could hardly be otherwise if they remain within the bounds of natural language. In the 'headgear' examples given above, for instance, *caps* are defined as *hats* and *bonnets, bonnets* as *hats* and *caps*, although periphrastic definitions are also attempted. One solution to this problem is the use of illustrations to replace language as the mediator between object and concept. However, this is hardly a practical solution for any extensive historical work, and will be less than helpful where meanings are uncertain. An alternative is the creation of an artificial metalanguage which can be ring-fenced like the terminologies of other disciplines so that meanings are agreed and constant. Attempts have been made to devise such metalanguages, notably by anthropological linguists faced with recording fine distinctions of meaning in languages and cultures which differ significantly from their own. A focus of interest in such work is often kinship terminology, which is crucial to the understanding of a society. The approach is generally to reduce words to their essential features of meaning, often referred to as 'components', which are criterial in distinguishing the meaning of one word from that of another. Thus Eugene Nida writes:

> The meaning of *father* contrasts with that of *mother* in that *father* is male and *mother* is female. Also, the meaning of *father* contrasts with those of *son* and *grandfather* in referring to a different generation, though it shares with *son* and *grandfather* the component of male sex ... We may thus define this meaning of *father* as consisting of three 'diagnostic' components ...: male sex, one ascending generation above ego, and direct line of descent. But this meaning can be known only by means of contrast with the meanings of words that share certain components with *father* but diverge from the meaning of *father* with respect to other components.
>
> (Nida, 1975: 33)

Procedures like these can be successful in analysing limited domains of language, and can produce taxonomies which are comparable to those used in classifying material objects, but their extension into more general areas of meaning has proved difficult. This is a problem to which there is no real solution.

Dictionaries and thesauri

One important point made by Nida is that words can best be studied in conjunction with the study of other words of related meaning. In order to do this, one requires not an alphabetically organized dictionary, however admirable, but a conceptually or semantically organized word-book – in other words a thesaurus. The purpose of a thesaurus, such as Roget's well-known *Thesaurus of English Words and Phrases* (Roget, 1852), is to display words in categories of related meanings, and the editors of such volumes will often claim that by so doing they cast light on socio-cultural factors. Spevack, for example, writes that the aim of his Shakespeare thesaurus 'is to mirror the world which is to be derived from Shakespeare's idiolect, as well as to give an impression of the surrounding contemporary world since Shakespeare accounts for almost half of the recorded words of his time' (Spevack, 1993: i). In similar vein, Fenton writes in his introduction to *The Scots Thesaurus*:

> In essence, the *Thesaurus* is a national culture in a nutshell. In particular, it encourages investigation not only into the individual themes, which is useful enough in itself, but also into the linkages between the various elements of that culture. It presents a picture of a world already becoming lost.
>
> (Macleod, 1990: xiv)

If such claims are true, and I would argue that they are, then a thesaurus of the Roget type holds considerable interest for historians as well as for linguists and stylisticians. Roget itself, which is re-edited and reprinted at regular intervals, yields much information of social interest. Between the 1962 and 1982 editions, for example, we may note that the heading for category 371 was changed from 'Mankind' to 'Humankind', and that the expression *male chauvinist pig* made its first appearance. If we look more closely at category 373, 'Female', in the 1962 and 1987 editions, we may see social trends in the new words and in those that are omitted, some of which I have italicized in the examples below (underlined words are italic in the original).

373. Female (1962)
woman, Eve, she; petticoat, skirt; girl, girlie; virgin, maiden; nun, unmarried woman, old maid 895n. spinster; co-ed, *undergraduette*; bachelor girl, *new woman*, career w., suffragette; bride, matron, dowager, married woman, wife, squaw 894n. spouse; mother, grand-mother, 169n. parent; wench, lass, nymph; lady, burd; filly 132n.

youngster; grisette, midinette; blonde, brunette, platinum blonde; sweetheart, bird 887n. <u>loved one</u>; moll, doll, bit of fluff, broad, mistress, courtesan 952n. <u>loose woman</u>.

373 Female (1987)

woman, Eve, she; girl, *little g.*, *young g.*, 132 youngster; virgin, maiden; nun, unmarried woman, old maid 895 <u>spinster</u>, bachelor girl, career woman; *feminist, sister, women's libber, bra burner,* suffragette; bride, married woman, wife, *'trouble and strife'*, woman, live-in, squaw, widow, matron 894 <u>spouse</u>; dowager 133 <u>old woman</u>; mother, grand-mother 169 <u>maternity</u>; *unmarried mother, working wife or mother, superwoman,* housewife; aunt, *auntie,* niece, sister, daughter, wench, lass, *lassie,* nymph; *colleen,* damsel; petticoat, skirt, doll, *chick,* bird; *honey, hinny, baby*; grisette, midinette; brunette, blonde, platinum b., redhead; girl friend, sweetheart 887 <u>loved one</u>; moll, *bint, crumpet,* bit of fluff; broad, courtesan 952 <u>loose woman</u>

One striking point here is the addition of various terms for different types of women, such as *working wife* or *superwoman*, and the disappearance of a few such as *undergraduette*, with its virtually obsolete suffix, and *new woman*, presumably no longer new. Another is the addition of words for liberated women, although this is balanced by the addition of *chick, bint* and *crumpet* to the earlier *petticoat* and *skirt*.

The Historical Thesaurus of English

Thesauri for particular periods or varieties of the language are likewise of interest, both intrinsically and for comparative purposes. It is, for instance, interesting to compare Shakespeare's colour terms (Spevack, 1993: 54–5) with the medieval terms in the Chaucer inventory compiled by C.P. Biggam (Biggam, 1993) or the listing in *A Thesaurus of Old English* (Roberts and Kay, 1995: 144–7), if only to note the degree to which this category has expanded in line with the increased sophistication of material culture, for example in dyeing techniques. Similarly, listings of words, even in isolation from their contexts, can be used to illuminate aspects of life in a past period. Roberts, for example, lists terms for musical instruments, playthings, burial practices, ships, crafts, armour, weapons and domestic implements, and relates these to the material objects of the Sutton Hoo ship burial and to practices described in literary and other sources (Roberts, 1992).

As yet, there is no historical thesaurus for the English language as a whole, but such a work is in preparation in the English Language Department at Glasgow University (Figure 4.1).[6] The *Historical Thesaurus of English* contains comprehensive, semantically organized lists of words recorded in English, including obsolete words, with their dates of use. It is based on data from the OED, supplemented by Old English materials prepared by Jane Roberts at King's College London (Roberts, 1992: 185, 192). The words are arranged hierarchically in a detailed taxonomy of meaning, and chronologically within each section, thus allowing the user to see the range of expressions for a given object or idea at any period of the language.

A sample of words for *sausage* is given below. The category comes from the very large section on food, which contains over 13,000 meanings in all. Each word is followed by its first date of use as recorded in the OED, and, as appropriate, its last date, or a dash to indicate currency up to the present, and any restrictive labels such as *slang* or *Scots* (not included in this sample). All Old English words are simply designated 'OE'. The dots in the subcategories represent the subordination of a category to one above it in the hierarchy. It should be noted that this sample may well be incomplete; we are saving until the last editorial stages any new words or words which have been redirected from other categories since this section was keyed in. (The structure of the classification is more fully described in Kay, 1994b.)

SAUSAGE

gehæcca OE; mearg OE; pudding c1305–1819; saucister 1347–1483; pot c1450 + 1777–; sauserling 1475 + c1570; sausage a1500–1650–; ising c1550–1706; gigot 1553 + 1656; gut-pudding 1697–1722; jegget 1736; pud 1828; dogs 1925–; snag 1941–; smallgoods 1969–; (**.division in chain of sausages**); link c1440–; link-hide 1895; link-meat 1895; links of love 1942–; (**.types of sausage**); herbelade c1390–a1500; franchemyle c1420–1483; haggis c1420–; livering c1460–1694; blooding c1460–1783; black(-)pudding 1568–; blood-pudding 1583–; Bologna(n) sausage 1596–; bloodling 1598; andouille 1605–1796; cervelat 1613–; mortadella 1613–; hog's pudding 1614–; swine's pudding 1647; blacking 1674; whiting 1674; hackin(g) 1674–1878; saucisson 1760/72–; Oxford sausage 1764–; polony sausage 1764–; white pudding a1800–; white hass/hawse 1818–; black-pot 1825–; German sausage 1837–; saveloy 1837–; Cambridge sausage 1840–; polony a1845–; boudin 1845–; chorizo 1846–; bologna 1850–; salame/salami 1852–; station-jack 1853; leberwurst 1855–; liver sausage 1855–; w(o)urst/worsht 1855–; blutwurst 1856–; bag(s) of mystery 1864–; blood-sausage 1868–; liverwurst 1869–; chipolata (sausage) 1877–; erbswurst 1885–; wienerwurst 1889–; red-hot 1892–; summer sausage 1893–; frankfurter 1894–; mettwurst 1895–; wiener 1904–; garlic sausage 1905–; weeny 1906–; hamburger 1908–; bratwurst 1911–; wienie 1911–; mealy pudding 1914–; banger 1919–; thuringer 1933–; pep(p)eroni 1934–; frank 1936–; kishke 1936–; sav 1936–; fish sausage 1937–; cocktail sausage c1938–; knackwurst 1939–; starver 1941–; boer(e)wors 1948–; kielbasa 1953–; Vienna sausage 1958–; tube steak 1963–; vienna 1963–; weisswurst 1963–; soya link 1965–; weiner 1965–; tripe sausage 1966–; schinkenwurst 1967–; soya sausage 1971–.

It will be apparent from the above that sausages of one kind or another have long formed an important part of the diet of English speakers, though the word itself, borrowed from French, is not recorded until the fifteenth century. John Ayto writes:

> The Romans introduced into northern and western Europe the cylindrical sausage of spiced minced meat stuffed into a skin of animal intestine ... This is the dry sausage (the French *saucisson*), often known in Britain as 'continental sausage' or, in the nineteenth century, 'German sausage' ... The wet sausage, however (the French *saucisse*, the sort that needs to be cooked), has become so much a part of the baggage of national sentiment that we use it as a term of endearment, as in 'You silly old sausage!'. Also, another sure sign of affection, it has several colloquial synonyms.
>
> (Ayto, 1993: 311)

The last point is amply demonstrated by the list above, as is the increasing contact over the centuries of English speakers with people from other cultures.

Equally striking is the shorter list of words for gin, taken from the 4500 words in the 'Drink' section. Although a relatively late import from Holland, gin 'caught on very quickly in England' (Ayto, 1993: 144), as the number of picturesque slang (*sl*) terms attests:

GIN
diddle c1700–1858 *sl*; geneva 1706–; gin 1714–; strike-fire 1725 *sl*; tittery 1725–1751 *sl*; royal bob 1729–1770; strip-me-naked 1751 *sl*; sky-blue 1755–1796 *sl*; lightning 1781–1851 *sl*; jacky 1799–1832 *sl*; max 1811–1851; daffy 1821– *sl*; ribbon 1823–; sweet-stuff 1835; bottled lightning 1839; (white) satin 1845– *sl*; tiger's milk 1850 *sl*; juniper 1857 *sl*; cream of the valley 1858; eye-water 1869– *sl*; cream of the wilderness 1873; twankay 1900 *sl*; mother's ruin 1937– *sl*; panther 1942–.[7]

Classification

It will, I hope, be evident from the above that the *Historical Thesaurus* is a potentially rich resource for historians of culture as well as for historians of the English language. One contentious issue, however, remains: that of classification. The categories chosen for illustration are relatively uncontentious, and can readily be related to real-world objects. It is likely that anyone faced with an array of food items, or the terms used for them in English, would come up with a category of sausages, although some might argue that such noble dishes as the haggis or the black pudding deserve better than to be dumped into this category. Extra subcategories can always be set up at the lower end of a

Section I The External World	Section II The Mind (in progress)
(largely complete)	1 Mental processes
1 The Earth	2 Emotion
2 Life	3 Good or bad opinion
3 Sensation and perception	4 Aesthetic opinion
4 Matter	5 Will
5 Existence	6 Endeavour
6 Relative properties	7 Language
7 The supernatural	8 Possession

Section III Society (largely complete)
1 Social groups
2 Habitation
3 War
4 Government
5 Law
6 Education
7 Religion
8 Communication
9 Travel and transport
10 Work
11 Leisure

Figure 4.1 *The* Historical Thesaurus of English: *summary of classification (Department of English Language, University of Glasgow, revised 1995)*

taxonomy to deal with words of very specific meaning should their number justify it.

Few categories, however, are as clear-cut as these. As previous discussion has indicated, even a category as obviously rooted in the material world as 'Clothing' has problems of indeterminacy of meaning and therefore of classification. Does one, for instance, try to distinguish *capes* and *coats*, as a modern taxonomy might, based on a binary choice of sleeved/sleeveless, or is a category of 'Outer garments' more suited to a historical thesaurus? This section has not yet been fully classified, so the question remains to be answered. Problems of a different but often perplexing kind arise when it comes to classifying the more abstract lexis.

Equally controversial is the overall shape of the classification: much depends on the starting-point, but who is to say where that is? As Roberts writes: 'Inevitably any thesaurus is just one of many possible orders in which its contents could be arranged. That is why the forthcoming *Thesaurus of Old English* can be regarded as "one snapshot" of the words that remain to us from Anglo-Saxon England' (Roberts, 1993: 1). The point from which that snapshot is taken may vary according to the purpose or scope of a particular thesaurus, and there is a certain interest in comparing the overall structures of the relatively few conceptual thesauri available. Although Roget-style thesauri dominate the market, the remaining specialized thesauri have more in common with each other than they do with Roget, tending to begin with the objects of the material universe rather than with abstract concepts (Kay, 1994a).

Problems of classification affect people in many disciplines, whether they are engaged with words or ideas or objects. As a conclusion to this chapter, therefore, the classification of the *Historical Thesaurus of English* is given in outline, in the hope that it may form a point of comparison with other taxonomies (Figure 4.1). It is the result of many years of collective effort, but no further claim is made for it than that it seems to us to be a suitable structure in which to display the words accumulated in English over many centuries.

Notes

1   For an overview and updating of the hypothesis, see Lucy (1992).
2   Some of the issues are discussed in Coseriu and Geckeler (1981), esp. pp. 48–50.
3   Recent developments in cognitive semantics are discussed in Taylor (1995).
4   This vocabulary is recorded in Roberts and Kay (1995).
5   An interesting account of the making of this dictionary is given in Murray (1977).
6   The project was founded by Professor M.L. Samuels in 1964 and is now a few years from completion, under the editorship of Christian Kay and Irené Wotherspoon. It will be published both in book form and electronically. Major financial support for the project has come from the British Academy, the Leverhulme Trust and the University of Glasgow.
7   Both of these sections were classified for the *Historical Thesaurus of English* by Irené Wotherspoon.

Bibliography

Ayto, John (1993) *The Diner's Dictionary*, Oxford: Oxford University Press.

Baugh, Albert C. and Cable, Thomas (1978) *A History of the English Language*, 3rd edn, London: Routledge and Kegan Paul.

Biggam, C.P. (1993) 'Aspects of Chaucer's adjectives of hue', *Chaucer Review*, 28(1), 41–53.

Biggam, C.P. (1994) *Hæwenhnydele*: an Anglo-Saxon medicinal plant', *Botanical Journal of Scotland*, 46(4), 617–22.

Coseriu, Eugenio and Geckeler, Horst (1981) *Trends in Structural Semantics*, Tübingen: Narr.

Fenton, Alexander (1974) 'Lexicography and historical interpretation', in G.W.S. Barrow (ed.), *The Scottish Tradition*, Edinburgh: Scottish Academic Press.

Hagen, Ann (1992) *A Handbook of Anglo-Saxon Food Processing and Consumption*, Pinner: Anglo-Saxon Books.

Kay, C.J. (1994a) 'A lexical view of two societies', in A. Fenton and D.A. MacDonald (eds), *Studies in Scots and Gaelic*, Edinburgh: Canongate Academic.

Kay, C.J. (1994b) 'Word lists for a changing world', in Werner Hüllen (ed.), *The World in a List of Words*, Tübingen: Max Niemeyer Verlag.

Lucy, John A. (1992) *Language Diversity and Thought*, Cambridge: Cambridge University Press.

Macleod, Iseabail (1990) (ed.) *The Scots Thesaurus*, Aberdeen: Aberdeen University Press.

Murray, K.M.E. (1977) *Caught in the Web of Words*, New Haven, CT, and London: Yale University Press.

Nida, Eugene A. (1975) *Componential Analysis of Meaning*, The Hague: Mouton.

Owen-Crocker, Gale R. (1986) *Dress in Anglo-Saxon England*, Manchester: Manchester University Press.

Pearce, Susan M. (1992) *Museums, Objects and Collections: A Cultural Study*, Leicester and London: Leicester University Press.

Roberts, J.A. (1992) 'Anglo-Saxon vocabulary as a reflection of material culture', in *The Age of Sutton Hoo*, Woodbridge, Suffolk: Boydell Press.

Roberts, J.A. (1993) 'A thesaurus of Old English: one snapshot of a vanished world', in Olga Fischer and Willem Koopman (eds), *Current Research in Dutch and Belgian Universities and Polytechnics*, Amsterdam: University of Amsterdam.

Roberts, J.A. and Kay, C.J., with L. Grundy (1995) *A Thesaurus of Old English*, London: King's College.

Roget, P.M. (1852) *Thesaurus of English Words and Phrases*, London: Longman, rev. R.A. Dutch (1962), S.M. Lloyd (1982) and B. Kirkpatrick (1987).

Spevack, Marvin (1993) *A Shakespeare Thesaurus*, Hildesheim, Zurich and New York: Georg Olms Verlag.

Stoppard, Tom (1967) *Rosencrantz and Guildenstern Are Dead*, London: Faber and Faber.

Taylor, John R. (1995) *Linguistic Categorization*, 2nd edn, Oxford: Clarendon Press.

Tilley, Christopher (1989) 'Interpreting material culture', in I. Hodder (ed.), *The Meanings of Things*, London: Unwin Hyman.

5

Virtual words, material worlds: the internet, language and reality

MARY McGEE WOOD

Introduction

'Virtual worlds' – what could be more different from the material world we have lived in until now?

> Real world cultures have mythic icons and forms which provide a 'common place' and shared patterns of thinking. I-net is in a position to consciously create things which are ordinarily an unconscious part of society. As people 'pretend' to believe these things and act them out we might see richer social forms emerging. They also have the potential of strengthening group identity. They may become a framework on which we can build richer social patterns than now exist. ...
>
> Those who spend time within this virtual universe may acquire new habits and techniques which they then inflict on the 'external world' thus giving this medium the power to transform all human affairs (a power which is only theoretical, far from actualization, but none the less real, this is a potential lever to move the world). ...
>
> Many will look askance at the above and decide it is only silly? But is it? I think not.
>
> ("ac", `alt.cyberspace`, 19 September 1995)

A more sober view comes from a serious researcher in virtual reality: 'There are some important things that it gives us that may bring about a completely new way of interacting with machines – far more about the psychology than the technology' (S. West, personal communication).

Virtual words: the internet

Let us stop to describe what we are talking about, before pronouncing judgement on it. What is out there on the internet, and how do we use it and relate to it?

For many years, electronic mail (email) has been a favoured means of communication among those few people – mainly researchers in computer science – who have had the resources to use it: a moderately powerful computer, with access to a connecting network allowing it to send to, and receive from, other computers. An email message is composed like any other document, and can be as long or short, impromptu or carefully revised, as the sender wishes. It can be a quick 'Hi!' or the complete text of a scholarly journal article. It can be sent to one specific recipient or to many, equally easily and cheaply. It will arrive within minutes or seconds (all being well: if any part of the network is 'down', it may never arrive at all). The recipient(s) will find it waiting whenever they next look in their computers' 'mailboxes'. The message can be read and re-read, printed out, edited, passed on to other people, stored in an archive for indefinite future use. Email combines (almost) the speed of telephone communication with (almost) the permanence of the written word. No wonder it is popular. No wonder, as increasingly powerful personal computers have become part of the furniture in increasingly many businesses and homes, their use for communication has mushroomed.

As email messages can be sent equally easily to any number of recipients, 'mailing lists' have grown up. These can consist of any number of individual addresses held as a list by a central 'server'. Mail sent to the server is automatically redistributed to every address on the list. For example, I can send a message to a server in Essex which sends it for me to the eight or nine other members of a working group advising one of the UK research councils on possible future directions for research funding. Or I can send a message to a server in the American Midwest, which sends it on to the KnitNet, a list of around 1000 knitters and hand-spinners from Antarctica, Japan and Australia through Europe to California and Canada (of which more later). Individuals subscribe to mailing lists, and then receive messages as if they were personal mail. If you get bored or overwhelmed (traffic on a mailing list can be a few messages per week, or dozens every day), you explicitly unsubscribe, and your address is removed from the distribution list.

More often, a large group will be set up as a 'newsgroup' or 'bulletin board'. As the name suggests, this is a central location where messages are held for users to look at if and when they wish, rather than being sent out as mail to each member. Indeed, there is no such thing as a 'member' of a newsgroup – anyone can read the messages 'posted' there whenever they wish. Typically, the newsreading software on one's computer allows one to keep a list of the groups one wishes to read regularly – selectivity is essential, as there are hundreds of newsgroups, covering a bewildering range of topics. Many are to do with computer hardware and software, but others are forums for discussion of society, politics and religion from all parts of the world; fan clubs for popular entertainers, musicians or television programmes; sport of all kinds, both professional (soccer, rugby, cricket and rowing results and many others are posted more or less as they happen) and amateur (people sharing advice on their own training methods and forthcoming events); all kinds of hobbies, leisure interests and crafts; anything you can imagine writing about, talking about or sharing an interest in. Again, more on this diversity later.

The most recent extension of this opening of access, this empowerment of anyone to share his or her knowledge and express his or her opinions, is the ability of organizations and individuals to post 'pages' on the 'World Wide Web'. Anyone with the right computing resources can set up their own Web page giving whatever information about herself or himself she or he wishes to make public. Thus, the University of Manchester has a 'Home Page' on the Web which gives general information about it. This has links which one can follow to find out about, for example, the Department of Computer Science, which in turn points to a page set up by the Artificial Intelligence group to describe its research interests, which in turn again points to pages set up by each person in that group. Those pages might have links to pages set up, on the other side of the world, by other researchers working on the same problems. Most importantly, we can all present ourselves in any way we wish. And this is even more true of pages set up by individuals outside any institutional structure.

The potential, the excitement of this vast new ability to share information is clear and compelling, even if we were still restricted to sharing information held as words and numbers. But recent developments in 'multimedia communications' mean that sound and pictures can be shared, too. The popular press have raised a largely uninformed and hysterical fuss about pornographic images available on the internet, out of all proportion to their actual prevalence. People post pictures of their lace-knitting techniques, their cockatiels, their babies. Academic groups can share diagrams or art reproductions. When the group alt.quotations had an argument some time ago about the exact phrasing of the first human words spoken on the moon, someone clinched it by posting a file which, given the right (widely available) decoding software, reproduced a recording of Neil Armstrong's voice.

This ability to handle, and integrate, sounds and visual images with language is rapidly becoming more sophisticated, and has begun to give us full-scale 'virtual reality' (VR) systems. VR helmets and gloves can put us in realistic three-dimensional worlds in which we can drive a car – our hand movements are relayed to the computer through the gloves, and the oncoming road and engine noise react appropriately in the input from the helmet. It is possible, of course, to create unpleasantly realistic war-games this way. It is also possible to learn to fly an airplane without risking the lives of passengers and dwellers below, or to practise and perfect surgical techniques before touching a patient, by interacting with a simulation, a 'virtual' copy of the material airplane or patient. Ultimately, our creative imagination can make virtual worlds which go beyond material worlds, which are no more tied to actual times and objects than are cinema and painting: a new medium for fiction.

So is there a real danger that virtual worlds will supplant the material world, as some critics fear, and some proponents seem to hope? Is the excitement just because all this facilitates fantasy? Is it just the fear of 'unreal', immaterial worlds? But myth and fiction have been doing that for as long as we can tell. Fantasy is right up there with language at the top of the list of candidates for the criterion that best distinguishes humans from other animal species. (And so is religion, which, for our present purposes, is a form of fantasy.) Virtual worlds and electronic language are only doing what the worlds of art and the language of the imagination have always done: taking us beyond the here and now, the material world under our feet and hands. I will argue that the languages of imagination and reality are fundamentally, provably distinct from each other; and then that in watching the ways in which we use language on the internet, virtual language, we can see that distinction with a new clarity.

The language of the abstract and the language of the concrete

There has always been a difference between words which are the names of things, language which refers to the here and now (*hand, tree, Pepper the tabby cat*), and words for abstractions, fictions or imaginations (*justice, amusement, basilisk*). It has been argued that one of the most important criteria distinguishing human language, as language, from the signalling systems of other animals is that they can only refer to the here and now. A gopher has different warning calls to alert the group to danger from different predators, but it can only utter each call when the appropriate predator is detected. Animals cannot lie. Nor can they discuss might-have-beens, or abstract concepts. Human language can do all of this and more. It is easy to sympathize with the claim that it is our ability, through language, to develop abstraction and imagination that has made possible human society, culture, technology and civilization.

Thus, from very early, we find a recognition that the language of myth is distinctive in one way, and the language of natural science in another. Plato was well aware of the power of myth, critical of the potential bad influence of stories which showed the gods as less than morally perfect beings. At the same time, he was not above inventing his own when it suited him, like the explanation of love as the efforts of originally four-legged, four-armed creatures to rejoin with their sundered other halves; and his characteristic use of Greek is rich in metaphor and tinged with poetry. Compare this with the solid realism of Aristotle, his careful factual writings on physics and anatomy, his plain, matter-of-fact, even cryptic prose. On one hand is the language of science, grounded in the material world, trying to understand and explain it: careful observation of biology and astronomy. On the other is the language of 'philosophy', reaching beyond the observable world to debate the nature of knowledge, of 'the Good', of government. Beyond this, from the priests and dramatists, is language which leaves the material world altogether for worlds of the imagination.

The distinction easily casts itself as between the language of science and the language of art (although with art we should include philosophy, fantasy and religion). It has evolved through the centuries of evolving Western thought, as more and more areas which for the Greeks were part of 'natural philosophy' have spun off to independent status as natural sciences. Let us put another name to this distinction, and refer to the characteristic words of the language of science, words which are labels for unambiguous parts of the real world, as 'terminology'.

'Terminology' may smack of technology, of the most abstruse corners of the sciences, of jargon: ironically, perhaps, of a specialist's view, far removed from ordinary people's perception of the everyday real world around them. That is because, in an area we know nothing of, the language is as baffling as the things it refers to, because they are unknown. If we don't know what *positron* means, or *perceptron*, or *mother-of-all*, we are liable to blame it on the words, rather than on our ignorance of particle physics or computer science or the design of spinning wheels. If we do know the area, then we do not perceive its language as terminology. But *shirt* and *blouse*, *fork* and *spoon*, *front door* and *cat-flap* identify specific objects in just the same way.

One possible criterion for determining whether a word is a 'term' comes from the use of computer models to hold our knowledge about (parts of) the world – 'terminology' can be defined as the vocabulary which labels such a model. Let me digress briefly to describe one such model and the lessons it offers about the nature of language.

GALEN (Rector *et al.*, 1993, 1995) is a European Community-funded research project building an advanced medical information system, based on a central concept model of medical knowledge which can support a range of clinical applications (diagnostic decision support, epidemiological surveys, and automatic generation of patient history summaries, for example), in a range of different languages, at levels of technicality appropriate to a range of different users (such as surgeons, general practitioners, nurses, and patients familiar or unfamiliar with their condition). Traditional medical terminology systems have been, at best, giant, semi-structured dictionaries: GALEN's distinctive central component is its Concept Reference (CORE) Module, a formal representation of medical knowledge, of anatomy, physiological function and disease. Coded into the computer are, for example, the fact that we have bones; that one kind of bone is a longbone; that there is a longbone in the thigh; and that this is labelled *femur*. Bones can break, and a break in a bone is labelled *fracture*; a break in the bone of the thigh is labelled *fracture of the femur*. Such labels are the 'terminology' of medicine in English. A separate component, the Multilingual Module, handles this labelling of concept entities in any number of natural languages. Similarly, a Code Conversion Module handles the mapping between concepts and other formal coding systems. These three modules together make up the GALEN 'Terminology Server', which gives us, sharply defined and unambiguous, the names of things.

Medicine is a field in which terminology abounds and its correct use is essential and life-preserving, but any slice of the real world and its nomenclature could be represented in the same way: families and varieties of plants, the components of an automobile or aircraft engine, clothing or food. We can point to a freshly picked tomato and identify it as Red Alert. We cannot, in the same way, indicate that it is fragrant and delicious, let alone that we approve ideologically of its organic cultivation. Subjective perceptions of scent, flavour and political correctness are not facts, and cannot be modelled.

Caveat

Let me sound a brief note of caution here, before taking the argument back to the internet. Our use of terminology, as native speakers of natural language, is not quite that straightforward.

> The assumption underlying the increasing internationalization of medicine is that there is a shared model of medical science and medical care which transcends local idiosyncrasies of language and usage. It remains a matter of controversy as to how far such a language-independent model of medical concepts is possible.
>
> (Rector *et al.*, 1993)

Even words which are firmly anchored to definable slices of the real world, we understand and use with a vast contribution from our knowledge of the world and common sense – and that is before cultural assumptions and connotations come into play.

'The signal underdetermines the message.' How often have you barely *heard* what someone was saying, in noisy surroundings, perhaps one word in four, yet understood perfectly what they were trying to communicate? How often have you 'heard' someone say what you expected, and realized only later that he or she had actually said something quite different? (Thus the – probably apocryphal – book review which began 'This book fills a badly needed gap in the field.')

Artificial intelligence researchers in the two disjoint fields of computer vision and computer speech recognition are well aware of this. An acoustic wave-form is highly ambiguous or indeterminate on many levels: a person receiving it, in a particular context, with particular background knowledge, interprets it so quickly that the ambiguities are never noticed. Or we may 'hear' something said to us, and only understand it after a few seconds, after we realize what the context is. Speech recognition research increasingly realizes that computers will need human-like world-knowledge and subtle powers of not wholly logical inference to achieve human-like understanding of natural speech.

Similarly in vision: the light waves which reach the human retina or a robot camera are a tiny part of the information and inference which allow us to recognize a familiar face, let alone the passing emotions expressed on that face. Look through a row of windows at a building opposite: how do we know that the building extends across the stretches of solid wall between the windows? I see a friend in t-shirt and shorts, red-faced, with wet hair, and know that she has just come back from a run, it is raining outside, and she would welcome a glass of water. Fifteen minutes later, I know that now her hair is wet because she has washed it in the shower, and a cup of tea might well be more appropriate. This kind of interpretation and inference is perhaps the greater part of our understanding of both vision and language, even of terminology.

Along these lines, although Umberto Eco's *Faith in Fakes: Travels in Hyperreality*, first published in 1985, pre-dates public consciousness of virtual reality or the internet, the observations in his essay 'Towards a Semiological Guerilla Warfare' on mass communications are entirely appropriate here too: 'Not long ago, if you wanted to seize political power in a country, you had merely to control the army and the police ... Today a country belongs to the person who controls communications' (Eco, 1995: 135). But the real control of that centralized message, Eco argues, lies not with its originator but individually with each receiver, who will interpret it in the light of his or her particular circumstances; and, the more widely these media reach, the more diverse will be their interpretation.

American scholars have realized what a Technicolor love movie, conceived for ladies in the suburbs, means when it is shown in a Third

> World village ... variability of interpretation is the constant law of mass
> communications ... For a Milanese bank clerk a TV ad for a refrigerator
> represents a stimulus to buy, but for an unemployed peasant in Calabria
> the same image means the confirmation of a world of prosperity that
> doesn't belong to him and that he must conquer.
>
> (Eco, 1995: 140, 141)

(We might think of Austin's (1962) distinction between locutionary
force – what an utterance inherently means – and perlocutionary force –
the meaning which is received – writ large.) And Eco urges us actively to
use our power to interpret individually the mass messages we receive:

> What must be occupied, in every part of the world, is the first chair in
> front of every TV set ... The battle for the survival of man as a
> responsible being in the Communications Era is not to be won where the
> communication originates, but where it arrives.
>
> (*ibid.*: 142)

One would expect the internet, with its openness of interaction, its
power of universal participation and right to reply, to take this
principle even further. In so far as it does not, it is because, as yet,
internet users are still culturally homogeneous. 'More than half of the
internet users in the UK are aged between 25 and 44, professional, and
90% are male' (Arthur, 1995). Women form a larger, and growing,
proportion in the United States (Miller, 1995), but on a global
perspective, compared to Eco's examples of Calabrian peasants and
Third World villagers, we are still talking about a small subgroup of
society which shares a sophisticated technology and the assumptions
built into that technology. (An early, and impressive, exception to this
restriction was the Zapatistas' use of the internet to keep the world
informed of the progress, and the dreams, of their insurrection in
Mexico (Berger, 1995).) We can hope, and indeed predict, that as
computer communications technology spreads more widely through the
world, and adapts to the new cultures and assumptions it meets, truly
global diversity of interpretation will spread with it.

Here, further, not only artificial intelligence, cognitive science and
cultural criticism but also virtual reality meet traditional epistemology.
A voice from the front line in virtual reality research says:

> Ultimately the world we experience has far more to do with our own
> projections and constructions than whatever objective reality may be out
> there at least as regards the more sophisticated concepts we form, and
> possibly in basic perception too – we heavily interpolate, extrapolate,
> fabricate and ignore things from the raw sensory input – to a far greater
> extent than we generally realize.
>
> (S. West, personal communication)

This long and wide-ranging caution is important, but – I believe – it does not undermine the distinction I am arguing for between terminology and abstract language. Even terminology is used and understood with vast resources of extra-linguistic knowledge, but it still comes down to material reality. A French and an English surgeon may use different words, and different cultural backgrounds, in referring to a disease of the human liver, but they will point to the same organ of the body and the same pathogen affecting it. A French and an English art critic, or high court judge, speak culturally unresolvable languages, where even approximate translation is difficult enough, and pinning to a common reference point in the material world is simply impossible, because there is none.

The internet as a test for reality

I have argued, first, that there is a fundamental distinction, as old as human language, between language which refers to the material world and is grounded in it – the language of science, 'terminology' – and language beyond the material, the language of art and philosophy. Second, a side-effect of building computer models of bits of the world and attaching words to those models gives us an objective diagnostic test to discriminate terminology from the vocabulary of the non-'material'. Third, some caution is needed even then, due to the vast resources of world-knowledge and inference which we bring to bear in processing even the most solid and unambiguous of terms. Finally, I want to suggest that watching the way in which language is used on the internet offers a new sharpness to the distinction between 'material' and 'abstract' language.

Browse – if you get the chance – through the long list of internet newsgroups available, and a clear pattern emerges. The newsgroup names set the groups up as a hierarchy. The first element indicates the most general area: comp for computer-related topics, sci for the sciences, rec for recreational interests, alt for 'alternative', uk for purely British concerns, and so on. The second element refines this further: the comp.sys groups are for computer systems, and so similarly sci.physics, rec.games, rec.sport, rec.pets. There is usually a third element which identifies the newsgroup uniquely, and in some cases there may be more: sci.physics.fusion, comp.sys. laptops, rec.pets.dogs.behavior (*sic*), rec.pets.dogs.breeds, and so on, and on.

The new urban legends of 'cyberspace', of souls lost by absorption into these virtual worlds, doubtless do have some foundation. Groups in the alt hierarchy (alt.culture ..., alt.society ..., alt. politics ... and so on) are particularly prone to be populated by people for whom they are world enough. Here the language of beyond-the-real is spoken, as it always has been in myth and fiction and philosophical speculation. Compare these people to the young men who walked through the Agora with Socrates, debating the nature of knowledge and beauty when they could have been practising estate management or the skills of war: the difference in technology is trivial compared to the similarity in motivation, and in the use and role of language.

On the other hand, there are newsgroups which clearly by their nature are about the material world, depend on it and feed back to it. Most of the rec groups are like this. On rec.pets.birds, for example, people exchange questions and advice on which sort of parrot is likely to talk best, or what to include in a varied diet for a cockatiel (dandelion leaves, but not chocolate). On rec.sport.running, the results of major races all over the world will be posted within minutes of happening. The next message may say 'I'm about to visit Montreal, can anyone recommend a good place to run?' This will almost always be followed by a number of answers, and, in the outcome, by the enquirer going out and running, probably a better route than he or she could have found independently.

Of course, it is too crude to say that some newsgroups speak in the language of the material world and others in the immaterial. There is always a mixture. But users are aware of the distinction, and of which is appropriate to which topic. rec.pets.birds discusses the ethics and ecological impact of importing wild-caught birds of rare species. talk.philosophy.humanism has been known to discuss the format and distribution of car-stickers with humanist symbols, and soc.religion.quaker the form of gravestones in old Quaker cemeteries. But this is felt to be out of character, and sooner or later – probably sooner – while the humanist goes back to discussions of Kierkegaard and the meaning of life, the runner will go back out on a new route, and the bird-lover will try again to teach the cockatiels to whistle 'Pop goes the Weasel'. The effect of the internet is to give them more and better-informed, not less, interaction with the material world. It is not a substitute for the real, but an enhancement of the real, an empowerment in dealing with it. If too much of the immaterial intrudes, it is likely to find its invasion side-stepped by a redrawing of the boundaries and terms of reference of the group.

An example which illustrates this well is the recent (and typical) history of the newsgroup rec.food.veg. Set up for discussion of all issues related to vegetarian food, the group rapidly became a wild miscellany within which some people debated the ethics of vegetarian living, some contested the health issues around various diets and dietary supplements, and some would ask 'Does anyone know good recipes for a veggie barbeque, or for the glut of beetroot in my garden?'

– and would usually have plenty of useful replies. After a while, discontent set in, and an ever-larger proportion of the traffic on the group was about what the group should be for, which of these themes should be discussed. Eventually the group split into several, including a group dedicated to ethics – which has since died – and a group entirely for the one person who most dominated the original group with hundreds of words every day of opinionated statements on any topic under discussion, which has been moved to the `alt` hierarchy. The two survivors are `rec.food.veg`, for general discussion, and `rec.food.veg.cooking`, which is just that: a forum for sharing or requesting recipes. And, for those of us who read it, this is not a substitute for cooking! On the contrary, we are likely to rush from the computer to the kitchen, and eat something new for dinner.

As promised, I will conclude with a closer look at one particular group – a mailing list, in this case – the KnitNet.

The KnitNet, as I mentioned earlier, is a group of (at the time of writing) about 1000 knitters around the world, who share technical questions and advice, leavened with a great deal of humour and personal chat. The atmosphere is that of a traditional knitters' face-to-face coffee-and-talk session, and indeed many such meetings have been organized through it, and solid personal friendships formed. Let me quote a small selection of (mostly) more technical recent messages – for a sense of scale, the total traffic normally runs at thirty or forty pages per day:

> My plan for the vest is a v-neck vest with each front having a cable (possibly two-color, I'll have to decide soon) the length of each front, the background (or rest) of which will be large blocks of color (I have about 7 balls at an ounce or two each). One color will change to another via three rows of k1A, k1B, vertically, and the cable and front buttonband will separate the blocks horizontally.

> Does anyone want to trade two bags of Reynolds Fiesta cotton/acrylic blend in primary green and primary yellow? It's lovely yarn, but the colors don't speak to me in quite the right way.

> Diane in Niagara Falls and I are planning a get-together in Toronto on Saturday, Sept. 16. This will include trips to Romni and the Yarn Mill, lunch and a show-and-tell of a favorite knitted item (big or small, doesn't matter).

> Just found out that I'll be in Rochester, NY, for the afternoon this coming Thursday. I may have time to visit one or two yarn stores while I'm there. Any suggestions? What stores are there in Rochester, NY?

> Thanks to everyone who advised me on how many balls of Fortissima for a pair of socks. Most said 2 balls will do with a few exceptions so I'll proceed with said sock and see how it goes.

Alpaca for socks? I've seen kits for alpaca socks but my own feeling would be: OK for the bottoms, 'cause it's a really warm fiber, but alpaca has no 'give' so I think they might slide down your ankle if you used it for the tops.

Someone asked about the accuracy of this pattern. I have knit them, and I do know that a correction needs to be made in the directions following the heel: It reads: 'You will have less sts than when you started' and the pattern says '12(12, 14)'. The *correct* number of sts for the *medium* size should be 14, not 12.

... mentions using hair conditioner for her socks. I use it when washing all my woollens. I also use shampoo for washing. With 16 and 18 year old daughters I always have a good supply (you know, constant changing of brands before using up what you have). I was also told to use it in the last rinse when washing fleece. Works great.

In my experience, Cascade 220 and Germantown worsted produce identical gage on size 7 needles (I get 5 st/inch).

And here are, again, a very few of the replies I received when I mentioned to the KnitNet that I was writing this piece, and asked for their response (with deepest thanks to these eight and many more, for their involvement and support, and for permission to quote their words):

I've been knitting for over 40 years, but never had anyone to learn from (learned from a book in the dime store) and though I loved it, did not really develop more advanced skills until I joined the Knitlist. I came to appreciate finer finishing techniques, began buying books on new stitches, patterns and techniques, started using new yarns and patterns that others recommended, and also began actually finishing what I started. Before, I felt isolated and that I was the only one who got bored with a project and let it sit for awhile – now I know it's just a UFO (unfinished object), and I realize that I knit for the enjoyment of the process, perhaps even more than for the finished product. This list has inspired me, taught me and most of all, provided support I never have had.

(Judy Sumner)

I also like the use of this new technology to further the ancient craft of turning one-dimensional yarn into three-dimensional garments. And another thing that you didn't mention: the (so-far) non-commercial nature of the 'Net', which inspires in people a matching altruism. Not only the pattern and yarn exchanges on the knit list (let alone the tons of helpful advice) but all the marvellous WWW sites that people create and maintain just for the hell of it. And the maintenance of the knit list, for that matter.

(Diana Foss)

My grandmother who knit is dead. This list has connected me with a whole community of grandmothers, sisters, and aunts (yes, even your crabby old aunt so-and-so shows up!) who knit and spin and dye. It is like being reconnected to a feminine world that was rapidly, and sadly, disappearing as our society got more mobile. (I don't mean to leave out the occasional man who shows up on the list, but they are the exception rather than the rule.) I knit every day now that I'm on the list. I have new friends with whom I keep in touch regularly. It's a great experience for me.

(Caroline M. McMillan)

I fit my knitting into my life, keeping a happy and healthy balance. But the KnitNet has helped me by being an outlet for the knitting and yarn side of my life. It has introduced me to a whole world that I would never have met without the internet.

(Arlene Williams)

Without this group I wouldn't have discovered Alice Starmore, or the peacock face cloth, or the Enchanted Forest sweater, or knitting backwards, or ... I always knitted, but I've learnt an incredible amount from this group, and I really do find it has enhanced things for me. And, largely thanks to the internet, I have taken up a whole new hobby, ice skating.

(Annabel Smyth)

I have knit for many years and was almost beginning to believe the retail stores, who said they were: (fill in the blank) closing, cutting back, not carrying yarn anymore, because no one knits. I was beginning to feel that I and a few close friends were the only ones out there. Of course, now I know differently. I found the Knitting Guild of America (almost sounds like a religion, doesn't it?), my friends and I formed our own guild, I got a computer system, and the rest, as they say, is history. I have found new friends from all over the world. I have learned many new things. And you're right! I have been inspired. The list also gives me ideas to share with the guild, and think of all the people who can answer my questions! I guess that's exactly what I'm working up to. The internet is a wealth of information, both on lists, such as ours and on bulletin boards. I don't believe people when they say that the internet is bad. Since when is information a bad thing? People in this country have a tendency to blame 'things' for their inability to use common sense. (I.e. 'The ladder is at fault because it fell over while I was standing on the top step reaching two feet off to my left.') That's a bit of an extreme, but you get the idea.

(Lynn Macquard)

From my perspective, many of the generalizations being made about the internet are based on a very limited sample of what actually is transmitted. Those samples are very male dominated, and I think some of the communication patterns are more about the gender of the participants than the technology. Knitlist is an interesting counter example, because it is a predominantly female list. I certainly think you are also right that it encourages 'involvement' with real stuff, rather than substituting for it – I buy more yarn and (more importantly) keep knitting in more challenging ways thanks to the list. Since there aren't many knitters here in Alabama, that is important. I do have a knitting guild, but it's small and once a month contact isn't as good for inspiration.

(Lynne Adrian)

Even though electronic communication is exclusive in some ways (one must be leisured enough to participate; relatively literate, both in the traditional sense and as far as computers are concerned; privileged enough to have access to a computer) within the cyber-community there is a powerful levelling effect which is unique to this type of communication. Differences that influence us in face-to-face communication (race, age, weight, accent, class, disabilities, sex, nationality, etc.) are hidden in electronic communication and need only be revealed when and if you wish. We are drawn together by our love for knitting and within our virtual community we form bonds based on this common interest. It broadens one's mind to find that the person you respect for their wisdom on the net belongs to some group of Others whom you fear or dislike in 'real life'. Even if one does not harbour actual prejudices, we are all, without exception, influenced to a degree by the outward physical attributes of people we meet. The virtual community sweeps these external differences aside. The question is, what is more 'real': the inner person whose thoughts, opinions, advice and dreams are expressed in email? Or the outer person you see and react to when you meet someone face to face? This is not to say that the world of email is free of all problems and prejudices of its own. However, it can force us to re-think our perceptions of what really is, and hence it can change reality.

(Laura Marple)

Conclusion

So, I would argue – as would many with working experience of the virtual worlds of the internet – that we have here, indeed, a new technology of great scope and power, but that what it does is reinforce and accentuate a distinction as old as human language itself, between the language of the material and the language of the immaterial, between language which is rooted in the real world and takes us back to it, and language which takes us beyond it.

The language of the material, on the internet, may lead me to order fleece from a Perendale sheep breeder in New Zealand, to establish a long-term friendship with an American couple who come to England for ten days every summer and to be taken to dinner by a knitter in Nashville, to knit a jacket for a friend's daughter's first birthday from a little-known pattern, to learn to spin.

Language beyond can go further beyond than ever before: the internet, and the technology of virtual reality, open new possibilities for the creative imagination, at least comparable to the excitement at the invention of cinematography, or still photography – which we take so much for granted now that it is hard to recapture that excitement. We need to see our new virtual words and worlds that way: not as a threat, but as an exhilarating creative challenge; and as a powerful way to reaffirm our open-minded, adventurous involvement in the amazing tangible diversity of our material world.

Note

Special thanks to Deborah A. Abbott, Jason Burton, John Frone, Rajeev Gore, Charles Sanderson, Suzanne Stein, Adrian West and the KnitNet. Apologies to all whose contributions I did not have enough space to use!

Bibliography

Arthur, C. (1995) 'Expert says internet is "cheapening" life', *Independent*, 10 August.

Austin, J.L. (1962) *How to Do Things with Words*, Oxford: Clarendon Press.

Berger, J. (1995) 'A dive into the pool of shared ideas', *Guardian*, 2 September.

Eco, U. (1986) *Faith in Fakes: Travels in Hyperreality*, Minerva edn, London: Mandarin.

Miller, L. (1995) 'Women are boldly going where few went before – on the internet', *USA Today*, 8 August.

Rector, A.L., Nolan, W.A. and Glowinski, A. (1993) 'Goals for concept representation in the GALEN Project', *Proceedings of SCAMC93*.

Rector, A.L., Solomon, W.D., Nolan, W.A. and Rush, T.W. (1995) 'A terminology server for medical language and medical information systems', *Methods of Information in Medicine*, 34, 147–57.

6

Old masters and young mistresses: the collector in popular fiction

KATHARINE EDGAR

Introduction: are collectors normal people? Do people think they are?

Our attitudes to collectors, as to anything else, are shaped by both our first-hand experience of the phenomenon and the representations of it that we come across in the media, fiction and art. It is the aim of this chapter to examine one particular class of these representations: the collector in popular fiction.

But is popular fiction really worthy of academic attention? Wouldn't there be more point, you might ask, in studying *real* literature? Well, naturally that depends on what you want to find out. A justification for this chapter might run as follows:

> *Millions* of people read popular fiction. Their attitudes to collectors, and by implication their attitudes to a good deal of the business of museums, are shaped by it; so it would be a good idea to find out exactly what it says, as that will help us to see what people really think about collectors.

Is that a sensible justification, or hopelessly naïve? Does popular fiction really hold the key to mass beliefs? In the course of this study I shall consider the question. I shall begin by stating what I mean by popular fiction.

The usual meaning of popular might be defined as 'liked by a lot of people'. But if that definition applied to fiction, then Kazuo Ishiguro or Peter Ackroyd would be popular fiction and an *unsuccessful* Mills and Boon novel would not; so this is clearly not what is meant. Instead, I am using the term 'popular' in the sense of 'non-literary'. Some fiction is considered to be 'literature', some is not. The arbitrariness of the distinction has been discussed many times elsewhere, for example, by

Terry Eagleton in the introduction to *Literary Theory* (1983: 1–16). He eventually arrives at an entirely relative definition, 'literature as highly valued writing' (*ibid*.: 11). The writing with which this chapter deals can, by extension, be described as fiction which is *not* highly valued. That this definition contains no information about what *kind* of writing this is causes no problems, since any writing about popular fiction is usually done with the aim in mind of examining work which, because of its low status, is generally neglected elsewhere.

This definition is not complete. Left as 'non-literary' fiction it would encompass fiction that, whilst trying to be literary, was simply so bad that no one would dream of dignifying it with the name of literature: the stories written by Adrian Mole, if he were real, or thousands of failed first novels. The other element in popular fiction is that it is commercially produced: bought or commissioned by a publisher and printed in large numbers for the primary purpose of making money – a Christian love story distributed in the hope of making converts would not, I believe, be 'popular fiction'.

There are certain internal characteristics which popular fiction tends to possess. They are also shared by some literary fiction, but this is excluded from my discussion by the 'non-literary' part of my definition. They are not, however, what *defines* popular fiction. A work which did not possess any of them but was commercial and non-literary would still fall under the 'popular fiction' heading. They are as follows:

1 the possibility of being categorized according to genre – e.g. detective story, love story, humour;
2 (and, following from this) a strong but essentially predictable plot – the stories are rich in incident, but it is taken for granted that at the end the mystery will be resolved or the lovers united;
3 stereotyped, simplistic, 'black-and-white' characters – human complexity is replaced by easily detectable good and bad.

As I have remarked, these characteristics are typical but not crucial. In fact, in the modern erotic novel the ending is far from certain – will the heroine end up with one or other or both of her boyfriends? And in some detective fiction – for instance, the 'Inspector Morse' books of Colin Dexter – motivation is complex and the criminal more likely to be an essentially ordinary person than a Sherlock Holmesian arch-villain. Why, then, have I felt it necessary to comment on these tendencies?

The answer is that they have major implications for the question I posed earlier: how the attitudes of the reading public relate to the attitudes inherent in the books. It is important, I think, to remember that just because fiction deals in stereotypes and extremes, readers do not necessarily do the same. If the typical fictional collector is not just someone with a hobby, but an obsessive, and his collection not just an album of first-day covers but a houseful of priceless works of art, this is a function more of the nature of popular fiction than of the beliefs of the readers, just as the beautiful heroine, rather than one that is merely rather pretty, and the evil murderer, rather than the maladjusted one, are. So the stereotypes I am going to extract, the patterns I am going to examine, should be approached with caution, and in context. It is the nature of popular fiction to take things to extremes, and this is both a problem to someone seeking to use it to detect readers' attitudes, and a blessing: it is because of these extremes that such clear patterns are visible, but in themselves they represent a distortion.

Before introducing concrete examples, I would like to add a note about the scope of my research. I have tried to work from a representative selection of modern popular fiction, while paying enough attention to certain genres to make comparison between different examples of them possible. Not all genres are represented – I found no collectors in science fiction or 'sword and sorcery' fantasy books. This is not to say that there are none, but reading the whole of popular fiction would take even longer than reading the whole of literary fiction. Since most of the books have so far been (and will probably remain) subject to little or no academic study, there is an unfortunate lack of indexes or concordances. I therefore relied on my own extensive reading in the area, and a number of tips from friends who would prefer to remain anonymous. Although most of the work I read was modern, I have also referred to older work, notably Sherlock Holmes, where this is still read very frequently. The three genres on which I have focused particularly are:

1 detective fiction;
2 crime fiction (the subject of the book is the perpetration of the crime, not its detection);
3 erotic fiction by 'women for women'.

There are essentially four characteristics that are attached very frequently to collectors in all these three sorts of fiction and which, when present, generally motivate the plot. They are as follows:

1 philandering;
2 difficulty in forming normal human relationships;
3 orderliness to the point of predictability;
4 a passion for the material collected, to the point of insanity.

I shall now discuss, with examples, these four qualities.

'Madamina, il catalog il questo': the collector as philanderer

Mozart's operatic hero, Don Giovanni, perhaps the most famous philanderer of all, effectively collects women: he even keeps a catalogue of his conquests. Again and again in popular fiction the parallel between collector and philanderer is made explicit: the collector of women also has an inanimate collection. The motif is repeated across all genres.

First, the detective novel: the most famous detective of all, Sherlock Holmes, is called upon in 'The Adventure of the Illustrious Client' to prevent the marriage of a collector of Chinese porcelain. Not only is Adelbert Gruner a murderer, he also has a history of seducing and abandoning women. And like Don Giovanni, he has a book:

> I tell you, Mr Holmes, this man collects women, and takes a pride in his collection, as some men collect moths or butterflies. He had it all in that book. Snapshot photographs, names, details, everything about them.
>
> (Conan Doyle, 1993: 1048)

In Roald Dahl's 'The Visitor' (Dahl, 1991: 332–3) the collection is actually an aid to seduction. 'Uncle Oswald' has two collections, arachnida and the walking sticks of the famous and infamous. The latter collection is 'displayed in two long racks standing against the walls of the passage (or should one call it the highway?) which led from the living room to the bedroom' (*ibid.*: 332) – a means of drawing the women closer to the relevant room!

> 'Take down the Tolstoy,' Oswald would say to a pretty visitor. 'Go on, take it down ... that's right ... and now ... now rub your own palm gently over the knob that has been worn to a shine by the great man himself. It is not rather wonderful, the mere contact of your skin with that spot?'
>
> (*ibid.*: 323)

The phallic symbolism of this collection is obvious, and the images evoked by the arachnida collection, spiders that spin a web and lie in wait for their next victim, no less vivid. Dahl then observes 'Nobody ever found it dull to be in Oswald's company, and perhaps that, more than anything else, was the reason for his success.'

In Jilly Cooper's light-hearted romantic novel *Bella* the father of Bella's new boyfriend is described as busy with 'Old Masters and young mistresses' (Cooper, 1980: 43), and the phrase is repeated on the cover blurb of Peter Marks's crime story *Collector's Choice*: 'Andor loved a beautiful nude, on canvas or off ... Andor was clearly a man to get what he wanted, whether it was an old master or a young mistress' (Marks, 1972: back cover).

In *Lace 2* by Shirley Conran, when a porn star, Lili, has been kidnapped, the first person to be suspected is the brother of her late husband, also a collector:

> Judy was also afraid because Spyros Stiarkis was a rich man, a careful, clever man, an obsessive art collector, and he was besotted by Lili. His other passion, as every gossip writer knew, was to acquire whatever and whoever had belonged to his dead brother.
>
> (Conran, 1985: 388)

In fact, Stiarkis turns out not to have been responsible for the kidnap. But when Lili is found, she is discovered, interestingly, to have been kept prisoner in what was once the harem area of a palace.

The philandering collector is not consistently either a hero or villain. Conan Doyle's Adelbert Gruner is evil and his book described as 'a beastly book, – a book no man, even if he had come from the gutter, could have put together. But it was Adelbert Gruner's book all the same' (Conan Doyle, 1993: 1048); and Conran's Stiarkis's ownership of an art collection seems to turn him into a potential criminal. But the authorial viewpoint is not always disapproving. Dahl's Uncle Oswald is an anti-hero, who is affectionately and certainly admiringly described but, like Don Giovanni, is punished: in his case, he discovers that one of the women he has slept with and whom he saw only in the dark is suffering from a particularly nasty form of leprosy. Marks's Andor, too, is an anti-hero: the story is told largely from his viewpoint, and although he is a criminal, the theft he plans to carry off is described (Marks, 1972: front cover) as 'the most beautiful heist ever'.

To collect women is, of course, to treat them like objects. Might one expect, then, that books written by or for women would tend to be disapproving of the philandering collector? The reality is otherwise. In *The Captive Flesh*, an erotic novel set in a harem, the hero can literally own women. Few details are given about his other collections, but the author makes it clear that Kasim was a connoisseur:

> Claudine and she were not Kasim's honoured guests at all. It all became clear to her. Kasim was a lover of beautiful things, a patron of the arts, and a collector. He had told her so himself, and she had not understood.
> She did now.
> Claudine and herself were Kasim's latest acquisitions.
>
> (Cordell, 1993: 54)

The plot of *The Captive Flesh* concerns not, as one might expect, the *escape* of the heroines Claudine and Marietta from the harem, but their learning to accept and even to love their imprisonment there. Kasim is presented as an attractive hero. The erotic novels published by Black Lace are emphatically not written as male fantasies, but are advertised and marketed as sexual fantasies written *by* and *for* women.

All the novels described above share one obvious similarity. The collector may not always be good or always bad, but he is always *male*. It is only in a very recent book, Susan Swann's erotic novel *The Discipline of Pearls* (Swann, 1995), that the pattern begins to be broken. Briefly stated, the plot is this. Marika, a beautiful but bored advertising executive, is approached in a car park by a strange man who hands her a box containing a pearl pendant and a card with a telephone number. On calling the number she is summoned to what turns out to be the first of many occasions where sexual scenarios are acted out. These she later discovers to have been stage-managed by a secret society dedicated to pleasure, the Discipline of Pearls. Towards the end of the book, Marika is summoned to the house of the head of the society, 'the Major'. The Major takes out some books: ' "These", he said, his gesture encompassing the bookcases which lined the walls, "are my pride and joy. The culmination of many years of collecting. I have many rare volumes. Would you like to look at some?" ' (Swann, 1995: 169). The Major's collection is, of course, erotica. Marika is impressed: 'Her eyebrows rose as she saw that he possessed a first edition of *One hundred and twenty days at Sodom*' (*ibid*.: 170).

Swann describes parts of the collection in loving detail: 'a large book ... bound in the most exquisite pale leather and had lettering of gold leaf on the spine'. The Major's relationship with his collection is almost physical: 'Feel the softness, the suppleness of the leather binding', he urges, and Marika is appreciative:

> Marika admired the book. It was indeed beautiful, the leather felt as soft as sueded silk. Inside it had marbled boards and end papers. She read the date – seventeen fifty-seven. Opening it she saw that the first illustrations were graphic in the extreme and skilfully executed. She sensed that this book was something to do with why she was there.
>
> (*ibid*.: 170)

Marika's intuition is correct. First, she is asked to choose an illustration from the book that she would like to re-create. This involves another piece from the Major's collection:

> Stephen unwrapped the scrap of red silk and drew out a carved ivory phallus. 'Scrimshaw. Made by whalers,' the Major said, hoarsely. 'Worth hundreds of pounds. Fine example.'
>
> (*ibid*.: 177)

Later, when the characters have recovered their breath after a few graphically described pages of sexual activity, the Major makes Marika an offer:

> 'I've been looking for someone to pass my expertise onto ... Occasionally an important work of erotica comes onto the market. In the past I would

pursue such a work and arrange any transaction personally, but I'm no longer a young man. I hardly leave the house these days.' He paused for effect. 'Would you consider acting as my agent?'

(ibid.: 181)

Effectively, then, Marika becomes a collector. Her initiation into the world, previously seen as properly a male one, of sexual adventuring, sexual liaisons without emotional commitment, mirrors her initiation as a collector – another pursuit seen as essentially male. The sensuous descriptions of the books contribute to the impression of Marika's awakening as a collector as paralleling her sexual awakening ('How extraordinary that she hadn't known that there were such heights to reach' (*ibid.*: 191)). It is also worth noting that the Major's presentation as a collector has the effect of making him, in spite of the doubtful context, more respectable. His collection demonstrates that erotic literature has a long history and sometimes enormous financial value. This is interesting when the context in which the book was written is considered. Although erotic literature does indeed have a long history, it is only now that it has begun to be marketed to the mainstream, placed in the fiction section of quite respectable bookshops and advertised along the escalators in the Underground. So the agenda is clear when Marika is told,

> 'My own great-grandfather was one of a group of individuals who started the society back in the eighteen-thirties,' the Major said proudly. 'The early Victorians weren't at all the prudes they were made out to be, you know. Great-grandfather was a true sensualist. He began the collection.'

(ibid.: 183)

Thus the positive side of collecting and connoisseurship – culture, erudition, developed aesthetic sense – is made to influence the reader's view of sexual activity.

It is arguable that the development in the presentation of collectors, whereby a woman is initiated into collecting by a man, relates to changed attitudes to male and female sexuality. But does the collector–philanderer stereotype, in itself, reflect a general feeling? On the contrary, the stereotype of which one is usually most aware is of the collector whose activities are a *substitute* for sexuality. This is the Freudian doctrine of sublimation. Freud wrote,

> When an old maid keeps a dog or an old bachelor collects snuffboxes, the former is finding a substitute for her need for a companion in marriage and the latter for his need for – a multitude of conquests. Every collector is a substitute for a Don Juan Tenerio, and so too is the mountaineer, the sportsman, and such people. These are erotic equivalents.
> (Freud to Fliess, 24 January 1895, quoted in Forrester, 1994: 110)

According to Freud the collector is a substitute for a Don Juan/Don Giovanni; according to popular fiction the collector frequently *is* a Don Giovanni. The philandering collectors of popular fiction use their collections as a means to more or better sexual activity, or they treat their two kinds of collection, the 'Old Masters and young mistresses', as interchangeable. The collecting certainly doesn't result from an insufficiency of sex.

At first sight the two ideas are opposed, but in fact they are very closely related. Both treat sex and collecting as being essentially similar, resulting from the same energy. Both treat collecting as in some way pathological, or at the very least abnormal: the philandering collectors are frequently seen as having an unusually high level of sexual energy, although in the erotic novel this is considered a good thing.

The social inadequate

He might be a stud, but can the collector in popular fiction really relate to people? Most of the time, it seems not. Sometimes the collector has a string of girlfriends, sometimes a family, sometimes no one at all, but rarely does he (or very occasionally she) manage this side of his life as well as his carefully laid out and catalogued collection. Collecting may not be presented as a substitute for sex, but it is frequently presented as a substitute for love.

At one level, the socially inadequate collector is simply a loveless character who happens to collect: no causal link is drawn between his emotional deficiencies and collecting activities. In E.F. Benson's comic 'Lucia' books, the eponymous heroine has a friend and eventual husband, Georgie, who collects 'bibelots'. Georgie has a horror of physical contact, presented at times as rather pathetic ('The two women kissed each other affectionately. Nobody kissed Georgie' (Benson, 1991: 688)), and when they eventually marry, he stipulates that 'connubialities ... should be considered absolutely illicit' (*ibid.*: 500) and will not accept Lucia's proposal until they have agreed on a place to keep his bibelots, 'which I simply can't get on without. Heart's blood' (*ibid.*: 502). The effect is simply meant to be comic; Georgie is old-maidish, and it is Lucia who dominates – it is she who proposes to him.

M.R. James, the ghost-story writer, writes about collectors several times, and the collector is always a single man. Solitude is perhaps helpful to ghost stories, but the tendency is striking even so. James Denton, in 'The Diary of Mr Poynter', lives with an aunt; Dennistoun ('Canon Alberic's Scrapbook') and Williams ('The Mezzotint') are, as James himself was, bachelor dons, who collect not for themselves but for the university; and Mr Dillett, who purchases 'The Haunted

Dollshouse', lives alone (James, 1992). I am not, of course, claiming
that living alone means social inadequacy, but it is none the less worth
marking, and certainly in the case of 'The Diary of Mr Poynter' gives a
comic effect of a henpecked nephew: 'Then the next thing will be
another parcel of horrible old books at some outrageous price ... it is
ridiculous, James, to look like that' (*ibid.*: 399). It could be argued, of
course, that it is living alone that makes James's collectors particularly
vulnerable to ghostly manifestations.

At the next level, there is an authorial disapproval of attaching too
much importance to material things, with the implication that it is this
that has *caused* the characters' emotional handicaps. *Tiger Eyes* by
Shirley Conran (1995) is the story of an artist, Plum Russell, and her
struggle simultaneously to break away from a loveless marriage and to
prove that a picture acquired by an acquaintance is a fake. If there was
any doubt at all about the authorial viewpoint, Conran attaches an
interesting postscript. Among her acknowledgements, she thanks Bruce
Chatwin, author of various books, including *Utz* and *The Morality of
Things*, which discuss collecting. Conran writes,

> Bruce knew that I collected West African tribal sculpture, among other
> things. After lectures on the dangers of acquisition and the treacherous
> nature of possessions, one day he brought me an elegant sculpture from
> Paris: the size and shape of a watermelon, it was hollow and made of
> heavy bronze with a slit down one side. I could not guess what it was.
> 'It's the ankle bracelet of a Benin chief's favourite wife,' Bruce said. 'And
> it's so heavy that she couldn't move when she wore it.' I stopped
> collecting.
>
> (Conran, 1995: 441)

Tiger Eyes is a strongly moralistic tale. Plum Russell's husband,
Breeze, is an art dealer – the motif of the male seller of women's art,
and by implication, their souls, echoes the male collectors of women's
bodies discussed above. The forged picture belongs to Suzannah, the
wife of Victor, one of Breeze's clients. The husband and wife have
different collections, Suzannah using art, including the fake Dutch
seventeenth-century still life, to create an elegant, traditional home, and
Victor preferring modern art and African tribal sculpture ('Victor's
office, which did not look that of a Hollywood tycoon, as Plum had
expected, but like a modern museum' (*ibid.*: 96)). Indeed, the couple's
tastes differ so much that Suzannah will not allow Victor to keep his
collection at home. Thus the reader is prepared for the fact that their
marriage, although it looks solid from the outside, is rotten, and their
daughter's attempted suicide comes as no surprise. Breeze, however, is
busily trying to stop his wife from pursuing her suspicions over the
forged picture in case the fuss damages his standing in the art world or

offends valued clients – thus money and possessions are presented as the enemy of truth. Plum preserves her integrity by leaving the wealthy Breeze, who represents material things, to live with a primary school teacher in rural France, while the disclosure that Suzannah's painting was indeed a forgery serves as a metaphor for the deceitful nature of possession.

In Jeffrey Archer's *Not a Penny More, Not a Penny Less* (1982), the multimillionaire conman Harvey Metcalfe has conned four men out of a total of one million dollars, and the plot concerns their various plans as they try to recover the money by whatever means they can. Metcalfe is a collector, and although devoted to his daughter, Rosalie, he is estranged from her: 'Harvey had three loves in his life: the first was still Rosalie, the second was his paintings, and the third his orchids' (Archer, 1982: 25). Having always been more interested in acquiring wealth and adding to his collections than in people, his manners are brusque: 'The telephone clicked into place. Harvey never said goodbye. He had never understood the niceties of life and it was too late to start learning now' (*ibid.*: 11). Metcalfe, of course, loses the million dollars. He also loses his daughter Rosalie, when she marries one of the four men Harvey has swindled, and, as a final bitter blow to Harvey, after the wedding his conservatory is stripped of his precious orchid collection.

More briefly, the father of a Jilly Cooper character is described as an inadequate father because of his absorption in his collection: 'Rupert hasn't had an easy life ... Charles [was] much too preoccupied with Old Masters and young mistresses. Rupert's pretty unstable as a result' (Cooper, 1980: 43).

There is a third level, however, at which the possessions are dangerous in themselves. In Peter Marks's *Collector's Choice*, the collector Harry Buchmann has 'bought' a wife: 'He learned he could buy beautiful porcelains; why not a good looking woman? A top-quality piece with no cracks, flaws or chips' (Marks, 1975: 95). But Jessica, his wife, turns out to be flawed after all. 'She had no illusions that Harry wanted her only for decoration but, seeing him dote on his porcelains, had wrongly assumed that he would grant her the same attention' (*ibid.*: 95). When he refuses to agree to a divorce, Jessica finds a way to force the issue:

> You've been extremely lucky that nothing's ever been broken. I mean, all those porcelains, the ancient glass you tell everyone is so priceless, even some of the bronzes are very fragile. I could get very careless, Harry.
> (*ibid.*: 124)

Her husband subsequently comes home to find that

> on the floor, beneath the glass shelves, was the Mayan terracotta figurine, smashed into a hundred pieces. On the shelf where the delicate

figure had stood was a note reading 'Darling – I am desolate about this. Can you ever forgive me?'

(ibid.: 125)

Harry Buchmann, enslaved by his possessions, is thus put at the mercy of a woman he had formerly considered only as an object – and pays the price for his inability to understand her as a person.

The two erotic novels discussed in the previous section, *The Captive Flesh* and *The Discipline of Pearls*, involve important characters too who have difficulty forming relationships: Marietta recognizes that her captor Kasim is 'enslaved by his own nature' (Cordell, 1993: 192) and the Major's heir, Stone, the tall stranger who presented Marika with the pendant, is described as 'remote and unwilling to form attachments with others – especially women' (Swann, 1995: 192). But Marika, being a rather more modern heroine than Marietta, is determined to change Stone: 'We've put our mark on each other, Stone, she thought, whether or not you want to face up to that fact. And I intend to make you acknowledge me' (*ibid.*: 192).

All this is fairly consonant with the popular stereotype of the socially inadequate collector. But what about the moral tone? Would we be justified in deducing from the frequent authorial disapproval of collectors that the activity generally is regarded as immoral? Again, I think the key to the question lies in the nature of popular fiction and its tendency to interest itself in excess rather than normality: of course people who are *only* interested in things have trouble forming relationships with people. But the fact that popular fiction stresses the extremes does not mean that its readers believe that life really is like that.

The fatal flaw: the predictable collector

Many of the fictional collectors discussed above suffer a downfall: from their seat atop a pile of priceless possessions they are brought low. Sometimes it is their inability to communicate with other people that causes their fall, as in the cases of Marks's Harry Buchmann and Archer's Harvey Metcalfe. But frequently there is another reason: they are easy victims of conmen or quarries for detectives because they are so completely predictable.

To be orderly in the way one cares for one's collection is, in popular fiction, normal for collectors. Shirley Conran's Victor had an office like a modern museum, which conjures up images of careful arrangement. Conan Doyle's philandering ceramics collector scrupulously records his unscrupulous (human) conquests in a catalogue, and in Roald Dahl's story Oswald's canes are displayed neatly in racks. Rarely do these collectors seem to live in the sort of chaos, or even the apparent chaos, that many real collectors enjoy. Sometimes this order extends into the way one's *time* is organized. Archer's Harvey Metcalfe, for example, 'rose at 7.30 am, a habit he could not break' (Archer, 1982: 113). Such order, particularly in someone who collects systematically or in a consistent area, turns the collector into a sitting duck for someone prepared to study his habits and tastes.

While I have suggested that overall the downfall of Harvey Metcalfe results from his putting possessions above people, one particular episode in the book, the plan which involves his collecting, relies very heavily on his predictability, both in his tastes in art and the timing, to the nearest second, of his actions. The plan, dreamed up by that victim of Metcalfe's who is also a Bond Street art dealer, is to sell Metcalfe a forged Van Gogh. Since it is important that no one else tries to buy the painting before Harvey, it has to be placed in the gallery window just before Harvey walks past, and to make the affair still more convincing and to appeal to Harvey's competitive instinct, another conspirator affects the clothes and accent of a German art dealer.

To begin with, the day goes according to plan: 'Harvey habitually spent the first morning of Wimbledon Fortnight visiting the Summer Exhibition at the Royal Academy in Piccadilly. He would then follow this with visits to most of the West End's major galleries ... This morning was no exception' (Archer, 1982: 115). After a few hiccups ('Oh no, damn it, he's gone into Sotheby's' (*ibid.*: 129)), and with the help of two-way radios, the picture is sold and Harvey relieved of £447,560.

In Peter Marks's *Collector's Choice*, the hero and art thief Andor has a devious plan for stealing a valuable Picasso from Harry Buchmann, the collector mentioned above who has problems with his marriage. When Jessica demands the Picasso as a divorce settlement, Andor offers to buy the picture from Harry temporarily to protect it until the divorce proceedings are complete. Actually he absconds with the picture to Switzerland. For the plan to be successful, Andor has to understand Buchmann's psychology. Buchmann must be sufficiently desperate to hand over the money without waiting for Andor's cheque to clear. He must be sufficiently attached to his antiquities collection to be prepared to risk the Picasso. Andor easily predicts Buchmann's reaction to his offer, and the $750,000 picture is his.

When Sherlock Holmes wants to keep Adelbert Gruner occupied while he searches for Gruner's infamous catalogue, the long-suffering Doctor Watson must pose as a fellow collector: 'Now, Watson, I want you to do something for me ... spend the next twenty-four hours in an intensive study of Chinese pottery' (Conan Doyle, 1993: 1052). Armed with his rapidly acquired knowledge of 'the hall-marks of the great artist-decorators, of the mystery of the cyclical dates, of the Yung-lo, the writings of Tang-ying, and the glories of the primitive period of the Sung and the Yuan' (p. 1052), Watson ventures forth armed with a piece of Ming 'the sight of which would drive a real connoisseur wild' (p. 1053). Holmes expects to have no trouble locating the book – Gruner has been described to him as 'a precise, tidy cat of a man in many of his ways' (p. 1048).

Gruner fulfils Holmes's expectations and admits Watson to his study. It is the unfortunate Watson, however, who spoils things; he arouses Gruner's suspicions by admitting to not having read Gruner's book:

> 'Dear me, this becomes more and more difficult for me to understand! You are a connoisseur and a collector with a very valuable piece in your collection, and yet you have never troubled to consult the one book which would have told you of the real meaning and value of what you held. How do you explain that?'
>
> 'I am a very busy man. I am a doctor in practice.'
>
> 'That is no answer. If a man has a hobby he follows it up, whatever his other pursuits may be.'
>
> (*ibid.*: 1055–6)

It is always possible to recognize a true collector, implies Gruner's speech – a claim that is the obverse of the idea that collectors' behaviour can always be predicted. And how can the true collector be recognized? Because he follows up his hobby *no matter what*. Is this another way of saying he is obsessed?

The collection mania

Gruner seems to be an obsessive. 'He has the collection mania in its most acute form', observes Holmes (*ibid.*: 1054). And obsession as a characteristic of the collector occurs again. In G.K. Chesterton's detective story 'The Curse of the Golden Cross' (Chesterton, 1976), an archaeologist discovering an ancient golden cross in a Middle Eastern cave is pursued by a collector who wants it too. Although the archaeologist knows the latter only as the shadowy figure who chased him through the cave and fired a gun at him and from the 'signs and symbols and queer impersonal messages' he has received, he is able to describe the collector thus:

> He does not seem to have any religious sentiment or fanaticism on the point; he seems to have no passion but the passion of a collector of curiosities. That is one of the things that makes me feel sure he is a man of the West and not of the East. But this particular curiosity seems to have driven him quite crazy.
>
> (*ibid.*: 104)

As if he was not mad enough already, the discovery of a duplicate cross in a Sussex tomb 'turned him into a demoniac possessed of seven devils' (*ibid.*: 104). So Father Brown investigates and solves the case; but not before the maniac collector has managed to murder a rector.

Spyros Stiarkis, the wealthy Greek who is a suspected kidnapper in Shirley Conran's *Lace 2*, is described, too, as 'an obsessive art collector' (Conran, 1985: 388) with a 'passion' for acquiring his late brother's possessions, as I mentioned above. The fact that this strikes fear into the kidnapped porn star's mother suggests that she thinks he may do something irrational – otherwise would not a family member be rather a lesser evil, as kidnappers go?

In one of M. R. James's best-known ghost stories, 'Canon Alberic's Scrapbook', a throwaway line indicates a belief that even if collectors are not mad, they are incapable of the same moral standards as normal people. When Dennistoun, collecting in France on behalf of his college, is offered an ancient manuscript for the absurdly cheap price of two hundred and fifty francs, James notes, 'Even a collector's conscience is sometimes stirred, and Dennistoun's conscience was tenderer than a collector's' (James, 1992: 12).

The ideas that collectors are predictable and that they are obsessive are of course closely connected: if someone is a monomaniac then at least you always know what he is thinking about!

Conclusion

Essentially four stereotypes of collectors, then, predominate in popular fiction: the philanderer, the social inadequate, the collector who is orderly to the point of predictability, and the obsessive. To return to the question I posed earlier: does this mean that this is how people see collectors?

My answer would probably be hopelessly vague: 'in a sense'. The philandering collector is contrary to the normal stereotype, but the link between sex and collecting has been considered to be true, albeit in a different form, at least since Freud. That collectors are socially inadequate, predictable or obsessive in popular fiction can be explained by the tendency of popular fiction to exaggerate everything, and the implicit moral disapproval can be interpreted as disapproval of the collectors in the books taking their collections too far. It seems a little unfair, of course, that the books set up collectors as creatures of excess only to punish them for it, but this is what fiction tends to do.

At this point you will no doubt be complaining that I haven't really achieved very much. I have looked at the stereotypes in the books, suggested that they can't be very accurate because people can't really believe them and anyway people don't, and decided that popular fiction isn't really much use as a mirror of attitudes. But if I already thought I knew what people thought, why did I bother reading the books at all?

I believe that reading fiction can help us understand what people do and think in real life by offering clear models that we can then go on to test, more analytically, on real people. The often simplistic nature of popular fiction makes it a source of quite clear stereotypes and so quite clear ideas. The books themselves cannot give us the answers, but they can help us decide what questions to ask.

Bibliography

Archer, J. (1982) *Not a Penny More, Not a Penny Less*, London: Coronet.

Benson, E.F. (1991) *Lucia Victrix*, London: Penguin.

Chesterton, G.K. (1976) 'The Curse of the Golden Cross', in *The Incredulity of Father Brown*, London: Penguin.

Conan Doyle, A. (1993) 'The Adventure of the Illustrious Client', in *The Case-Book of Sherlock Holmes*, Ware: Wordsworth.

Conran, S. (1985) *Lace 2*, London: Penguin.

Conran, S. (1995) *Tiger Eyes*, London: Pan.

Cooper, J. (1980) *Bella*, London: Corgi.

Cordell, C. (1993) *The Captive Flesh*, London: Black Lace.

Dahl, R. (1991) 'The Visitor', in *The Collected Short Stories of Roald Dahl*, London: Penguin.

Eagleton, T. (1983) *Literary Theory*, Oxford: Blackwell.

Forrester, J. (1994) 'Freud and collecting', in J. Elsner and R. Cardinal (eds), *The Cultures of Collecting*, London: Reaktion Books.

James, M.R. (1992) 'Canon Alberic's Scrapbook', 'The Mezzotint', 'The Diary of Mr Poynter', 'The Haunted Dollshouse', in *Ghost Stories*, Ware: Wordsworth.

Marks, P. (1972) *Collector's Choice*, New York: Dell.

Swann, S. (1995) *The Discipline of Pearls*, London: X-Libris.

7

Mr Cropper and Mrs Brown: good and bad collectors in the work of A. S. Byatt and other recent fiction

HELEN WILKINSON

Introduction

Collectors recognize the power of the impulses which drive them to collect. The potency of the need to make collections is eternally apparent to those who do it. Non-collectors also have strong and culturally pervasive opinions about the activity. One of the television advertisements for the National Lottery broadcast in the summer of 1995 featured two sets of flat-dwellers. A couple with a taste for loud music and late nights are seen keeping awake the resident in the upstairs flat, a middle-aged single man in a single bed. The scenario of the advertisement hinges on the transformation of this lonely individual's life by a lottery win. Above his bed is a framed butterfly collection. In the late twentieth-century cultural vocabulary, his collection is as much a shorthand for virginal isolation as are his striped flannel pyjamas. While we may wish to deny or contradict the validity of those opinions, those of us who study collectors, or who wish members of the public to visit institutionalized collections in museums, would do well to consider popular images of collecting. Moreover, such stereotypes are obviously part of the mind-set of the collectors themselves, and so may serve to shape collecting practice: perhaps it is in response to negative stereotypes such as these that so many collectors seek external validation for their collecting practice in collecting clubs, or in museums through People's Shows.

For this reason, the portrayal of collectors in contemporary culture is a rewarding field for study. This chapter sets out to consider the portrayal of collecting and collectors in the modern novel.

In my work on recent fiction, I have identified a number of recurring themes, and a consideration of each of these forms the structure of this chapter. These themes are concerned with the importance of the material in people's lives, and with the ways in which its significance is explored in fiction; with portrayals of the collector in society, and with the use of collections in defining a status, or a self-image; with the relationship between collecting and creativity, and with the ways in which novelists reflect current thinking about the influence of gender and sexuality on collecting practice.

The discussion will focus on A. S. Byatt but will also consider the work of other novelists, including John Fowles, whose portrayal of Frederick Clegg in *The Collector* (Fowles, 1989) is perhaps the best known and most compelling handling of the theme. Fundamentally, this novel harnesses a set of ideas about collecting similar to those implicit in the National Lottery advertisement. Byatt's writing on collections, on the other hand, is particularly absorbing because her fiction attempts an analysis of the impulses which lead individuals to collect. Moreover, collections in Byatt's work may be negative and sterile, but they may also be positive and life-affirming. Nowhere is this dichotomy more directly presented than in the short story 'Art Work'. This story encapsulates many of Byatt's ideas about collecting and touches upon all of the themes mentioned above. An analysis of it provides a convenient way in to Byatt's work.

'Art Work': a case study

The Matisse Stories (Byatt, 1993b) is a collection of three stories each growing out of a painting by Matisse. In 'Art Work', Byatt contrasts the repressed and self-conscious art of an unsuccessful painter with the startling installation produced in a London gallery by his family's cleaner, Mrs Brown.

In his art, the painter, Robin Dennison, explores ideas about colour, and the anxieties of representation:

> Robin was a neo-realist. He painted expanses of neutral colours, wooden planks, glass table-tops, beige linen, crumbling plaster, and somewhere, somewhere unexpected, not quite in a corner ... he painted something very small and brilliant, a glass ball, a lustre vase, a bouquet of bone-china flowers (never anything alive), a heap of feathers.
>
> (Byatt, 1993b: 52)

Robin has a collection of such objects which he paints repeatedly. He keeps them on a special table in his studio, and to confirm their status as hallowed objects, he refers to them as fetishes:

> Robin Dennison's 'fetishes' have a table of their own, a white-painted wooden table, very simple. Once they were mantelpiece 'things' but as

they took on their status as 'fetishes' they were given this solidly unassuming English altar. What they have in common is a certain kind of glossy, very brightly coloured solidity. They are the small icons of a cult of colour.

(ibid.: 62)

Robin's is an art of precision, and selecting exactly the right representative of each colour for his collection causes him considerable anxiety. Mrs Brown's lack of order causes him even more anxiety: 'Mrs Brown is chaotic and wild to look at and a secret smoker and represents – even while dispersing it or re-distributing it – filth' (*ibid.*: 58). However, Mrs Brown's 'dirty' attitude to objects comes to represent creativity and potentiality, opposed to Robin's sterility and impotence. She defies conventions of taste, but it is her way of seeing and mode of collecting which are finally endorsed.

The story is an exploration of the relationship between collecting and creativity. Elsewhere, the act of collecting is used as an analogy for the creative act, whether written or visual. Here both artists *literally* make art out of their collections: Robin's collecting is as repressed as his art, but Mrs Brown's collecting is part of an ongoing process of transformation and transfiguration. The dynamics of her collecting do not stop with the moment of acquisition. In this, she is perhaps the epitome of a good collector for Byatt: her need for objects goes beyond the mere fact of ownership.

It is highly significant, of course, that Mrs Brown is a woman and Robin is a man. Robin's collection is kept apart on its own 'altar', and he resents Mrs Brown's cleaning and rearranging, which have the effect of denying the collection's special status and treating it simply as part of the home. Mrs Brown's collection is synthesized, not into a home but into her art, which is a kind of bizarre parody of the 'home' which society expects women to create. In this, Byatt exploits the different collecting modes often identified as being typical of men and women. Women's collections are often defined, by both themselves and society, as trivial or domestic, part of the home. Men's collections are much more likely to be taken seriously by society and set apart by the collector from the domestic milieu. The objects *in* the two collections equally constitute a kind of paradigm of male and female collecting practice: Mrs Brown's clothes are a foreshadowing of the soft sculptures which are canonized as art in the gallery at the end of the story:

> She makes all her own clothes out of whatever comes to hand, old plush curtains, Arab blankets, parachute silk, his own discarded trousers. She makes them flamboyantly, with patches and fringes and braid and bizarre buttons. The epitome of tat, Robin considers.

(ibid.: 58)

The phrase 'whatever comes to hand' is crucial. Mrs Brown's objects are transfigured from everyday life. Robin's objects are removed from their everyday context, and deliberately stripped of their associations. Indeed, it worries him that one of his objects may be read for its associations rather than as a representative of its colour:

> [The collection] began with the soldier who cost 5/6 when Robin was little, and is made of painted wood with red trousers and a blue jacket and a tall, bulbous black wooden bearskin ... Robin does not often paint him now – he cannot clear him of his double connotations of militarism and infantilism, and he loves him for neither of these, but because he was his first model for slivers of shine on rounded surfaces.
>
> (*ibid.*: 62)

Mrs Brown's objects are those she encounters in her work as cleaner and mother, and her collecting of the lost and discarded and their transformation into art are a kind of triumphant apotheosis. She is revealed to have had a troubled and dramatic life, and to have suffered domestic violence. Her installation is read as a feminist critique of the tyranny of home-making, but with a note of redemptive humour in the bizarre excess of creativity:

> The cavern has a crazy kind of resemblance to a lived-in room. Chests of drawers, made of orange boxes covered with patchworks of wall-paper, from vulgar silver roses to William Morris birds ... reveal half-open treasure chests with mazy compartments containing crazy collections of things. White bone buttons. Glass stoppers. Chicken bones. Cuff-links, all single. Medicine bottles with lacquered labels, full of iridescent beads and cod-liver oil capsules. Pearlised plastic poppet beads and sunflower seeds, doll's teaspoons and drifts of variegated tealeaves and dead rose-petals. Sugar mice, some half-chewed. String, bright green, waxed, red, hairy brown, running from compartment to compartment.
>
> (*ibid.*: 78)

The triumph of Mrs Brown's vision over Robin's way of seeing the world is consummated by the fact that it is his lost cufflinks and discarded items from his house which are transformed into her art. Mrs Brown, with her cipher-like name, also represents the ordinary collector, rather than a collector operating in privileged artistic mode. Byatt celebrates not only the attitude of women to objects, but also the part objects play in everyday lives. The ethos of the story is ultimately redemptive, however, in that, inspired by Mrs Brown, Deborah resumes her long-neglected art work and Robin begins to paint images which are daring and vibrant. The materiality of human experience, social determinants, gender difference and sexuality are all addressed in 'Art Work'. I intend now to consider each of these themes in turn, with primary reference to Byatt, but casting the net more widely when appropriate.

Materialism, modernism and recent fiction

'Art Work' illustrates how the *material* may be a central concern of fiction, from its opening image of a still, contained Matisse painting to the climactic description of Mrs Brown's ebullient sculptures. The place of material culture in the novel has been a contentious issue in the twentieth century. Nineteenth-century novelists found it natural to use rich descriptions of physical settings and were alive to the possibility of conveying abstract concepts and nuances of character through distinctions of possessions, surroundings and dress. However, the modern movement largely saw such mundanities as barriers to the portrayal of character and individuality, condemning writers who made use of them as materialistic. One of the most scathing onslaughts was made by Virginia Woolf, who in doing so invokes another Mrs Brown. In her essay 'Mr Bennett and Mrs Brown', she imagines a meeting on a train between Arnold Bennett and an old woman whom she names Mrs Brown, and describes how Bennett would set about describing her appearance, and by dwelling on extraneous details would miss the real Mrs Brown, the essence of her character:

> He ... would observe every detail with immense care. He would notice the advertisements; the way in which the cushion bulged between the buttons; how Mrs Brown wore a brooch which had cost three-and-ten-three [three shillings and tenpence three farthings] at Whitworth's bazaar; and had mended both gloves – indeed the thumb of the left-hand glove had been replaced ... What can Mr Bennett be about? ... He is trying to make us imagine for him; he is trying to hypnotize us into the belief that because he has made a house, there must be a person living there. With all his powers of observation, which are marvellous, with all his sympathy and humanity, which are great, Mr Bennett has never once looked at Mrs Brown in her corner.
>
> (Woolf, 1992: 78–80)

An exception to this modernist trend is, of course, Joyce's *Ulysses*, which famously shows a fanatical desire to accumulate realistic detail. We learn more about the physical setting of Bloom's life than that of any previous literary protagonist:

> Milly was a kiddy then. Molly had that elephant grey dress with the braided frogs. Mantailored with selfcovered buttons. She didn't like it because I sprained my ankle first day she wore choir picnic at the Sugarloaf ... Happy. Happier then. Snug little room with the red wallpaper, Dockerell's, one and ninepence a dozen. Milly's tubbing night. American soap I bought: elderflower.
>
> (Joyce, 1993: 148)

Such references in Joyce acknowledge the *materiality* of human consciousness, and the importance of objects in an individual's self-definition. Joyce enshrined the material in the most influential fictional work of the twentieth century, and enabled the kind of alertness to the material in later twentieth-century fiction which Woolf would have us believe to be outmoded. Indeed the book itself is a kind of collection, full of lists, accumulations, an impulse to compendiousness, containing birth, death and everything in between.

The novel has, at various times in its history, been regarded as a predominantly female form. It is certainly an ideal vehicle for an examination of the thousand petty domestic tyrannies which govern the lives of many women, and has been used as such from Jane Austen to Anita Brookner. In her novels, A. S. Byatt uses details of the domestic objects which surround her heroines to examine the way women's lives in particular may be shaped and constrained by material. Objects in Byatt have an *active* role: they are not merely used, but play a part. The extreme example of this is the death of Stephanie in *Still Life*. It is perhaps a rather heavy-handed piece of symbolism that the heroine who fails to reconcile her intellectual and emotional needs, and who settles for confining domesticity, should be killed by her own refrigerator. Other female characters show the capacity to be dominated by their environments. Winifred, whose son suffers an acute breakdown and flees from home, contrasts her perceived failure as a mother with the surviving accoutrements of housewifery and motherhood, now a kind of parody:

> She had been pleased to acquire, to be given, most of these things, she remembered sourly. They made her life appear to correspond with some ordered, ideal form, some series of ceremonies to which the proper utensils lent authenticity and grace ... But Marcus's flight brought terror. The home was not a home if he screamed and wept at the thought of returning to it.
>
> (Byatt, 1985: 147)

Maud, the main female character in *Possession*, is a supremely efficient academic. But in spite of her formidable intelligence, she feels oppressed by some objects, perhaps precisely because they are outside her control. Her house is pristinely ordered and her memory of the turmoil wreaked on mind and spirit by a former lover has a material focus: 'Her mind was full of an image of a huge, unmade, stained and rumpled bed, its sheets pulled into standing peaks here and there, like the surface of whipped egg-white' (Byatt, 1991: 56). Her refuge from this, her 'clean white sheets', is both a metaphor for purity and calm, and a provider of it in its physical reality. The concern of characters in *Possession* with collections and souvenirs or 'sacred objects' is in a sense merely a specialized form of the sensitivity towards the material shared by many of the characters in the novel. The plot concerns two researchers, Maud who works on Christabel Lamotte and Roland who works on Randolph Ash; both their subjects are fictional Victorian poets. The chance discovery of a letter leads Roland and Maud to uncover a relationship between the two poets, documented in an extensive correspondence. Their interest in the collection of letters is in competition with that of Mortimer Cropper, an American scholar, obsessed with building up the complete Ash archive. Differing attitudes to collections and objects are thus at the heart of the novel. Moreover, objects have an active part in its narrative. Christabel has a collection of stones, gathered during the brief time she spent with Ash as his mistress. She keeps them in the house she shares with her companion Blanche, and uses them as doorstops and paperweights. Blanche sews these stones into the hem of her dress when she commits suicide in the Thames, to stop her skirts giving her buoyancy. Since Blanche's suicide is a direct response to Christabel's rejection, implicit in her holiday with Ash, the connection is highly significant. The stones move from the narrative in which they were placed by Christabel, a record of a joyful holiday, into a new narrative of Blanche's making. They become instrumental in destroying Christabel's idyllic memories of that holiday, memories which she had sought to authenticate by her retention of these souvenirs.

A strength of Byatt's novels is her sensitivity to objects, which gives her writing an unusual depth and resonance. Her writing on collecting should be seen in the light of the importance of all material culture to her fiction.

The collector in and out of society

The most famous and most explicit treatment of the collector in the novel is surely John Fowles's *The Collector* (1989). A socially inadequate insect collector wins the pools and sets about collecting the perfect specimen, a young woman with whom he has become obsessed. The pools win is significant because this sudden acquisition of a fortune enables the collector, Clegg, to sever all normal connections with the outside world. He no longer needs to work, and his remaining relatives are despatched on an extended holiday to Australia. In this way, the collector's stereotypical social inadequacy is literalized in a complete divorce from society.

The connection between Clegg's insect collecting and his depraved kidnapping is explicit to his captive:

'Tell me about yourself. Tell me what you do in your free time.'
I'm an entomologist. I collect butterflies.

'Of course', she said, 'I remember they said so in the paper. Now you've collected me.'

She seemed to think it was funny, so I said, in a manner of speaking.

'No, not in a manner of speaking. Literally. You've pinned me in this little room and you can come and gloat over me.'

I don't think of it like that at all.

(Fowles, 1989: 44)

Yet the similarity of the impulse to collect butterflies and to acquire his chosen woman in this most repressive way is revealed through the collector's language.

Seeing her always made me feel like I was catching a rarity, going up to it very careful, heart-in-mouth as they say. A pale Clouded Yellow, for instance. I always thought of her like that, I mean words like elusive and sporadic, and very refined – not like the other ones, even the pretty ones. More for the real connoisseur.

(*ibid.*: 9)

Throughout the novel, collecting as practised by the protagonist is seen uniformly as repressive, negating and sterile:

I am one in a row of specimens. It's when I try to flutter out of line that he hates me. I'm meant to be dead, pinned, always the same, always beautiful. He knows that part of my beauty is being alive, but it's the dead me he wants.

(*ibid.*: 203)

The logical conclusion of the negating impulse of collecting comes at the end of the novel. Miranda dies, and the collector is left plotting another kidnap now that his possession of Miranda is complete.

The butterfly collector offers a particularly potent symbol of collecting as a negating activity, because in order to be collected, butterflies must first be killed: 'I'm thinking of all the butterflies that would have come from these if you'd let them live. I'm thinking of all the living beauty you've ended' (*ibid.*: 54–5). The killing jar is a recurring image in the novel, and ultimately Miranda's subterranean prison becomes her own 'killing jar': after her death she is more completely part of Clegg's collection. The novel seems to offer an alternative mode of collecting when Miranda attempts to persuade Clegg to become an art collector:

Look what you could do. You could ... You could collect pictures. I'd tell you what to look for, I'd introduce you to people who would tell you about art-collecting. Think of all the poor artists you could help. Instead of massacring butterflies like a stupid schoolboy.

(*ibid.*: 76)

This vision is not ultimately affirmed, Miranda coming to concur with her lover and mentor's denunciation of collectors: 'They're anti-life, anti-art, anti-everything' (*ibid.*: 123). Nevertheless, in its suggestion of a distinction between art collecting and insect collecting, the novel harnesses the social convention which sees art collecting as an upper-class, high-culture activity, and insect collecting as a banal, lower-class activity with little cultural cachet, and associations of obsession and inadequacy.

The Collector is a profoundly disturbing novel. As a portrait of an unbalanced and obsessive personality it is staggering in its depth and power. However, it has surprisingly little to offer the student of collecting. In a sense, the collector of Fowles's novel is simply the lonely and repressed trainspotter of popular culture developed to its logical conclusion, albeit with unnerving vividness. It successfully exploits a stereotype and has perhaps been instrumental in fuelling the dissemination of that stereotype. But it tells us little about the millions of ordinary collectors who balance their enthusiasm (or even obsession) with a job, a social life and conventional expressions of sexuality. Byatt's collector Mortimer Cropper in *Possession* bears a marked similarity to Frederic Clegg in some respects. However, her exploration of collecting is ultimately richer than that of Fowles because the sterility of Cropper's collecting is contrasted with the activities of good collectors, like Mrs Brown. Byatt offers an enlightening exploration of the dynamics of a widespread phenomenon, whereas Fowles presents a singular portrayal of deviance.

Because two of Byatt's recent works have a Victorian setting, her fiction also allows for an exploration of collecting in different societies. The activities of her Victorian collectors belong to an altogether more serious and respected mode of collecting. Randolph Ash in *Possession* is a poet, but collects natural history with seriousness and dedication. A fictional portrait of him by Manet is described as showing him in front of his collection: his activities as artist and scientist are seen not as contradictory, but rather as complementary. The protagonist in *Morpho Eugenia* (published as one of a pair of novellas in *Angels and Insects* (Byatt, 1993a)) is a professional natural historian and collector. For both of these Victorian collectors, the collection is a way of structuring a new understanding of the world and the individual's place in it, in the light of Darwinism. The potential of the collection is not limited to a personal narrative, but offers a way of looking at the world, a microcosm. Ash's display cases housing his collection are 'sealed worlds' (Byatt, 1991: 447). Crucially, collecting for Ash and his contemporaries and the collectors in *Morpho Eugenia* is not only about personal definition through collecting, possibly in defiance of, or isolation from, society. Collections may also be a way of *presenting* oneself, defining one's status or character to the outside world.

Collections have different meanings, according to whether they exist in a public or a private domain. The crossing of the boundary between the two territories is a moment of enormous significance, and it occurs when a collection is shown for the first time by an individual to an audience.

In *The Game* Byatt contrasts two sisters, Julia, a novelist, and Cassandra, an academic. Both had a disturbing relationship during their adolescence with Simon Moffit, a natural historian and snake collector. Both Simon and Cassandra, the academic, are collectors, Simon professionally. One of the key moments in the novel is when the young Simon shows Cassandra his collection of snakes, marking a new phase in their relationship: 'Today he showed me the snakes. I hoped he might, as I imagine he would not show them to most people' (Byatt, 1992: 73). This apocalyptic act of 'showing' the collection also constitutes a defining moment in *The Waterfall* (Drabble, 1969), and will be discussed later.

Collecting, identity and gender

Collecting practices reflect external personality traits. More than that, they may be used as ways of shaping one's personality, a deliberate reconstruction of one's identity. The dangers for one's sense of self inherent in the potential of collections to do this are explored by Byatt through characters who collect material associated with an individual. A major theme of *Possession* is the relationship between a scholar or biographer and the subject of his or her enquiries. The lives of Roland and Maud reflect the lives of their subjects in a very obvious way, and all the scholars experience anxiety that their life is being subsumed in that of their subject. This anxiety is most acute in Cropper, with his obsession with acquiring objects associated with Ash. Remembering his first encounter with an Ash 'relic' he experiences the sense that his life is nothing beyond his encounters with Ash, 'as though he had no existence, no separate existence of his own after that first contact with the paper's electric rustle and the ink's energetic black looping' (Byatt, 1991: 105). Roland experiences a similar *frisson* when he finds a lost letter of Ash's in a book which had belonged to the latter, a discovery on which the plot hinges. The emotional power of objects with historical or personal associations is acknowledged and celebrated by the novel. What is seen as dangerous and negative about Cropper's relationship with Ash is not his feelings of excitement and awe on handling objects which Ash had owned, or even his desire to possess them. Rather, his *response* to those objects is flawed. Whereas Roland's encounter with Ash's objects inspires him to creative action, Cropper's collection is ensconced in airless sterility, and his writing on Ash does not gain insight from his possession of those objects. This distinction is the key to understanding the novel's ethical judgements about collecting. Souvenir-hunting is distasteful, but collecting can be liberating and creative:

> [On Roland's desire to keep the letters:] He had always slightly despised those enchanted by things touched by the great: Balzac's ornate walking stick, Robert Louis Stevenson's flageolet, a black lace mantilla once worn by George Eliot. Mortimer Cropper was in the habit of drawing Randolph Henry Ash's large gold watch from an inner fob pocket, and arranging his time by Ash's timepiece. Roland's Xeroxes were cleaner and clearer than the originals ... But he wanted the originals.
>
> (Byatt, 1991: 23)

Roland is puzzled by his response because he habitually feels nearest to Ash when following 'the twists and turns of his syntax, suddenly sharp and clear in an unexpected epithet' (*ibid.*: 20). The objects he describes with scorn are precisely like those prized by Cropper's family in a private cabinet of curiosities, even down to the detail that it had contained Balzac's walking stick. His response to the letters is approved, however, because it spurs him to a genuinely deepened response to Ash. The night before Ash's funeral his wife anticipates the intrusions of future biographers and collectors with horror: 'He shall not be picked by vultures' (*ibid.*: 443). The emotional force of this condemnation of collectors can only be balanced in the ethics of the novel if the collector makes use of the collection as a starting-point for a personal act of definition or creativity, not merely appropriating the collector's identity for his or her self.

Roland's own life is enriched through his encounter with Ash via his letters. He begins a new, more positive relationship, a new career, and begins to write poetry. By contrast, a characteristic of those with a merely acquisitive attitude to relics, literary or otherwise, is a failure to live except through their original owner. Recently Michael Palin has presented such a collector in his novel *Hemingway's Chair* (1995). The protagonist is a post office clerk in Suffolk, obsessed with Ernest Hemingway, and with a desire to possess his fishing chair. The clerk is a stereotype with few social skills, who bizarrely *becomes* Hemingway when in contact with his possessions: he is sexually inexperienced, but has considerable sexual prowess when he 'is' Hemingway; he is naturally timid, but becomes assertive:

> [Sitting in the chair] Martin became slowly and perceptibly more substantial. His face lost the earnest frown with which he had arrived, his eyes grew wider but softer, the line of his jaw grew stronger, his slim chest widened. Even the sight of his toes barely able to touch the ground did not detract from the remarkable display of possession.
>
> (Palin, 1995: 185)

'Possessions' here, as in Byatt, is a multi-layered concept: Martin achieves *self*-possession only through possession of Hemingway's objects.

In these acts of self-definition through collecting, there are certain discernible gender differences. Men and women collect in different ways, and so the collections of Byatt's male and female characters reflect this. Frequently her women synthesize into their home, while her men have more professional or institutionalized collections: Cropper's collection is professional, as well as a personal obsession, defining his status as an academic, *the* academic expert on Ash. *The Virgin in the Garden*, the companion novel to *Still Life* (Byatt, 1981), contains an example of such gender difference. Lucas Simmonds is a biology master whose bizarre religious obsession and fixation with Marcus (Winifred's son from *Still Life*) causes Marcus's breakdown. He has a gruesome collection in the biology lab, containing images of deformity and incompletion. The collection is highly formal, ordered in a scientific manner and given a professional status:

> Dozens of foetuses. Tiny creamy-pink rats, blunt-headed, blind-eyed, with minute stumps of feet and tails, all rolled together and surely slightly crumbling like cheese in the surrounding liquid. Larger, round-bellied ratlings, cord and placenta still attached, flat-headed unborn cats, pallid flesh, unformed eyes closed against the glass wall and the light. Snake embryos, preserved in strings, like beads on a chain, coiled and forever undelivered.
>
> (Byatt, 1981: 123)

This style of collecting contrasts with that of another character, Felicity Wells, whose collection furnishes her room:

> Miss Wells' room was tiny, decorated, perched in and temporary. Black Victorian bookcases, with machine-cut Gothic beading ... supported a bitty collection of objects.
>
> (*ibid.*: 109)

Collecting is also used as an image in the work of Byatt's sister, Margaret Drabble, and although the theme does not have the same prominence as in Byatt's work, Drabble offers some telling insights. Emma Evans, the protagonist in *The Garrick Year* (Drabble, 1966), fills the family home obsessively with Victorian clutter, transports her collection to Hereford when the family moves there for a summer, and uses it to transform their ultra-modern flat. In this, she might be said to be typical of a female collector who makes her collection an integral part of her home, without explicitly elevating it to the status of a collection enshrined on its own 'altar' (Byatt, 1993b: 62). Her husband David's failure to recognize the emotional significance of her collection is a symbol of their estrangement: he calls it her 'filthy clutter'

(Drabble, 1966: 125). The decisive moment of the novel comes when David finds Emma's new purchase, a small marble pillar which she had felt compelled to buy:

> I knew that I was even going to pay fifteen pounds for it if he made me, as I had already worked out that it would look good under my marble bust of Lady Mary Wortley-Montague. I felt crazy, and horribly in touch with my own craziness.
>
> (*ibid.*: 123)

Enraged, he throws it down the stairs of their flat, barely missing their baby, an action confirming the finality of the breakdown of the couple's relationship. It is not only that men and women collect differently, but that this gender difference can cause a breakdown in sympathy, a failure of each to understand the other.

The short story 'The Changeling' (from *Sugar and Other Stories* (Byatt, 1988)) concerns a novelist, Josephine, who once wrote a novel about a disturbed schoolboy, Simon Vole, modelled on her own unhappy childhood. This story appears to reveal sympathy with teenage despair, but her own son runs away from home. She fails to help another teenage boy who is entrusted to her care precisely because of the sensitivity she showed in that novel.

Josephine is a collector who aspires to the creation of a perfect home. However, her inadequacy manifests itself in a failure to use collected objects to shape her surroundings. Her home-making reveals the kind of deceit implicit in her construction of herself through her stories as a sympathetic counsellor of teenage problems. She has created an 'ideal home', but it is not a true image of her character:

> The warm and welcoming place, which now existed, was not, she knew, a true expression of herself. It was what she knew must be. What she was, was the obsessive hider in the boiler-room dust.
>
> (Byatt, 1988: 157)

As a child she had a retreat in the school boiler room. She furnished it with a collection of objects secreted there in a kind of parody of the home she later fails to create: 'She collected things: a blanket, a bicycle lamp, an old sweater, a biscuit tin, a special box for pens' (*ibid.*: 154). Worrying about her son's disappearance she agonizes over his response to her home: 'Had he, later than his father, sensed that it was all made up, the warm firelight, the clean clothes, the open door, the smell of cooking?' (*ibid.*: 158).

Josephine is just one of the collectors in Byatt's work whose failure to collect constructively reveals profound personality weaknesses. These personality flaws are more specifically manifested in the collector's sexuality.

Collecting and sexuality

To use a collection to decorate a house is to make use of it, to need it for more than the moment of acquisition. For Byatt, this is the essence of a 'good collection': the dynamics of possession do not end with the moment of acquisition. It is a balanced, rational, social use of a collection. Failure to use a collection in this integrated way leads to the accusations of obsession associated with the popular image of the collector as a sexually repressed or inadequate individual. One of Margaret Drabble's novels from the 1960s offers a classic statement of frustration in possession and links it explicitly to sexual disappointment. Collectors who do not synthesize their collections into their lives may experience a similar failure to synthesize relationships. When the protagonist meets her cousin Lucy for the first time as a child she shows her collection of marbles to her:

> Lucy liked the marbles ... I knew each one, as it were, by face and name.
> I don't think I minded showing them to Lucy: I was not a secretive child,
> merely unhopeful. Lucy looked at them for some time, picking up first
> one and then another, and then she looked at them with something like
> suspicion, and said, 'Do you do anything with them? Or do you just
> collect them?'
>   'I just collect,' I said, and started to put them away again into their
> box. But her question, although I did not show it, had filled me with
> unease, because it was something I had always worried about: For what,
> after all, did one do with things when one had got them? ... I felt there
> was always something left undone, some final joyful possession of them,
> some way to have my having of them more completely. I felt this with all
> games – there was a particular one that I used to play, later, with ration
> books and an old handbag of my mother's, a game of shopping that at
> the outset seemed to promise each time bliss beyond belief – some
> violent orgasmic moment, perhaps, where we would *become* adults,
> where we would *be* our mothers; but the moment never happened, it
> would fade and drop away from us ... leading us nowhere, each time
> by-passing its rightful end. And so it was with sex. Ah well, it is too clear
> to state. But what at the age of seven had I done wrong, to suffer so in
> later life?
>
> (Drabble, 1969: 126)

Sexual disappointment and a failure to collect in a balanced and integrated way are indications of the same character flaws. In this novel, neither is seen as the cause of the other. In Byatt, the link may be more explicit. Cropper's collecting practice, for example, is certainly connected with his sexual repression. He has a classically repressed sexuality with the hall marks of an Oedipus complex. He is in awe of his mother, with whom he lives, and shies away from writing his own biography because he is diffident of writing about her: it is perhaps for this reason that he seeks refuge in writing about another's life:

> In his dreams of her Professor Cropper always lost his sense of proportion, so that she loomed large as his capacious entrance hall, or stood hugely and severely astride his paddock. She expected much of him, and he had not failed her, but feared to fail.
>
> (Byatt, 1991: 102)

He seeks sexual satisfaction not through direct human contact, but through masturbation and the distancing medium of photography:

> [He] drew out those other photographs of which he had a large and varied collection – as far as it was possible to vary, in flesh or tone or angle or close detail, so essentially simple an activity, a preoccupation. He had his own ways of sublimation.
>
> (*ibid.*: 111)

Just as his sex life manifests a failure to engage with other people, his collecting practice embodies a kind of sterility. His collection of Ash's objects is hermetically sealed in a room removed from the world. Its physical separateness embodies his failure to synthesize it into his own life:

> The needle case and the curl of hair would be enshrined in the hexagonal glass room at the very centre of the Stant collection, where Ash's relics and those of his wife, family and acquaintances accumulated in the still desert air ... [He] was briefly visited by a vision of his white temple shining in the desert sun, enclosing cool courts, high staircases and a kind of glass honeycomb of silent cells.
>
> (*ibid.*: 106–7)

Clegg, the eponymous collector in Fowles's novel, has a sexual obsession with his victim. He is also virginal and inadequate. However, it is significant that he does not actually rape Miranda but indulges in more indirect forms of sexual humiliation. Like Cropper, he is happiest indulging his fantasies at one remove, and forces Miranda to pose for obscene photographs.

Both collectors in *The Virgin in the Garden* display a kind of repression. Felicity Wells, usually referred to as 'Miss Wells', is a kind of stereotype of spinsterhood, who even lives in the vicarage. Lucas Simmonds's repression takes a more extreme form. He has a bizarre castration fantasy. He removes the genitals from the pictures of men and women in the biology lab, and later attempts to castrate himself. Other bad collectors in Byatt are also celibate. In *The Game*, Cassandra, who has a dangerously obsessive attitude to objects, is a don at an Oxford women's college, a very traditional image of celibacy. Simon, a snake collector, has chosen a lifestyle – collecting in dangerous foreign locations – which precludes normal sexual contact. Cassandra has a series of rituals which protects her from the outside world. One of these is her rather hysterical Anglo-Catholicism. Her sister wonders what the responses of a religious service mean to her sister: 'form, certainty? She could remember Cassandra's chanting voice from their childhood. Cassandra had always been one for ritual' (Byatt, 1992: 120). Simon has lost his Anglo-Catholic faith, but has developed a quasi-religious obsession with the formlessness and privation of the Amazon. Obsessive, secretive collecting, ritual and celibacy are all interlinked for Simon and Cassandra. Mrs Brown is of course a good collector, but her collecting and art are a kind of sublimation of her sexual self, exorcising as they do the terrors of domestic violence.

In this area perhaps more than any other, Byatt's fiction reflects traditional ideas about collecting rather than prevailing current practice. Certainly some collectors do develop an obsession with their collection in the absence of strong sexual bonds, or as a refuge from unhappy sex lives. But collecting is far too widespread a cultural phenomenon for all its practitioners to have such a warped sexuality in practice. Not all Byatt's collectors are sexually frustrated: Roland and Maud in *Possession* achieve sexual happiness together. Both have had unhappy past sexual experience, and it is significant that they are brought together through a shared involvement with a collection. In this novel, collecting practices are a reflection of character – those with balanced characters collect successfully and couple happily.

Collecting, recreation and creativity

This section sets out to explore the reasons why collecting offers such a potent theme for the novelist, and to explain the frequency of its occurrence in recent fiction. It is of course a widespread cultural phenomenon and one which raises interesting questions of psychology. But then, so are role-playing games, yet it would be difficult to cite significant examples of their appearance in contemporary fiction.

Without resorting to a purely formalist reading, it may be argued that collecting as a theme appeals to the writer because it offers an image for the creative process. In 'Art Work', visual art is both an image for collecting and, in the case of Mrs Brown's creations, a kind of collecting. In *Possession*, biography and criticism are seen as analogous to collecting. Both written and visual creative expression and the formation of a collection are ways of making sense of the world, of forming a narrative of personal or public experience.

An individual's collection forms a kind of personal narrative. Like written narratives, it is exclusive and closes off possibilities, attempting to enshrine a particular version of the past. Collections in novels therefore offer the writer an opportunity to present an alternative narrative, a view of the collector which the main narrative may affirm or subvert. They also deepen the novel, shifting its forms of story-telling from the merely verbal to the material, thus more richly presenting life.

The collector has a psychological need to own the object of his or her enthusiasm, just as a writer needs to control, to appropriate his or her subject. Both are a kind of possession; both may be a reduction. Cropper's writing on Ash, like his collecting, is a strategy of control and appropriation. He reduces the possibilities of Ash by his intrusive, knowing narrative style:

> All this raises the question of the feelings of the ardent poet-lover, now aged thirty-four, for his innocent bride, now no young girl, but a mature thirty-six-year-old aunt, devoted to her nephews and nieces. Was his innocence as great as hers? How had he endured, the twentieth-century mind suspiciously asks, the privations of his long wait?
>
> (Byatt, 1991: 110)

He makes Ash in his own image just as he gathers the properties of Ash for his own collection. It is significant that Roland, one of the 'good' scholars/collectors, becomes a poet at the end of the novel. Poetry, unlike Cropper's proprietorial style of biography, is a creative use of what one has garnered of the world, which extends rather than closes its possibilities.

In 'The Changeling', Josephine in her childhood collected and wrote in secrecy in her boiler-room retreat. In adulthood, she continues to see her writing as an essentially secret activity. She writes to 'exorcise' memories, without reference to a future audience: 'There are writers, believe it, and Josephine Piper was one of them, who can only function by imagining no reader' (Byatt, 1988: 156). Josephine feels oppressed by her house guest, Henry Smee, and suffers acutely from his invasion of her privacy (*ibid.*: 158). Yet her writing exploits him, and after his suicide she draws on his experience for her next work:

> The ghost of those limp yet skilful hands, just that, attached itself to the form of the present Simon (whose name was in fact James) but not so that anyone would have noticed.
>
> (*ibid.*: 160)

This theme of the writer as exploiter, appropriator of her or his subject, occurs also in *The Game*. The title itself carries sinister overtones of prostitution. Julia prostitutes her sister by her exploitative style of writing. She writes a novel based closely on her sister's sequestered academic lifestyle and personal habits, an act of creation that destroys the subject on whom it had fed, driving her sister to suicide. Cassandra likens her experience of appropriation and distortion to the activities of those professional collectors and appropriators, museum curators:

> What was missing was filled in by her with dotted lines, pieces of new string to jerk the joints, or wood to replace limbs as they do in museums, and never a footnote to say, this material is conjectural. This is an eclectic and conflated text.
>
> (Byatt, 1992: 230)

Good collectors, like good writers, do not appropriate their subject in this reductive way, but synthesize. Collections are a deeply serious aspect of Byatt's work: they are both an image for, and part of a process of, creativity and regeneration that her work celebrates.

Conclusion

Novels use words as their medium, but Byatt's novels are enhanced by her sense that the human medium is not merely verbal, but also material.

At the end of *Possession*, Cropper's obsession with acquiring all of Ash leads him to desecrate the poet's grave to retrieve a box placed there by Ash's wife. In the box are a final letter from Lamotte to Ash, unopened, containing a photograph of the couple's daughter, who was being brought up in Norfolk as Christabel's niece. There is also a lock of hair. The protagonists, finding that Ash's wife kept the letter from him, conclude that he never found out about their daughter, and that the lock of hair is Christabel's. But in a postscript to the novel, the reader discovers that the hair is their daughter's, taken by Ash on a journey to Norfolk when he met her secretly:

> There are things which happen and leave no discernible trace, are not spoken of or written of, though it would be very wrong to say that subsequent events go on indifferently, all the same, as though such things had never been.
>
> (Byatt, 1991: 508)

Thus the novel ends with a subversive object, eluding the analysis or categorization of the collectors, a souvenir of an event which they believe never happened, mutely undermining the version of history which is 'spoken of or written of'. Yet the novel also ends with happiness and a new beginning for Roland and Maud, consummating a relationship initiated by their shared exploration of objects and remains. They have participated in the act of regeneration and creation that is successful collecting.

Collections and objects are prominent in these novels because the novelists have recognized their potency in individuals' lives. Novels may not always accurately reflect current collecting practice, as it is understood. The value of Byatt's novels for a student of material culture lies in the reminder that it is not only specialists who are moved by collections. These novels illustrate how the processes of creating, remembering and narrating enacted by a collection may be at the heart of our human experience.

Bibliography

Byatt, A. S. (1981) *The Virgin in the Garden*, Harmondsworth: Penguin (first published 1978).

Byatt, A. S. (1985) *Still Life*, London: Chatto & Windus.

Byatt, A. S. (1988) *Sugar and Other Stories*, Harmondsworth: Penguin (first published 1987).

Byatt, A. S. (1991) *Possession*, London: Vintage (first published 1990).

Byatt, A. S. (1992) *The Game*, London: Vintage (first published 1967).

Byatt, A. S. (1993a) *Angels and Insects*, London: Vintage (first published 1992).

Byatt, A. S. (1993b) *The Matisse Stories*, London: Chatto & Windus.

Drabble, M. (1966) *The Garrick Year*, Harmondsworth: Penguin (first published 1964).

Drabble, M. (1969) *The Waterfall*, London: Weidenfeld & Nicolson.

Fowles, J. (1989) *The Collector*, London: Picador (first published 1963).

Joyce, J. (1993) *Ulysses*, Oxford: Oxford University Press (first published 1922).

Palin, M. (1995) *Hemingway's Chair*, London: Methuen.

Woolf, V. (1992) 'Mr Bennett and Mrs Brown', in *A Woman's Essays*, Harmondsworth: Penguin (first published 1924).

8

Towards a critique of material culture, consumption and markets

SØREN ASKEGAARD and A. FUAT FIRAT

Introduction

Many discourses concerning modern and/or capitalist/bourgeois consumption culture, which is admittedly highly materialistic, and mass (because the capitalist market system requires such massification), consider the needs of the consumers to be given. The almost unquestioned status of this assumption is clear from the fact that even many critics of modernity and the capitalist economic system accept this premise. For example, in his chapter 'Ruin and Rebus – History of the Arcades Project', Madsen (1993), a comparative literature scholar, while providing a critical analysis of consumption in bourgeois society, nevertheless says: 'the bourgeoisie exploited the newly developed technological potentials for the fulfilment of their needs (which is what capitalism is about)', talking about the needs of the bourgeoisie as if they were there to be fulfilled and it took new technologies to do so. Yet the greatest success of the bourgeoisie (or capitalism) may in fact have been that instead of fulfilling or even reiterating needs, people's dreams, wishes, etc., it (re)constructed them. Capitalism could not be, itself, without such construction, by simply fulfilling needs that 'were there'. Much of this (re)construction may have been, and indeed was, in the image of the old, but the old was completely recast in the imaginary and the imagery of the new culture that was partially signified and built by the technologies[1] and their cultural impacts. And, of course, many a consumer need, wish, want and dream was completely newly constructed.

The construction of needs in modern society is well documented in a large volume, *Consumption and the World of Goods* (Brewer and Porter, 1993), in which various renowned scholars trace the growth of consumption culture in sixteenth- and seventeenth-century Europe, especially England and France. This consumption culture not only depended on the continual (re)production of material goods, but also found its expressions in terms of material wealth. Ability to have (accumulate) and consume material goods became the sign of achievement and success, of having accomplished goals in life. Consuming, refusing to consume, and making different combinations of consumable items became the primary means of expressing self, social position (McCracken, 1988), worldviews and, in some cases, rebellion (Breen, 1993). Our purpose in this chapter is to explore the reasons for the growth of material culture and its impacts upon modern consumption and the constitution of the market. Then we intend to bring to attention some major fallacies of material culture and its emphasis on the functional in order to shed some light on the possibilities for change in human society.

Material culture

Modernity's beginnings are largely linked to a transformation in the dominating ideas regarding the role and position of the human individual, especially in what are now called 'Western' cultures (Rorty, 1979; Russell, 1945/1972). Specifically, modern society arrived when belief systems that depicted humans as subject to higher and spiritual powers – as well as living fates that were predetermined by such powers – began to loose ground to ideas that gave the human individual much greater powers in determining her or his own fate. Modernity entrenched itself when ideas depicting the human individual as the *knowing subject* – that is, an individual who inquires about her or his material environment and conditions of life by using science to gain an objective and valid knowledge of them – dominated the social choices and decisions made in the public domain. In trying to establish their rule, the proponents of modern culture and its core institution, science, juxtaposed the 'real' presence of the material against the spiritual, clearly demarcating the two and opposing them to each other. When the forces of modernity won the combat, the material was privileged as the domain of knowledge – where the truths of the conditions of human existence lay – and the spiritual was disprivileged as the domain of ungrounded beliefs and dogmas. The struggle became historically framed as a battle between two irreconcilable systems, both of which required universal and total commitment.

It is understandable, therefore, that modern consumption culture is a material culture. There is more to it, however. Modernism has, indeed, been keen on separating domains of life into categories and often opposing them, as in the case of the material versus the spiritual. The principal purpose of such structuring of life seems to have been to develop order and normativity. Modernism opposed and disintegrated the feudal or aristocratic order to free individuals from serfdom – which helped to free labour for the industrial capitalist organization of society – and rendered the order of the religious organizations largely ineffective in the political affairs of nation-states – which helped to free consumers to seek material rewards. However, modernism did not oppose the idea of order. Order is inherent in the project of modernity.[2] After all, without orderly progress, it is not possible to realize a precise goal such as the modern project. Since the norms of the old order were defeated, however, the norms of the new order had to be established (Steuerman, 1992).

As Habermas (1983) elaborates, following Max Weber, in its quest for normativity modernism separated the spheres of science, morality and art. Each sphere, then, had its own norms.[3] The sphere of science was considered to be the most important and consequential one in the quest for realizing the modern project and had to be free of contamination by the norms of other spheres. Contamination would cause failure in developing true knowledge of the human condition.

Similar to the demarcation of these three spheres, and to the opposing of the material to the spiritual, modernism also opposed culture to nature. Nature included all that was given to being human, which represented limitations and impositions on humanity. Initially, culture represented all that was humanly created, the potential for humanity to take its fate in its own hands and to control and manipulate nature and its effects. Consequently, given the modernist tendencies previously mentioned, culture was privileged over nature.

Indeed, this impulse to develop clear demarcations among categories and then oppose them to each other for the purpose of establishing order is very much a modernist one. The more recently flourishing postmodern sensibility is, on the other hand, one of multiplying and exploring categories. Consider, for example, the modern treatment of gender. Modernism construed the cultural significations of the sexes into two opposing categories: feminine and masculine. This not only recognized the existence of the two sexes[4] but imposed a rather polarized existence for both – to such an extent that males and females have been greatly (re)produced in the images of the masculine and the feminine. Such treatment of categories ignores and largely eliminates the potential overlaps and the multiple similarities between the opposing categories, as well as the multiple differences within the categories. The measurement instruments, techniques and dominant methods of modern science reflect this consequence. Instruments of modern science are built on the premise of discovering smaller and smaller distinctions. On the other hand, modern analytical tools (for example, statistics) are largely based on measures of central tendency (such as means, proportions, modes, distributions and medians). The result is that once a difference is 'found', no matter how small, exclusive and 'distinct' categories are form(a)(u)lized.

Postmodern sensibility does not disregard difference. On the contrary, a lasting postmodern slogan has been 'long live differ-(e)(a)nce!' Yet postmodernism also recognizes the blurred edges in each distinction, the paradoxical alikeness of almost all difference, and the overlaps in every demarcation. As a result, postmodern sensibility urges critically playing with momentary balances among the differences and the similarities rather than trying to render them permanent and/or universal. For a system of thought that uses transgression only in terms of a progressive search for a better order, such as modernism, the postmodern sensibility may be seen as antithetical and scary. This is interesting, especially since postmodernism is not a break with the modern but a call to recognize the conditions that permeated modernity, and that were exacerbated by modernity, while rejected and repressed by modernist discourses. The postmodernist call is, further, to practise these conditions, critically yet playfully, and unabashedly.[5] Thus, postmodernism is not so much a radical opposition to but rather a radical development of modernism; in the sense of an 'increased profusion and speed of the circulation of cultural artefacts, postmodernism is not so much a critique or a radical refusal of modernism, but its radical exaggeration. It is more modern than modernism' (Lash and Urry, 1994: 3).

However, in modern society, the impulse to demarcate domains to impose greater structure and order into society resulted in further separation of culture into its elements. Specifically, culture was separated into the social, the political and the economic. Each domain or sphere of cultural activity[6] then developed its own norms and institutions through which affairs were regulated and performed within that sphere. For the political, the fundamental norm was that of (representational) democracy organized through the nation-state. The fundamental norm of the social was the civil society, its basic institution being the family. The economic was guided by the norms of material resource efficiency,[7] and its medium (its institution) through which these norms operated and economic interactions were organized and performed was the market.

Eventually, modern culture signified the economic as the engine of society, and the market has become the foremost – and increasingly the only – locus of legitimation in modern society. Almost all affairs of society are now mediated by and through the market. Whether resolving political issues or settling social relationships, the principles and the rationale of marketability tend to dominate the process. In electing political leaders or in waging wars, the campaigns are run as marketing campaigns.[8] Underlying marketization is the symbolic articulation and signification of consumption through the market.

Material consumption and the symbolic

An historical review of consumption trends tends to indicate its transformation from a reliance on activities performed for and during consumption to a reliance on the presence and utilization of products acquired in the market (Fırat and Dholakia, 1982; Fırat, 1986). The consumer of even the nineteenth century relied much more on his or her own labour while consuming. To eat, for example, he or she had to cook from scratch; washing clothing items largely meant sitting or standing by a water source (a river or a sink) and scrubbing, rinsing and wringing by hand; and cleaning the house was largely a day's labour of sweeping, dusting and scrubbing furniture, floors, etc., by hand. Even clothing required more knitting and sewing at home. With the maturing of modernity and its mass-production technologies, all such consumption categories, as well as newly created ones, increasingly have come to depend on purchasing products already available in the market: pre-cooked meals or pre-prepared food ingredients, washing machines, vacuum cleaners, microwave ovens, refrigerators and the like. By the 1950s and 1960s, consumption in Western economies basically meant acquiring and using or devouring market products. When, for example, one asks historians of popular culture, studies period literature, or interviews people of different generations about their consumption experiences in their youth, a similar pattern stands out: consumption in earlier periods is expressed in terms of activities whereas in later periods, especially beginning with the period between the two world wars, it is expressed in terms of products (Fırat, 1986). When contemporary generations talk about their consumption experiences, their narratives are replete with mention of products, such as the automobile, the microwave oven, the telephone, the television, the sound system and the video machine, among others. National and international statistics also tend to show that these products are diffusing to larger and larger proportions of households, especially in the 'market economies'. The high aspirations and diffusion rates for such products are further clearly evidenced in research conducted in the 'transforming economies'. It is important, therefore, to develop an understanding of the almost universal allure of these products for consumers across the globe.

The modernist explanation for the diffusion of all these products among larger and larger proportions of households was a functional one: that with changing patterns of life, due to industrialization, urbanization, etc., these products became increasingly necessary or needed – that they fulfilled utilitarian purposes. Such explanations do not provide a substantive understanding of why the same products became sought by all consumers for the satisfaction of these needs when alternative products also existed. Why, for example, did the car command such allure for so many[9] when public transport could fulfil the same need more cheaply and with less nuisance? Why was the television so much sought after when films, social gatherings and other entertainment activities provided for the same need at better prices, with greater variety – at least originally – and greater human contact? Clearly, there were reasons beyond the simple explanations built on a concept of needs.

One such answer may be that of the symbolic significance of these products. Modernist discourse, having established the ideological hegemony of the material, suppressed the symbolic in favour of the functional or the utilitarian. As expressed by Sahlins (1976: 134): 'History [was] accordingly suppressed by the iron logic of practicality.' Rational people, as consumers, would not waste their time, energy or money for images and symbolic purposes unless a material utility existed in these symbols and images. They understood that unless such a purpose was served, no 'true' – to be interpreted as material – end would be reached. The result would be solely illusory and ephemeral. In this spirit of reasoning, modern sociology and marketing/consumer research were willing to co-opt concepts such as conspicuous consumption and ideas such as the representation of social status through consumption. Indeed, in these cases the products represented symbolic meanings more than immediate utilities, but these meanings served consumers in reaching tangible goals in the material world: improving their lives by situating them in better positions in society and providing greater consuming abilities.

Such subjugation of the symbolic to the material and the functional is indicative of the need to suppress the symbolic for the purposes of extending the modern experiment. It recognizes and simultaneously rejects the symbolic. In fact, when the characteristics of the products in question are studied more closely, they do reveal underlying symbolic meanings along dimensions that they share. These products – the car, television, refrigerator, washing machine, dishwasher, microwave oven, personal computer, air conditioner and the like, each at a different level of diffusion but all very much sought after by large majorities of households around the world – are perceived to represent a move towards consumption that provides greater individuality and privacy with a sense of greater affluence. This is based on the idea that these products are eliminating the chores of life – eliminating labour during consumption – and, at the same time, suggesting a sought level of achievement in life through the mere fact that they – these specific representatives of affluence – can be afforded. These tendencies in consumption are imbued with symbolic meanings, both constructed and emphasized by culture (Fırat and Dholakia, 1982). It is these symbolic meanings that have enticed modern consumers to be seduced by these products representing the symbolic pattern even when a 'rational', 'functional' and 'economic' assessment of their 'necessity' did not justify their adoption by many consumers (Fırat, 1987).

The contradictions between rational consumption and adoption of the modern products do not readily expose themselves when economically affluent consumers are observed. These contradictions surface, however, as irrational consumption choices when relatively low-income, poor or disadvantaged consumers are concerned (Caplovitz, 1963; Irelan, 1967). It is then that we begin to encounter households and individuals who forgo adequate nourishment or health care in order to possess a car or a television set or designer clothing. In such circumstances, the impulse of the modernist researcher has been to lay the blame on the consumer, charging her or him with irrationality or ignorance, rather than recognizing the strong cultural symbolic systems at work.

Maybe the most important symbolic character of consumption arises from the history of its signification in modern society. Was it merely a coincidence that the term 'consumption' was also popularly used in the seventeenth-century English-speaking countries to refer to one of the deadliest diseases of the period: tuberculosis (Porter, 1993)? Tuberculosis was called consumption to indicate that it wasted people away. In the vernacular, therefore, consumption was largely equated with waste. Symbolically, the activity was assigned to destructive and negative images. It destroyed value that was created in production, the sacred activity. Consumption was profane – in every sense of the word. Such symbolism has resulted in many paradoxical emotions and behaviours for the modern consumer. Consider that the major product of consumption is the consumer's maintenance and growth.[10] The symbolic meanings replete with negative nuances attached to consumption have reflected on its product too, resulting in many a consumer's feelings of worthlessness. Throughout the modern period, consumption has been regarded as a necessary activity, necessary for (re)energizing the individual in order for him or her to attend to higher-order activities and purposes in life. On the other hand, savings and investment are necessary for growth in the capitalist mode of production. As demonstrated by Douglas and Isherwood (1978) in their grid/group analysis, it is exactly the weakening social bonds and pressures that permit the pursuit of individual economic success through savings and investment. Therefore, consumption was not to be overdone or become excessive, but held under control and performed in a prudent manner. Consumers were not to become engrossed in the sensations of consumption and engage in it with zest or excess. Furthermore, consumption was signified as a private activity to be performed largely in the private domain, the home. It was not to be displayed or exhibited. It is understandable, therefore, that the sociologists of consumption did not look upon it favourably when they realized that some powerful and wealthy consumers were not heeding these tenets of the consumption game.[11]

Consumers, the underprivileged as well as the privileged, continued to live in their symbolic universe of consumption even though it was not recognized as such by the social scientists. They used consumption not only to indicate their social statuses, as maybe the powerful and wealthy consumers mostly did, but to register resistance or other social and political states they were otherwise unable or powerless to make known (Breen, 1993). But even more significant is what may be the most symbolic act of consumption of all: that of signifying and representing selves or identities in the image of the images sought.

Consumption as production

The modern significations of consumption as the use or destruction of value that is created in production have been largely questioned and deconstructed. The argument has been put forth, by Baudrillard (1970, 1972), for example, that instead of value being determined in exchange-value based on the inputs during production, as theorized by modern economists, it is articulated and formulated in sign-value, during consumption. As a postmodernist theoretician, Baudrillard has, thus, reconstrued the meaning of consumption and production, in effect switching the positions of the two and recasting consumption as the important sphere of human activity. There is, however, in this re(de)construction, a tendency to perpetuate the separation of the two spheres, as now consumption is considered to be the value-creating human activity, as opposed to production.

Yet a logical extension of the reconstruction of the two categories leads to their merging into one activity. The recognition arises that if value is created in consumption through sign-value, as Baudrillard argues, then consumption is a productive activity; it is production. In effect, it becomes obvious that the signification of the two activities as separate and opposing categories was, indeed, a construction, not self-evident in or fundamental to the nature of human activity, but so determined in the modernist culture. This construction is highly related to the modern reorganization of society into separate public and private domains, where the valued activities – that is, activities which resulted in products that commanded value in the marketplace – were socially organized in the public domain, to afford them greater economic rationality and efficiency – that is, greater profitability and capital accumulation.

As a result, people's lives have become largely divided into workplace and home, working hours and leisure hours, production and consumption. Yet, as the modern economists who were mainly instrumental in these separations were aware, consumption existed in every moment of production, and production existed in every moment of consumption. It was on the basis of their understanding or definition of value that the same process was at times called or deemed production and at other moments deemed consumption. Specifically, this process was called production when it was productive in the sense of contributing to the accumulation of economic surplus (Sweezy, 1947); in capitalism, capital accumulation. In modern society and modern thought the definitions of categories and descriptions of 'reality' were, indeed, tightly consistent. Productive (that is, value-creating) activities were those that were contributing economically; the economy was considered to be the engine of society in reaching the goal(s) of the modern project; and the institution of economic interactions, the market, became the dominant, if not the sole, medium through which society's affairs were resolved or performed. The strength, resilience and endurance of capitalism and the market economy can, therefore, be partially understood in this internal consistency of the modern cultural narrative and the absence of another competing narrative as consistent in its elements.

Yet this consistency depends largely on the definitions themselves; on the definition of value, for example. Were we to consider human life and growth as valuable products of human existence, independent of whether or not the human that is produced in the acts of consumption – such as eating and drinking, wearing clothing, driving cars, watching television, reading books, using electricity, and the like – finds economic worth in the market, the modern narrative of production and consumption would collapse; because now, a human being sitting at home and eating and reading would have to be considered to be involved in production.

Would anyone who was asked whether human life is valuable (or should be valued) respond in the negative? That is unlikely, given the modernist rhetoric of the importance of the human being and the modern narrative that puts the human being in the centre of the modern project as the knowing subject for whom life was to be improved. But many may say that human life is not valued around the world, either sarcastically or with sober reference to how human beings are still treated. And this is an indication of the differences in what modern culture says it is about in its rhetorical discourse and what in actuality takes place. Indeed, today many may agree that the health of the economy takes precedence over individual human lives.[12] One might wonder how modern culture, which in its rhetoric values human life, has come to consider its production as not production, and how anything else could take precedence over human life.

A good example of how this may happen is the life experiences of women in modern culture. On the one hand, women are revered in modern literature as mothers and sisters and wives, but on the other hand it is now well understood that they have simultaneously been rendered powerless and have been discriminated against, having fewer rights than men, being treated as possessions of men, and being greatly dependent on men (Chodorow, 1979; Saffioti, 1978). How is this possible? If women are so praised in modern rhetoric and literature, why, then, has this hype not become a reality?

The semiotic and the symbolic articulation of the modern condition may provide the answer to this when a straight materialist answer may not exist. Social reality is, indeed, constructed through hype and simulation; however, this hype and simulation are not only represented in words, but communicated by signs of all kinds. In the case of women, for example, what it is to be a woman is socially represented not only in what is said or written about women but in how they are remunerated for their work, how they are presented in the arts and the media, how they are 'placed' in law and politics, etc. Messages regarding who women are and ought to be are displayed through multiple means, some more forceful than words and rhetoric. Social reality is built upon a semiotic system that is much larger than verbal language, in the demeanours, acts and, very often, nuances which construct symbolic meanings for and make symbols of all objects, including the human being. Mostly, significations occur through the valuation practices in society; that is, acts that promote or demote, reward or condemn, dignify or degrade, glorify or oppress, remunerate or exploit people and their roles in society. The interesting thing about the human individual is that whereas she or he has the potential to contribute to this semiotic system and actually does so through her or his activities and speech acts, the modern world has been dominated by mass media and other powerful top-down communication and power systems.

Thus, in modern society, the individual, so central in modernist rhetoric, has been rendered secondary and unimportant in the semiotic system. At the same time as modernism declared that everything was for the improvement of life for the human individual, and that the human individual was sovereign, many aspects of the modern organization of social life and work communicated modernity's distrust in the abilities or the intellect of this individual. In effect, modernity tried hard to structure social institutions to ensure a framework for individual 'rational' behaviour. This is well represented in modern architecture, for example, where buildings were structured to urge people to move in functional, utilitarian ways, or in Fordism, where workstations were structured to make workers 'productive'. The distrust of the human being is clearly exhibited in these efforts to control his or her actions rather than allow the individual to be in control. It is understandable, therefore, that in such a society, where the rhetoric exalted the individual, he or she would be made subservient to the economy. In effect, the consumer became the consumed in modern culture. The production of the consumer through consumption was largely to prepare him or her for this role: to be able, ready and willing to be consumed for the purposes of a healthy economy.

Consumption, therefore, in contrast to how it was conceived in modernity, is not simply a destruction of value but a production of the human being and her or his experiences in the world. Recognizing this creates a completely different perspective on the consumption–production dichotomy; that, in effect, it is not a dichotomy but a unity. It is only our perspective on the phenomena we encounter which may result in our articulation of one or other aspect of the process or cycle of consumption/production. Consumers seem to be increasingly looking consciously at their consumption activities as the means for producing or customizing themselves in their images. It may be useful, therefore, for social scientists to change their traditional perspective and begin to study consumption as production.

Material culture: beyond the dichotomy of the functional and the symbolic

The idea that consumption is production, beyond the Marxian notion of reproduction of labour, has not been acknowledged by the major part of the social sciences until very recently. The domination of neo-classical economics within the academic social sciences and social policy-making has meant that the assumptions of the rational, utility-maximizing individual prevented other ideas about the constitution of the individual from having more than a peripheral impact. Thus, the sciences dealing directly with the market, consumption and the exchange of material goods have, from their very beginnings, tried to exclude any considerations about the symbolic dimension of human life in their search for recognition as exact sciences. Even the disciplines addressing consumption directly – marketing and, more specifically, consumer research – have been rather slow to move beyond the *Homo economicus*.

Within the marketing literature, for example, Levy (1959) was one of the first to point out the relevance and relative importance of the meaning of objects in relation to their function. Since then, there has been an increasing interest in what has been called 'symbolic consumption' (cf. Hirschman and Holbrook, 1981). Yet in these and more recent discussions of symbolic consumption, there has been a tendency to distinguish between symbolic consumption, consumption of the sign-value of objects, and functional consumption of the utilitarian value of objects. This tendency also seems to dominate among scholars within the field of cultural studies. Often, the symbolic and the functional are treated as extremes on a continuum, where certain consumer goods are considered to be more or less symbol-laden than others. At the 1980 Conference on Consumer Esthetics and Symbolic Consumption, one of the foremost representatives of studies in symbolic consumption in marketing stated that

> [T]he symbolic meaning of a product may, in some product classes, overcome or dominate its technical performance as a determinant of consumption. This is especially likely if the product is frequently used to signify social position and/or self identity. Falling into this 'conspicuously consumed' product category are such diverse products as automobiles, apparel, home furnishings, educational institutions, hairstyles and leisure time activities.
>
> (Hirschman, 1981: 4)

Symbolic consumption thus seems to have been studied mostly in the realm of the so-called 'cultural products', where the product is consumed predominantly for the artistic or aesthetic pleasure it arouses, as in the case of books, concerts, theatre and the arts.

Consider the difference between this approach and the following passage from the philosopher who proposed the name '*animal symbolicum*' for the human being:

> No longer in a merely physical universe, man lives in a symbolic universe. . . . No longer can man confront reality immediately; he cannot see it, as it were, face to face. Physical reality seems to recede as man's symbolic activity advances. Instead of dealing with the things themselves man is in a sense constantly conversing with himself. He has so enveloped himself in linguistic forms, in artistic images, in mythical symbols and religious rites that he cannot see or know anything except through this artificial medium. His situation is the same in the theoretical as in the practical sphere. Even here man does not live in a world of hard facts or according to his immediate needs and desires. He lives rather in the midst of imaginary emotions, in hopes and fears, in illusions and disillusions, in his fantasies and dreams.
>
> (Cassirer, 1970: 27)

Following Cassirer, a theoretical distinction between the functional and the symbolic seems unfortunate, since it tends to ignore a basic trait of the human being: that this species has no access to the world other than through its own interpretations. Hence, this distinction hides the important fact that functional and utilitarian objects are symbolic, while reflecting a basically modernist idea that goods are functional before they become symbolic. However, there can be no functionality or utility without a specific goal for these, and such a goal cannot be but cultural and, hence, symbolic. As Castoriadis (1986) underlines, it already takes some kind of imagination to grasp the 'toolishness' of a tool, an imagination that several animals also demonstrate. But it takes the symbolizing ability, which may only be found in the human mind, to imagine the abstract notion of a 'tool', to free it from its immediate and concrete use and conceive of it as 'functional' or 'useful' in an abstract sense.

In modern society, the symbols of 'function', 'utility', 'mastering of nature', 'efficacy', etc., have been some of the most important symbolic constructions and, as such, they have dominated the discourse on material culture and consumption, what Baudrillard (1972: 168) has called the rationalizing, reductionist and repressive metaphysics of utility. However, from the early modern perspective these symbolic constructions are not perceived as such. In the utility-based approach to material culture, the material world is seen as being increasingly liberated from significations pertaining to non-scientific or non-functional aspects of the object. Only with the rising criticism of modern philosophy by the nineteenth-century philosophers and sociologists is this belief in what Max Weber called the disenchantment of the world beginning to fade. This is an ongoing process, which may lie at the heart of the idea that the postmodern is indeed a 'post' phenomenon. Increasingly, it is acknowledged that since we do not perceive the things in their 'natural' state of being, but rather as representatives of a certain (cultural) relationship between society and nature, the notions of function and utility represent such a symbolic relationship.

Lash and Urry (1994: 14) indicate that '[i]n the symbolic exchange ... of traditional societies the object of exchange was "peopled, so to speak" with the gods and demons, with the social and political relations of society.' They add that, later, utility becomes dominating 'as the functionalism of the object takes over from its symbolic significance'. The more abstract notion of exchange-value becomes the standard measurement of the quality and nature of this functionalism. But their phrasing reveals an unwillingness to reconcile the functional and the symbolic. It would have been more appropriate to say that functionalism *becomes* the predominating symbolic significance rather than replaces it. Thus, only the first half of the process is reflected upon by Lash and Urry. The objects are repopulated with new gods and demons named function and utility, both related to a supreme god named rationality.

For Lash and Urry, the development of modern into postmodern society is, then, marked by the weakening of the functionalistic attitude to objects and the increasing production of signs rather than material objects, where the postmodern sign-value is held as even more abstract than the exchange-value. Interestingly, since Lash and Urry's purpose is to present an alternative to the pessimism prevailing in much of postmodernism, this misses a liberating aspect of postmodernism. Instead of underlining that sign-value may be more abstract than exchange-value (a dubious statement), the replacement of sign-value, which is inherently cultural, puts the agency and the foundation of meaning back in the hands of humans from the 'natural' and 'external' forces of function and utility. We will elaborate this point towards the end of our discussion.

As one of the major critics of modern thought, Baudrillard (1972) expresses the fall of the modern conception of consumption in his thesis that use-value is only a rationalization; it is the value in terms of exchange of signs that is decisive in a sociology of consumption. He reveals the 'functional simulacrum' by referring to the inscription of any functional judgement in a social morality rooted in a work ethic. Thus, a meaningful understanding of objects and consumption is not to be founded on a theory of needs and their satisfaction, but on a theory of social performance and signification.

This is in opposition to the modern ideology of consumption, where the system of needs is regarded as an extrinsic phenomenon and, as such, a given and natural system. By deconstructing the concept of needs, Baudrillard helps to show how this legitimizing system of needs is actually a consequence of the production–consumption logic itself. Baudrillard (1972: 95ff.) goes on to problematize the critique of consumption and material(istic) culture based on the Marxian notion of fetishism. He argues that the concept of fetish in its colloquial use designates the magic ascribed to some kind of metaphysical aspect of the product as opposed to some kind of 'real' and 'objective' status, which would represent its true character. But, as we have argued, nothing permits us to assume that we can have access to this 'real' ontological status of the object.

Summing up Baudrillard's argument, use-value is, in itself, a social relationship based on the system of needs instituted by society. The common code becomes utility, and the symbolic exchange of signs as conceived by modern thinkers is also a utility-based discourse. Our argument is, then, that if sign-value is utility, following the Baudrillardian analysis, then utility is also a sign-value. This relationship is what is neglected by many scholars in consumer research, who maintain a fundamental distinction between the two domains. Baudrillard's point of view in this respect remains unclear. At one point he states that in modern societies, the object is rarely a pure fetish since there is a technological and functional imperative which imposes itself (Baudrillard, 1972: 46). What we argue here is exactly that technology and function have been the predominant fetishes within the modern conceptualization of the material culture. Elsewhere, he comes closer to the point of view suggested here, namely in his treatment of the concept of design. He argues that Bauhaus, the movement within design that firmly established the unity of form and function so that this unity in itself became the criterion for good artistic work, is the one single movement which marks the 'universal signification of the environment' in terms of function as well as signification in general. Bauhaus represents the 'practical extension of the exchange value to the whole area of signs, forms, and objects' (Baudrillard, 1972: 231). The notion of consumption, then, expresses exactly this state of things where the commodity is immediately produced as sign and the signs are produced as commodities (Baudrillard, 1972: 178).

This hints at a problem in the standard approach to luxuries, which are often defined as goods with an elaborated sign-value beyond the sphere of the basic, utilitarian consumption. Appadurai (1986), for example, suggests that luxury goods should be qualified not so much in an opposition but rather as extremes in a continuum, indicating the degree of rhetorical and social use of the goods. Such goods, he states, are incarnated signs (1986: 38). However, the distinction between necessity and luxury is replete with problems. 'Luxury' is the term traditionally used to designate the consumption sphere beyond the necessities, a distinction which may have its borderline set anywhere from the absolute minimum necessary for biological survival to a more socially defined minimum necessary for a normal social existence, that is, defined in relation to existing norms and practices in society. The uncertainty regarding the fundamental categorization is, however, only a first and obvious problem. Furthermore, if we are witnessing a change in the economic sphere from a production of material goods to a production of signs, then, following the argument of Appadurai, this would indicate a spreading of a 'logic of luxuries' to the entire material culture, in which case the distinction between luxury and necessity abolishes itself.

Along a similar line of argument, Lash and Urry (1994) propose that the economy is increasingly producing signs and not material objects. They use the term 'reflexive accumulation' to designate a situation where the economic and symbolic processes in society are increasingly interrelated. Thus, these discussions all point to the standard assumption that we live in a period which can be described by references to the rise of the symbolic on behalf of the functional. While we surely agree that we witness profound changes in the organization of economic and symbolic processes towards the end of the twentieth century, the terminology used by Lash and Urry and others to describe the change is based on the unfortunate distinction between material objects and signs or, in other words, functional and symbolic objects.

What we argue is that these changes – the spreading of the logic of luxuries and the production of signs rather than material goods – express not a symbolic order replacing a material one, but the (re)discovery of the capacity of goods to communicate beyond their inscription in a single hierarchy between luxury and necessity or high and low symbol value. The markets today are filled with a multiplicity of symbolic meanings, going across and against traditional status hierarchies. Goods of all kinds are becoming consciously used as cultural markers or means of expression whose individual and social importance in any context goes far beyond their utility. As Douglas and Isherwood (1978: 62) underline, '[t]he essential function of consumption is its capacity to make sense'. Both consumers and marketing communications contribute to carrying this argument to its extreme, to the point where the consumers' choice of anything, from their car and house to their breakfast cereal and their toilet paper, can be used for expressing a certain cultural value.

To many, such developments are only possible in economies which have reached a given level of development and can afford the luxury of spending so much time and energy on the symbolic meaning of things rather than their usefulness. This is completely missing the point of our argument. What is basically at stake here is a *critique* of the modern idea that all pre-modern and so-called primitive societies are first and foremost concerned with their own physical survival and, therefore, do not have the surplus to develop technology and production. This is the myth of all humankind's origin in a subsistence economy totally governed by the problem of survival, most developed by Marxist materialism (Sahlins, 1976). But, one may ask with Baudrillard: 'Do human beings organize themselves first and foremost in order to survive or as a function of the individual and collective meaning they ascribe to their existence?' (Baudrillard, 1970: 50).

The anthropological evidence provides us with the answer to this question. For example, Lizot's (1985) analyses of the Yanomami and their choice between social and economic life, Sahlins's (1976) critique of Marxist materialist historical theory, Mauss's (1950) analyses of exchanges as total social events rather than as economic transactions, or Bataille's (1949) underlining of the importance of waste and destruction in economic life all point to the symbolic importance of any economic activity in any society. As stated by Appadurai:

> From the point of view of demand, the critical difference between modern, capitalist societies and those based on simpler forms of technology and labor is not that we have a thoroughly commoditized economy whereas theirs is one in which subsistence is dominant and commodity exchange has made only limited inroads, but rather that the consumption demands of persons in our own society are regulated by high-turnover criteria of 'appropriateness' (fashion), in contrast to the less frequent shifts in more directly regulated sumptuary or customary systems.
>
> (Appadurai, 1986: 32)

This development is a consequence of the changing imagery concerning goods and their ability to convey meaning.

In this connection, we would refer to Campbell's (1987) interesting attempt to link the hedonic aspect of modern consumerism and the Romantic Movement of eighteenth-century Europe. According to Campbell, the classical theories on the origin of wants cannot account for their explosion at that given point in time. Hedonic consumption in its modern form is linked to the growing importance of fashion, luxury and leisure time and the consequences of these phenomena in terms of the construction of a self based on consumption. This process, Campbell argues, is reinforced by the Romantic Movement's leitmotif: the search for the lost identity. The emotional benefits offered by consumption activities pave the way for a new self-consciousness, and for a self-consumption and self-construction rooted in imaginatively created pleasures offered by material culture and the growing communicative systems attached to the production/marketing sphere.

Postmodernism, as discussed earlier in this chapter, might then be understood as the dominance of 'micro-Romanticism' as opposed to the classical 'macro-Romanticism' described by Campbell, founded on grand narratives of origin, the heritage, the land, etc. The patterns of identification under micro-Romanticism are sought in a much more fragmented and piecemeal environment of market communications, where styles and tastes reflect no longer just class and status distinctions but also autonomy from such patterns. The market, instead, is the carnival place where everybody is free to search for goods in a context of what Lash and Urry (1994: 108) call 'expressive individualism'. They suggest the term 'allegory' to signify such a symbolism liberated from grand social schemes and projects, a more postmodern, anarchic and heterotopian consumption signification system.

Allegorical consumption, in this sense, points to changes in the power structures concerning supply and demand in the marketplace.

Morin (1962) wrote that the dialogue between supply and demand within mass culture is an unequal one, since it is the dialogue between a very well-formulated person and a mute. One may wonder whether postmodernism signifies the breaking of the silence of the latter. The concept of allegory hints at such new possibilities. But to be able to exploit these possibilities fully a new concept of the market is necessary.

The development of the market and the possibility of theatre

There are different definitions of the term 'market'. Some of these relate to space, such as 'the place where people come together to trade or exchange entities of meaning'. This may have been an early definition based on the experiences of barter and trade that occurred even very early in history among and within tribes, where often ceremonial sites were selected for exchanging items. These sites have come to be called markets, which later developed into regular meeting and exchanging places, such as the agora in ancient Greece. Yet even in calling these sites 'the market', there is the development of the idea of exchange with a certain mentality or purpose and goal in mind. In early markets, as just mentioned, the exchange was mostly ceremonial and spiritual or representative and signifying of relationships, even when and if the items exchanged were of use to both parties. The principal purpose guiding the selection and/or offering of items exchanged was neither enhancement of economic value, nor even the perception that these items were useful or 'needed'. It was the spiritual and symbolic meanings of these items that made these exchanges significant (Sahlins, 1976).

With the development of modern society and, especially, the industrial, capitalist organization of this society, the principal purpose that guides exchanges has transformed from the spiritual to the material. The symbolism of exchanges in the market is representative no longer so much of relationships that members of society have to spiritual entities or even to each other, but rather of those relationships to the material/economic values that the products exchanged for can provide to the buyers. In other words, in contemporary modern markets, the prevailing idea of the principal purpose of the market is not to express or communicate relationships but to increase the economic value of one's assets, possessions, acquisitions or appropriations. However, this is, in effect, a symbolically signified seeking of an end that is interpreted as material betterment of human life. The idea, that is, that life will be improved, better and happier if one accumulates more and more goods and services is largely the result of symbolic meanings that these goods and services became imbued with culturally.

The meaning or definition of the 'market' has also gone through a change from signifying a site to representing the total demand in society or the total amount of purchase activity (quantity or volume of exchanges) in economics. In business or management disciplines, especially in marketing – that discipline which is most concerned with the market – it has come to be defined as the set of actual and potential consumers of a product (a product being anything which there may be a desire to consume: a good, a service, a person, an idea). In this conceptualization of the market is also the transformation of the human individual from a subject in search for meaning in her or his life to an object upon whom are exercised the strategies for regulating, enlarging, stabilizing, developing, organizing, etc., the market. No longer is the consumer the one for whom a market operates; she or he is the market.

Earlier we have discussed the view that the market was the medium or institution through which modern society sought to exercise its economic interactions. The brief discussion immediately above, regarding the definitional transformations the market has gone through, represents the institutionalization of the consumer in modern discourse. The modern construction of the market and its becoming the sole locus of legitimation in society – and/or the sole medium through which all affairs of society are organized – along with the identification of the consumer (the human individual) as or with this medium (or institution) has led to two important consequences. One is the sub-ordination of the human individual, as the consumer, to the interests of the economy. That is, instead of the economy being in the service of the consumer, the consumer is often present in circumstances that enable the economy (that is, the activity of entities that yield economic value) to be healthy. This consequence is well evidenced in the fact that in all affluent economies of the world today (specifically, the G7), we find large proportions or numbers of homeless and/or underprivileged and 'excluded' individuals who are sacrificed for the healthy economy.

The second consequence of the market becoming the sole locus of legitimation is the *unidimensionalization* of the cultural construction of life's experience for the human subject, and of social choice. This is, as discussed before, the determination of all relationships on the criterion of material resource allocation efficiency. Yet this unidimensionaliza-tion and the subordination of the human being to the economy have disenchanted life, taking many other dimensions of being human out of life, and limiting the choice of the human subject to considerations of the economic, to trying to be 'rational' in only an economic sense.

The universalization and globalization of the market furthermore instils the illusion that all human relationships are relations of exchange. In modern market systems people have increasingly come to think of all their interactions with others in terms of exchange,

exchange that will somehow enhance their condition. The mentality that came to dominate the exchanges in the market has, therefore, increasingly dominated all relations. As a result, a friend giving a gift to another expects something in return that will also make his or her life better, and a parent giving to his or her child expects something in return. There is nothing in the 'nature' of any relationship that requires such a mentality of exchange. Rather, it is the historical development of the market and its role in modern society which instils this mentality into relationships.

If this development has, indeed, disenchanted human lives, and as people are, therefore, looking for a change, what can be expected and/ or what is likely to re-enchant human life? The conditions we have been discussing, in fact, point to the possible answer to the above questions. The discussions indicate that the market and its hegemony in contemporary society are the major reason for the unidimensionaliza- tion and economization of human interaction that disenchant human life. The answer, therefore, seems to be in multidimensionalizing the interactions and relationships in human life.

The difficulty is with imagining the workings of another medium, which operates through criteria that represent multiple dimensions of being human, not just the economic one. While inadequate in helping accomplish an enchanted life, the market does seem to work or is conceptualized as working, through mechanisms of monetary units and demand and supply, to arrive at some equilibria that tend to realize the rationales of economic growth and resource allocation. Theories of such mechanisms or workings of the market have been developed throughout three centuries, at least, and provide much force to belief in the successes of markets. Yet, while achieving economic growth, the free workings of the market are now largely considered also to cause problems along other dimensions, namely ecological, social and political, among others. But the answer in most cases tends to be interventionism, that is, political interventions into the workings of the market. These interventions are assessed by many, with some justification, as causing further problems, inequities, imbalances and, especially, political 'antidemocratic' practices. The recent seeming victory of market economies in world politics has tended to strengthen the righteousness of these assessments – drowning out the issue of imbalances of political power based on economics.

While the problems of the market are increasingly understood, there is not yet a conceptualization of another mechanism or medium that works or could work as seemingly independent of constant interference or intervention as does the market. On the surface, at least, it seems as though the market works by itself when there are demand and supply present to enable exchanges, and, given the 'universal' units of money, some equilibria tend to be reached resulting in some allocation of the material economic resources of the world. Generally, the question of what mechanism that has such a seemingly automatic way of working could replace the market is raised when the ills or problems of the market system are pointed out. What, indeed?

In this question there are, already, the biases of our general belief in the market system. There is, clearly, intervention in the market system, except that it is an intervention through the use of money. That is, when demands are made, requesting that the resources of our planet and society be allocated in certain ways, by using our buying power (that is, our financial assets, or money), this is an intervention into how things are to be done economically. The interesting thing is that we conceptualize and signify our interventions in the market through the use of our wealth or incomes as non-intervention, as the 'natural' flow of things. That is, the only 'natural' and, therefore, readily acceptable form of expressing our demands in and from society is considered to be through our economic means (money we have). Furthermore, there are ways of thinking we generally seem to have fallen into, which support the continuing hegemony of the market. One such is the assumption that when we are involved in the market, we are doing our individual thing, not trying to impose preferences and/or decisions upon others, but merely making choices for ourselves. And, as we make these choices that impose upon no one else, the market works its magic and allocates society's resources in efficient ways that further improve the lives of all involved. What could we replace the market with that could work so magically, and so automatically maximize society's goals?

When the prevailing beliefs about the market are as above and at a time when other forms of intervention into the workings of the market – such as economic planning or political guidance as, say, in the former Soviet Union and the People's Republic of China – seem to have failed so badly, not only in an economic but also in a social and political (such as human rights) sense, it indeed seems very difficult to think of anything that could replace the market as the working mechanism of human society. For one thing, any considerations other than the principles of demand and supply (working through exchanges based on the availability of money or something else to trade) seem to distract the workings of the market and, therefore, the maximization of social welfare. It seems that, for another mechanism to work as the market can, we need constructs similar to demand and supply, but which involve dimensions other than the economic, and/or a unit of exchange (a medium/mediator of exchange?) similar to money, but which integrates qualities of human individuals other than their economic resources (i.e., wealth and incomes).

Before we go on any further, we should comment on one fallacy of the beliefs in the workings of the market. When an individual who has much money or an organization that controls large financial resources makes market choices, these choices are not purely or merely individual choices and not imposing upon others, as the proponents of the market system tend to believe. These choices in the market do impose upon others, by increasing the availability of certain things in the market (and the society as a whole) and diminishing the possibility of alternatives. We find good examples of this in the United States, for example, in the area of transportation. The market choices of, most notably, the car industry, together with other rich and powerful groups in favour of private (car) transportation, have resulted in the great dilapidation of public transportation and in its unavailability in safe and reliable forms for those who need and desire it.

What is needed, then, is a medium that integrates the different dimensions of human life, including the economic, social, political, ecological, psychological and biological, among others. And this medium must ideally weave these seamlessly, where they do not interfere with or eliminate each other, but find agreeable balances in the resolution of human desires toward the construction of meaningful lives. A tall order, indeed! But what is the alternative to seeking and constructing such a medium, as the market has been historically constructed? The alternative is the continuation of the hegemony of the market and, consequently, further disenchantment of human lives and loss of meaning in life, in exchange for flourishing economies and material welfare − which, in the end, may paradoxically deplete the economic and material resources of the earth.

A possible medium that will serve such a multidimensional balancing of meanings in human life may be the *theatre*, in the sense of a symbolic space (a stage) where all human interaction occurs, and the purpose of this interaction is not to maximize any singular goal of human society (such as the maximization of economic value) but to negotiate all goals. The theatre, in its original sense that we have just expressed, was the medium of culture before culture got separated into its elements in modernity and the *stage* became separated from everyday activity. With the relegation of culture to only a single dimension of what it used to be − that of specialized forms of expression and exposition of human seeking and experience (such as art, literature and performance) − the stage also became specialized, available and accessible to only those specializing in high culture, instead of being the space for theatre in which everyone participated in their everyday activities. Theatre became, indeed, a 'staged' event where most of the people were left out as the audience or spectators.

In this separation, the separation between art and science also plays a part, because it represents the separation between the observer and the performer. As the large majority of human beings have been ejected from the stage, they have been limited to expressing themselves only through their purchases and votes, letting it be known which performances offered they like(d), so to speak, but not having the chance to become full participants in the performances. Given that we have lived the modern experiment for over three centuries, and given that, therefore, its effects cannot immediately be erased, the only way that an inclusion of all on (in) the stage can be achieved may be through providing the means for all to become performers, as people who can express and communicate their meanings sought and experiences desired in multiple ways, beyond their purchases and votes. For a re-enchantment of our lives, we must put considerable effort into imagining and constructing the means for making everyone a performer, as well as into recognizing the shifting configurations of power that may make such means possible.

Notes

1 The technologies themselves were, however, culturally signified and (re)construed. That is, while their invention processes may have been *relatively* autonomous, once invented, their meanings, uses, selection for development or discarding were all culturally determined.

2 The project of modernity is generally considered to be the improvement of human lives by controlling nature through scientific technologies (Angus, 1989).

3 The norms of the sphere of science were reason and truth, the norms of art were aesthetics and beauty, and the norms of morality were normative-rightness and justice (Foster, 1983).

4 While extremely few, there are people who are sexless – in the sense of not belonging to either the male or the female population, or who biologically belong to both. Nature and culture seem to collude to keep such people to a minimum.

5 These conditions have been explored elsewhere (see Fırat, 1986) as hyperreality, fragmentation, reversal of consumption and production, decentring of the subject, and paradoxical juxtapositions (of opposites).

6 Ironically, through this separation, the cultural came to represent only part of what it was. The term 'culture' was assigned to a 'superstructural' role, that of values and tastes, which were considered to be largely determined by 'infrastructural' elements, mostly the economic.

7 In capitalism, this meant the criteria of capital accumulation: rationales of profitability and return on investment.

8 Here we are thinking of the presidential campaigns in the United States of America or, increasingly, other countries, and the handling of the Gulf War in the media in 1991.

9 By the 1980s more than 96 per cent of all households in the United States owned one or more cars.

10 Still, the popular thinking on the products of consumption carries mostly negative meanings. The consumer is generally not thought of as a product of consumption. Rather the products of consumption are usually considered to be rubbish, litter, junk – waste in general – and, lately, pollution and resource depletion.

11 Thorstein Veblen (1899) and his followers, as well as many contemporary social scientists – for example, Kenneth Galbraith (1971) – have this disposition towards consumption.

12 We must acknowledge that today there are increasing anti-modernist (sometimes postmodernist) discourses which argue that human life ought not be considered to be any more important than any other life on earth, and that such self-importance in humans often leads to ecological or other forms of disaster.

Bibliography

Angus, I. (1989) 'Circumscribing postmodern culture', in I. Angus and S. Jhally (eds), *Cultural Politics in Contemporary America*, New York: Routledge.

Appadurai, A. (1986) 'Introduction: commodities and the politics of value', in A. Appadurai (ed.), *The Social Life of Things: Commodities in Cultural Perspective*, Cambridge: Cambridge University Press, pp. 3–63.

Bataille, G. (1949) *La Part maudite: essai d'économie générale*, Paris: Editions de Minuit.

Baudrillard, J. (1970) *La Société de consommation*, Paris: Gallimard.

Baudrillard, J. (1972) *Pour une critique de l'économie politique du signe*, Paris: Gallimard.

Breen, T.H. (1993) 'The meanings of things: interpreting the consumer economy in the eighteenth century', in J. Brewer and R. Porter (eds), *Consumption and the World of Goods*, London: Routledge, pp. 249–60.

Brewer, J. and Porter, R. (1993) (eds) *Consumption and the World of Goods*, London: Routledge.

Campbell, C. (1987) *The Romantic Ethic and the Spirit of Modern Consumerism*, Oxford: Blackwell.

Caplovitz, D. (1963) *The Poor Pay More*, New York: Free Press.

Cassirer, E. (1970) *An Essay on Man*, New Haven, CT: Yale University Press. (first published 1944).

Castoriadis, C. (1975) *L'Institution imaginaire de la société*, Paris: Seuil.

Castoriadis, C. (1986) 'L'imaginaire: la création dans le domaine social-historique', in *Domaines de l'homme*, Paris: Seuil.

Chodorow, N. (1979), 'Mothering, male dominance, and capitalism', in Z. R. Eisenstein (ed.), *Capitalist Patriarchy and the Case for Socialist Feminism*, New York: Monthly Review Press, pp. 83–106.

Douglas, M. and Isherwood, B. (1978) *The World of Goods*, New York: Norton.

Featherstone, M. (1991) *Consumer Culture and Postmodernism*, London: Sage.

Fırat, A.F. (1986) 'Towards a deeper understanding of consumption experiences: the underlying dimensions', in M. Wallendorf and P.F. Anderson (eds), *Advances in Consumer Research*, Vol. 14, Provo, UT: Association for Consumer Research.

Fırat, A.F. (1987) 'The social construction of consumption patterns: understanding macro consumption phenomena', in A.F. Fırat, N. Dholakia and R.P. Bagozzi (eds), *Philosophical and Radical Thought in Marketing*, Lexington, MA: Lexington Books, pp. 251–67.

Fırat, A.F. and Dholakia, N. (1982) 'Consumption choices at the macro level', *Journal of Macromarketing*, 2 (Fall), 6–15.

Foster, H. (1983) 'Postmodernism: a preface', in H. Foster (ed.), *The Anti-Aesthetic: Essays on Postmodern Culture*, Seattle: Bay Press, pp. ix–xvi.

Galbraith, J.K. (1971) *The New Industrial State*, New York: Mentor.

Habermas, J. (1983) 'Modernity – an incomplete project', in H. Foster (ed.), *The Anti-Aesthetic: Essays on Postmodern Culture*, Seattle: Bay Press, pp. 3–15.

Hirschman, E. (1981) 'Comprehending symbolic consumption: three theoretical issues', in E. Hirschman and M. Holbrook (eds), *Symbolic Consumer Behavior*, Proceedings of the Conference on Consumer Esthetics and Symbolic Consumption, Ann Arbor, MI: Association for Consumer Research, pp. 4–6.

Hirschman, E. and Holbrook, M. (1981) (eds), *Symbolic Consumer Behavior*, Proceedings of the Conference on Consumer Esthetics and Symbolic Consumption, Ann Arbor, MI: Association for Consumer Research.

Irelan, L.M. (1967) *Low Income Life Styles*, Washington, DC: US Department of Health, Education and Welfare.

Lash, S. and Urry, J. (1994) *Economies of Sign and Space*, London: Sage.

Levy, S.J. (1959) 'Symbols for sale', *Harvard Business Review*, 37 (July/August), 117–24.

Lizot, J. (1985) *Tales of the Yanomami*, Cambridge: Cambridge University Press.

Madsen, P. (1993) 'Ruin and rebus – history of the Arcades project', *Orbis Litterarum*, 48 (2/3), 68–82.

Mauss, M. (1950) 'Essai sur le don. Forme et raison d'échange dans les sociétés archaïques', in *Sociologie et anthropologie*, Paris: Quadrige/PUF, pp. 143–279. (first published 1924).

McCracken, G. (1988) *Culture and Consumption*, Bloomington, IN: Indiana University Press.

Morin, E. (1962) *L'Ésprit du temps*, Paris: Grasset.

Porter, R. (1993) 'Consumption: disease of the consumer society?' in J. Brewer and R. Porter (eds), *Consumption and the World of Goods*, London: Routledge, pp. 58–81.

Rorty, R. (1979) *Philosophy and the Mirror of Nature*, Princeton, NJ: Princeton University Press.

Russell, B. (1945/1972), *A History of Western Philosophy*, New York: Simon and Schuster.

Saffioti, H.I.B. (1978) *Women in Class Society*, New York: Monthly Review Press.

Sahlins, M. (1976) *Culture and Practical Reason*, Chicago: Chicago University Press.

Shultz, C.J., II, Belk, R. and Ger, G. (1994) (eds), *Research in Consumer Behavior, Vol. 7: Consumption in Marketizing Economies*, Greenwich, CT: JAI Press.

Steuerman, E. (1992) 'Habermas vs Lyotard: modernity vs postmodernity?' in A. Benjamin (ed.), *Judging Lyotard*, London: Routledge, pp. 99–118.

Sweezy, P.M. (1947) *The Theory of Capitalist Development*, New York: Monthly Review Press.

Veblen, T. (1899) *The Theory of the Leisure Class*, New York: Macmillan.

9

A sinister way of life: a search for left-handed material culture

NIGEL SADLER

Introduction

One of a museum's roles is to hold a collection that is relevant to its potential users, and in recent years this has meant expanding the collecting policy to include all sectors of the community, especially the minority groups. One section of the community that is often forgotten is left-handers, one in ten of the population. Just for one moment consider a range of objects in everyday use. Most are designed for right-handers and by their teens most left-handers have had to adapt to using right-handed equipment. Today it is easier to come across items specifically designed for the left-hander, ranging from a potato peeler to a high-powered rifle. However, a search through collections and reminiscences makes it apparent that there are many items that should have gone to museums. Why don't more museums hold these collections? Before we can look for items we need to understand why people are left-handed, and the history and discrimination of left-handedness, and whether we can predict careers that left-handers are likely to undertake.

Why is the world right-handed?

In tests with cats, rats, mice and monkeys, results have shown that on average half of the animals use the left paw and half the right. In mammals other than humans, there is no predisposition to either side. To decide why most humans became right-handed we need to look closely at areas where we differ from other mammals.

Humans can create and design a wide range of tools. It is argued that before we started to have specialist tool-makers at the dawn of agriculture we were neither left- nor right-hand dominant. The introduction of agriculture and specialist tool manufacture led to right-hand predominance, as harvesting crops with sickles was more efficiently done all in the same direction, and specialist tool makers soon found that they could make more tools if they used the same pattern, mould, etc. Looking at hunter-gatherer societies that still exist today, there appears to be a slightly higher number of left-handers than in the population as a whole but nowhere near an equal split between left- and right-handers. Another difference between humans and other mammals is our highly developed language skills. It can be argued that as the main centre for speech control is in the left hemisphere of the brain, this side has become dominant and favoured development in the right side, notably the hand and foot. To understand this we will need to look at brain development and genetics.

The human brain has two hemispheres and each dominates different functions:

Left hemisphere (right-handed)	*Right hemisphere (left-handed)*
Speech	Looking/non-verbal memory
Thinks/plans/deduces	Acts/feels (emotions)
Sings the words	Sings the tunes
Logical	Imagination/day-dreaming/fantasies
Mathematical	Creativity

Popular belief is that those with a predominant 'thinking' brain will become right-handers and are usually verbal, analytic and good at maths and will think linearly. Those with a dominant 'feeling' brain become left-handers and are intuitive, mystical, have a strong visual sense and are more apt to think holistically. Most scientists agree that the two hemispheres have different predominant functions, but are not as different as we would like them to be in order to label people, especially using handedness as a criterion. The regions in the brain that produce and comprehend speech are usually predominant in the left hemisphere of the brain, with the right hemisphere having a smaller language area. Studies show that 97 per cent of right-handers and 68 per cent of left-handers have language in their left hemisphere, 19 per cent of left-handers and 3 per cent of right-handers have language in the right hemisphere, and 12 per cent of left-handers have language in both hemispheres.

Two of the leading theories for causes for left-handedness are testosterone levels and 'birth stress' (Coren, 1993). A pregnant woman produces testosterone, which slows the rate of the development of the left hemisphere of the brain and suppresses the growth and development of other organs like the thymus gland, which is important for the development of the body's immune system in a foetus. 'Birth stress' theory suggests left-handedness is due to some level of brain damage in the womb or at birth. One study concluded that left-handers are on average shorter and weigh less than their right-handed counterparts (Coren, 1993: 165), an indicator of birth stresses (and somewhat of a surprise to the writer, who is a left-hander, 6ft 7in tall and weighing over 16½ stone). These suggest that left-handedness is not the cause but a symptom of a bigger issue. Some scientists have even suggested a link between left-handedness and alcoholism, attempted suicides, criminality, depression, drug abuse, emotionality, epilepsy, juvenile delinquency, mental retardation, a predisposition towards aggression, psychosis, schizophrenia, sleeping disorders and school failure, in which higher percentages of left-handers can be found. Left-handedness should be seen as a possible marker for the above conditions but not the cause. Other research has shown that the average age of death for right-handers was 75 years and for left-handers 66 years, and that left-handers are 78 per cent more likely to have an accident (Coren, 1993). An increased risk of accidents would be one cause for left-handers having shorter life expectancies, but is also one symptom of the greater problem that includes the question of why left-handers are more likely to have allergies and immune deficiencies, which can, singly or combined, cause reduced life expectancy.

It is interesting to note that the probability of a left-handed child being born to parents who are both right-handed is 10 per cent, and that there is a 10 per cent chance if the father is left-handed, a 20 per cent chance if the mother is left-handed, and a 35 per cent chance if both parents are left-handed (Coren, 1993: 85–7), which indicates that left-handedness is genetic in part.

Careers

One in four American *Apollo* astronauts were left-handed, and four out of the last five presidents of the USA – Gerald Ford, Ronald Reagan, George Bush and Bill Clinton – are left-handers. Does handedness make a person more prone for certain careers? Geschwind argued that left-handers had greater spatial awareness and would therefore enter jobs such as architecture (Brightwell, 1985). Surveys showed left-handers ranged from 16.3 per cent to 29.4 per cent in some architecture companies and amongst architecture students. For other careers it is only casual observation rather than analytical study that suggests a higher ratio of left-handers: for example, I have noticed that in archaeology and museum work there appears to be a higher percentage of left-handers.

Sport is one notable area where being left-handed has distinct tactical advantages. Some surveys suggest that at any one time around

20 per cent (Paul, 1990) of top tennis players are left-handed, including John McEnroe, Martina Navratilova and George VI (who played in the 1924 Wimbledon doubles). Cricket is another game where there is a higher percentage of left-handers.

The clumsy child

If left-handedness is just a genetic or biological condition, why does it attract so much discrimination? As Langford has put it, expressing the general social condition of left-handedness: 'Religious taboo, social stigma, primitive superstition and a general dislike of the unusual have branded left-handers, at best, mildly unfortunate, and, at worst, as social outcast' (Langford, 1987: 7). Even psychologists have shown discrimination. Theodore Blau saw left-handers as stubborn, over-sensitive, impulsive, embarrassing to the family, having difficulty following directions, having trouble completing projects, and more likely to have speech problems. Abram Blau was of the opinion that left-handers were just anti-social and used the 'wrong' hand as a deliberate challenge to the otherwise natural and normal state of right-handedness.

Some of the worst discrimination is during early school years. Victorian children were chastised for writing or using their left hand for everyday tasks, which may sound barbaric but continued well into this century. It is clear that teachers are not specifically advised on dealing with left-handers, and many do not see left-handers as needing special assistance or even equipment. Left-handers are often made to feel different in a negative way, usually via ridicule, the need for special tuition, or constant complaints of clumsiness and untidiness. Language reflects this discrimination against left-handers. For example, in Latin *rectus* (right) means straight, just and a position of honour, whereas *sinister* (left) means evil, awkward, wrong and unfavourable. In English today, 'right' means 'correct' or 'in a proper manner' and 'a right-hand man' implies a person of trust, whereas a 'left-handed compliment' means an insult. There are over forty derogatory English terms for left-handedness, the most common being 'cack-handed', taken from the French word *caca* (excrement), whilst there are none for right-handedness. These terms are in everyday use and many people are unaware of their true origins.

Discrimination in the workplace is generally based on the equipment used. There may be no left-handed scissors in the office, or more probably most machines and heavy equipment may be built and designed for right-handed use, which means left-handers using their less-able hand. As a left-handed curator, I have found problems in my job. For example, when re-sleeving photographs I started to insert them in the sleeves with my left hand. I soon realized that all these photographs were sleeved in the opposite direction to the rest, which had been done by right-handers.

Right-handers might say 'What harm does this do?' Apart from the obvious inconveniencing of left-handers, and suggesting that there is something wrong with us that needs correcting, it does lead to a more serious problem. Cyril Burt, a psychologist, said about left-handers: 'They squint, they stammer, they shuffle and shamble, they flounder about like seals out of water. Awkward in the house, and clumsy in their games, they are fumblers and bunglers at whatever they do' (Burt, 1937: 287). These views are still commonly held today. The accepted stereotype of left-handers, which includes being clumsy, socially inept, untidy and lazy, is reinforced by parents, teachers and work colleagues. Few right-handers have even considered why left-handers are untidy or clumsy, and think complaints about equipment are just cases of a bad workman blaming his tools. All they need to do is watch left-handers struggle with right-handed scissors and tin-openers to see the awkward positions the hands get into.

Children of the devil

In Christianity the devil is always on God's left (we throw spilt salt over our left shoulder for good luck because it is supposed to hit the devil). In the Roman Catholic church all rituals are carried out with the right hand, including the blessing, the sign of the cross, and taking and offering the wafers and wine during communion. The Bible mentions the right hand or right side eighty times and the left hand or left side twenty-one times, the latter in most cases to indicate dishonour or evil (Coren, 1993: 18), as for example in St Matthew's parable of the sheep and goats. He claims that in the vision of judgement all nations will be divided before the Son of Man when he appears, with the sheep on his right and the goats (sign of the devil) on his left. Those on his right will inherit the kingdom and those on the left will be cast into hell. A politically correct Bible released in August 1995 by an American group did consider left-handedness. In their version people no longer sat on the right hand of God, as this was leftist. They now sit 'beside' God.

Following on from the belief that the devil controls the left side, during witch hunts marks or indications of left-sidedness would be enough to condemn people. This was taking the prejudice to its extremes, and Joan of Arc probably was condemned because of this (many paintings show her holding her sword in her left hand).

Christianity is not the only religion to show this discrimination. The Talmud (rabbinical law of the Jews) states the chief adversary is called Samael (which derives from the Hebrew Se'mol, meaning 'left side'), who was on the left side of God until he was expelled from Heaven. In

Buddhism the path to Nirvana divides in two: the left-hand road is the wrong way of life and should be avoided.

Left-handedness and its effects on museums

Exhibitions

Have you ever wondered why most people prefer to go in one direction around a museum exhibition? There is a general tendency to turn right (with the body turning in a clockwise motion) and therefore an exhibition can feel odd if a visitor is forced to go left. For left-handers the opposite is more likely to be true, and they are two and a half times more likely to turn left than right-handers. This means that most museum exhibitions are laid out for the benefit of right-handers.

Objects

There is a distinct lack of left-handed objects in museum collections. This might be because:

1 they don't exist because they were never made;
2 they don't exist today because they have not survived;
3 they have never been collected;
4 they are held by museums but not recorded properly.

Some objects are easy to identify as being made by left-handers, either from the knowledge that the creator was left-handed or by using a specialist to identify a left-handed trait, such as handwriting (graphologists suggest that certain criteria can show whether a letter has been written left- or right-handed). Below is an eclectic list of areas where I have found examples of objects made by or for, or adapted by, left-handers or that show left-handedness. It is clear that it has been easier to find items made in the Western world. Further research would hopefully indicate a diversity of items held in ethnographic collections as well.

- **Advertising**: In some advertising material, including Victorian and Edwardian, people are shown using their left hands. This may not be an indication of left-handedness, in fact, but more probably what looks right in the composition (or the result of a right-handed image being reversed in printing).
- **Archaeological material**: Archaeologists working on 122 skeletons from the eleventh to the sixteenth century at Wharram Percy suggest that a study of the arm bones indicates that 16 per cent used their left hand for load-bearing tasks (Denison, 1995). This assumes the load-

bearing arm will be slightly longer. Unfortunately these statistics mean little in a search for the history of left-handedness, as the sample is too small and only studies one function of handedness. Even though 16 per cent may have carried heavy objects in their left hand this may have been the only thing they did left-handed, as the dominant hand is not necessarily the stronger. In tests 13 per cent of right-handers had a stronger left hand and over 50 per cent of left-handers had stronger right hands (Coren, 1993: 39). A full study of pottery, tool manufacture and wear on tools is needed.

Paul Sarasin, a French archaeologist, studied early stone implements and noticed that some Neolithic tools were sharpened on the left side and others on the right. He concluded that there was no conformity to one pattern and the tools revealed an almost equal division between right- and left-handedness (Langford, 1987). However, S.A. Semenov, an anthropologist, has carried out micro-wear analysis on flint tools dated from 35,000 to 8000 BC which indicates that 80 per cent had greater wear on the right side, suggesting they were used right-handed (Semenov, 1964).

- **Archives**: In 1860 people who wrote left-handed were said to represent 2 per cent of the population; by 1957 this was 7 per cent; and in 1992 the Centre for Left-Handed Studies (CLHS) suggested that 11 per cent of children wrote left-handed.

Given the discrimination against left-handers, it is likely that many records will hold accounts, generally negative, of left-handedness and its treatment. Unfortunately, there is no easy access to these records. We know from many stories and anecdotes that during Victorian times children were chastised for being left-handed. A cursory look through some local school log-books shows records of caning for absenteeism, rudeness, etc., but as yet no local records of the treatment of left-handed children have come to light. This may be because individual teachers carried out the punishment or corrective treatment and it was not reported to the head teacher who wrote the school log. Personal diaries may also record individuals' feelings about their treatment at school or in the workplace, but again it will be a matter of luck to identify these sources.

Many left-handers start to write right to left and quite often in mirror image, and one estimate suggests that 93 per cent of mirror writing is by left-handers. Some famous left-handers are renowned for their mirror writing, notably Leonardo da Vinci, who kept notes in mirror image, and Lewis Carroll, who mentions mirror writing in *Alice in Wonderland*. Once taught to write the 'right' way left-handers progress from pencil to ink pen. At this stage they quite often smudge their work, as their hand trails over what has just been written (the introduction of the biro has done away with some of these problems). Is it possible to look at passages of text, especially by schoolchildren, and identify from the smudges whether they were written left- or right-handed? This will require further research. Researchers have shown already that left-handers push pens and are therefore more prone to cramps and muscle fatigue and are much more likely to write illegibly when writing fast than right-handers, and in exams will slow down to appear neat. This could explain why in one study of exam papers the left-handed students usually gave shorter answers.

- **Art**: Left-handedness can also be indicated by a difference in perception. Some psychologists argue that as the right hemisphere is more dominant in left-handers they will be more artistic. It is argued that left-handers are more likely to draw faces in right profile and right-handers in left profile. Many of da Vinci's works show people in right profile, e.g. portraits of Isabella d'Este (1500) and the *Madonna and child with a yarn winder* (1501), but there are also examples of people in left profile. In some of da Vinci's sketches for the *Mona Lisa* he has the left hand over the right, a natural pose for left-handers (Paul, 1993: 103), but this was altered in the final painting (McMullen, 1975). Right-handed artists have also painted images of people carrying out tasks left-handed. The *Spanish Singer* by Edouard Manet, in the New York Metropolitan Museum of Art, is shown playing the guitar left-handed (Carr-Gomm, 1992). In one study of 10,000 works of art ranging in date from 15,000 BC to AD 1950, 1180 had unambiguous figures holding something in or using a hand (Coren, 1993), and 93 per cent of these people were carrying out tasks with their right hand.

Cave and rock paintings are an area of great discussion. Anthropologists studying remains of Native Americans in the United States in the late nineteenth century found 33 per cent of early rock paintings were by left-handers (Paul, 1993: 160). Elsewhere studies of hand stencils show fewer right hands; for example, in the Ice Age site at Gargas there are 136 left hands compared to 22 right hands (Bahn and Vertut, 1988: 104). This probably denotes a much higher percentage of right-handers; but these stencils are not very good evidence of handedness, as the dye for them may have been spat out, not applied by the dominant hand. Other research on cave paintings shows equal numbers of animals in left and right profile (Langford, 1987: 10).

Art is also an indicator of prejudices. In D. Rychaert's painting, the alchemist producing life in a glass vessel is portrayed as left-handed, and Pieter Bruegel the Elder portrays a number of alchemists as sinistral. As alchemy was not understood, many believed that alchemists were in league with the devil; they are therefore portrayed as left-handed (Blake-Coleman, 1982), just as the devil is.

- **Buildings**: The Kerr family of Scotland, famous for the numbers of left-handers in their family, gave their castles left-handed (anti-clockwise) staircases so they would be easier to defend.

- **Cartoons/puppets**: It is not clear whether cartoon characters shown left-handed indicate a left-handed artist drawing from experience, a right-handed artist drawing the person mirror image to themselves, or the character being drawn to fit into the overall composition. Bart Simpson, from *The Simpsons*, is shown left-handed in most of the tasks he carries out. He might just be left-handed to fit in with the stereotype that left-handers have a rebellious nature.

  Most of the Muppets are left-handed, but this is not because their creator Jim Henson was left-handed. The Muppet operators are mostly right-handed and use their predominant hand for the more difficult task of operating the head, leaving their left hand free to operate a subsidiary activity, such as the Muppet's left hand.

- **Cheque books**: The introduction of a left-handed cheque-book by Lloyds Bank in 1995 was probably no more than an expensive marketing gimmick rather than a realistic attempt to aid their customers. They claimed that amongst their 6.5 million customers 900,000 were left-handed. Other banks do not appear to want to follow suit due to the cost implications of such an action.

- **Clothing**: It is clear that most people prefer to use one foot rather than the other for specific tasks, for example, kicking a ball. In most cases the predominant hand and foot are on the same side (Gillett, 1983). One study showed 88 per cent of people were right-handed, 81 per cent were right-footed and 84 per cent had their dominant hand and foot on the same side (i.e., were congruent). Generally the shoe on the predominant foot will scuff and wear down faster than the other. As there is a strong link between left-footedness and left-handedness, various assumptions could be made about increases or declines in the number of left-handers by assessing wear on shoes.

  Most clothing is designed for right-handed use. Trouser zips, which have a small flap of material covering them attached on the left-hand side, give easier access from the right-hand side, and single-pocketed shirts that have a pocket on the left give easier access for right-handers. If clothing shows opposite signs to these, it is likely to have been made by or for a left-hander. An easier area in which to identify left-handed manufacture is knitted and crocheted clothing; in knitting a left-hander will hold the stitches on the right needle, and not the left as is common practice, which gives a distinctive twist to each stitch in the finished garment.

- **Cups**: Often a passing comment can lead to extensive work trying to seek out an item. One such is a left-handed moustache cup. On the *Antiques Roadshow*, 24 December 1995, a right-handed moustache cup was shown. The expert said there were rare examples of moustache cups for left-handers, but so far they have eluded me.

Modern mugs that have a single image usually have this on the side that faces the drinker when the cup is held right-handed. At one friend's house I am often given a cup with a picture of a pig's face on one side and its bottom on the other side (guess which side a left-hander will be looking at). Today specialist mugs are produced with images to favour a left-handed drinker.

- **Customs**: There are some objects that are related to the left hand but by themselves do not indicate left-handedness. One of the best examples of this is the wedding ring. Placed by English tradition on the weaker hand (the left), it was originally used to protect the wearer from evil.

- **Electrical equipment**: Early flat irons were ambidextrous but, with the introduction of electricity, irons had the cords coming out of the right-hand side, making them awkward for left-handed use. Today many companies are producing irons with the cord coming out from the end rather than from either side, and, like many new kettles, steam irons have water gauges on both sides so a left-hander doesn't risk injury by trying to turn the hot kettle or iron round. In fact much of the new kitchen equipment is being designed for ambidextrous use. Unfortunately, there is still a right-handed bias for heavy electrical equipment, ranging from where the on/off button is to where the safety guard or the operating handles are located.

- **Figureheads**: Like other objects, figureheads can illustrate left-handedness rather than left-handed manufacture. The figurehead on the *Cutty Sark* represents one of the coven of witches in Robert Burns's poem 'Tam-O-Shanter'. As Tam escapes from the witches, one gives chase and pulls out the horse's tail. The figurehead shows the witch holding the tail in her left hand.

- **Furniture**: Desks with side-mounted writing surfaces again don't show the 10 per cent of left mountings needed to cope with left-handers. Many places that employ these desks rarely think about a left-hander's needs. A left-hander using one of these desks ends up sitting in a twisted, uncomfortable position when writing.

- **Mechanical devices**: In the sixteenth and seventeenth centuries, these display a definite preferred clockwise direction in rotation (Blake-Coleman, 1982). This could have been due to the designers being right-handed, to superstition or to prejudice. It is interesting to note that in Leonardo da Vinci's drawings of mechanical inventions most cranks could only be operated by the left hand.

- **Movie industry**: The movie industry has produced many films in which famous or infamous left-handers are portrayed right-handed. In some cases they have been unable to do this; for example, in *The Babe* (1992), the story of Babe Ruth (played by John Goodman), the hero has to be portrayed as left-handed, as he was famous for being a left-handed batter. In other cases this has not been so. How many films show characters as well known as Alexander the Great or Jack the Ripper as left-handed? Recent research has brought one to my attention: *The Left-Handed Gun* (1958) was the story of Billy the Kid. Films can also show left-handers, such as Robert De Niro, Marilyn Monroe, Judy Garland, Rock Hudson and Betty Grable, in action. A good example is in *Limelight*, where Charlie Chaplin, a left-hander, plays the violin left-handed.
- **Musical instruments**: Most musical instruments are designed for right-handers, with the exception of the French horn, which is valved for the left hand. This predominance is probably meant to introduce conformity: imagine how confusing it would be to have a violinist playing left-handed in an orchestra, where not only would it look odd but bows would clash. Some musicians have overcome this problem, notably the guitarists Jimi Hendrix and Paul McCartney.

  There are also several pieces of music specially written for left-handers, including Ravel's Concerto in D Major for the Left Hand for piano and orchestra (written for Paul Wittgenstein, who lost his right hand in the First World War), Prokofiev's Concerto No 4 for the Left Hand and Bax's Left-handed Concertante, written for Harriet Cohen, whose right hand had been injured.
- **Oral history**: Given the lack of tangible items it becomes more apparent that we need to capture reminiscences. In the oral history records kept at Vestry House Museum, numbering over 230 interviews, the compilers, the Waltham Forest Oral History Workshop, were unable to recall a single reference to handedness. They have now agreed to try and include a question on handedness when asking about schooling and working life. It is hoped that this will create a record of local life for left-handers.
- **Photographs**: There are two areas where photographs are going to be helpful. The first will show famous sports stars, performers and musicians at work. For example, a photograph of the Beatles would show a left-handed guitarist (Paul McCartney) and a left-handed drummer (Ringo Starr). Second, social history photographs can either be used positively to indicate left-handers or as a negative record, such as a Victorian school photograph where the children are posed holding their pens in their right hand. It must be remembered that a photograph is only a split second in time and even if a person is holding something in the left hand it does not necessarily indicate left-handedness.

- **Scissors:** Right-handed scissors have the cutting blade cutting upwards and are biased so that the blades press together during the cutting operation. A left-hander using a right-handed pair of scissors will have the cutting blade cutting downwards and obscuring the cutting line, and the right-hand bias forces the blades apart slightly so that the material being cut slips between the blades. Left-handed scissors are biased in the other direction to right-handed scissors.
- **Sporting memorabilia:** In most sports the equipment used will be the same for right- or left-handers. However, some will obviously be different, such as golf clubs or padding for cricketers.
- **Tools:** One good example of a left-handed tool is a medieval carpenter's side- or broad-axe, held by the Museum of London (London Museum, 1940), which is flat on the right face. The use of a similar axe was illustrated in the *Building of Noah's Ark* in the *Nuremberg Chronicles* (1493), which shows right- and left-handed carpenters working on the same piece of timber (Ungar, 1991).
- **Trade catalogues:** These are a very good source for left-handed equipment, but they have drawbacks. Some companies that have been supplying equipment and tools for left-handers for many decades do not necessarily carry them in their catalogues. For example, a company that has produced leather-making tools in Walsall since the 1860s is proud that it produces specialist tools for left-handers, but at no stage has it recorded this fact in its catalogues.
- **Typewriters and keyboards:** One of the few items in general use today that favours left-handed use is the QWERTY keyboard. It is estimated that 57 per cent of the work on a typewriter is done by the left hand. The introduction of keypads for computers has seen the introduction of a right-hand bias with the number pads on the right. Specialist keyboards are now available with the number pads on the left.
- **Weaponry:** This is one area where there are good examples of left-handed equipment. The collection held by the Royal Armouries is one of the few that I have come across that holds records indicating left-handedness, probably because instances are so easy to identify. For example, in their inventory of guns they list as left-handed an 1868 sporting rifle, a 1975 German target pistol, a cross-eyed stock (right shoulder, left eye), and a 1770 flintlock. In the Royal Armouries' new museum in Leeds a case in the hunting and sporting gallery is to include left-handedness. In Germany, the manufacturers Feinwerkbau, Walther and Anschutz carried out a survey of German target shooters, which showed that between 5 per cent and 10 per cent were left-handed. These companies now have 10 per cent of their total production committed to left-handed guns (Paul, 1990).

Swords generally indicated handedness by the position of the guard for the hand. Left-handed swordsmen had a major advantage over right-handers, and even today this is clearly shown by the number of top fencers who are left-handed. In the 1984 Olympics the first eight places in the men's foil were left-handed. In 1747 Captain John Godfrey is quoted as saying 'I cannot help taking notice that the left-handed Man has the advantage over the right-handed, upon an equal footing ... In both Small and Back-Sword, I would rather contend with the right-handed Man with more judgement, than the other with less' (Coren, 1993: 53).

Other left-handed items associated with weaponry include daggers used in conjunction with a sword (as most swords would be held in the right hand, the dagger would have to fit into the left hand); boomerangs; and two First World War postcards showing equipment for left-handed soldiers.

Conclusion

The real problem left-handers face is the ignorance of right-handers. Ask most left-handers to name famous left-handers and they will be able to come up with a list, as it is something that they notice. Ask right-handers and they will often struggle. The left-hander is invisible. Left-handers generally don't complain about the problems they face and therefore right-handers don't know that they exist in proportions large enough to matter.

The comments and thoughts written here are only the initial part of a more detailed study on left-handedness being carried out for an exhibition held at Vestry House Museum, Walthamstow, during 1996. Initial research shows left-handers are clearly discriminated against in museum collecting, with no active collecting policy or even adequate recording for retrieval. Museums must hold items specifically made or adapted for left-handers, but have either misrecorded or failed to identify these objects' left-handed origins. Hopefully museums will be able to help the left-handed cause by making it part of their collecting policy to record handedness. As people become aware of the items in their collections, more knowledge can be gained about life for left-handers in the past and about items made for or by them, or adapted by them.

Bibliography

Agass, G. (1995) 'Slowly tackling the problem in hand', *Waltham Forest Guardian*, 17 August.

Bahn, P.G. and Vertut, J. (1988) *Images of the Ice Age*, London: Bellew.

Bannister, J. (1994) *Brian Lara: The Story of a Record Breaking Year*, London: Stanley Paul.

Blake-Coleman, B.C. (1982) 'The left heresy and directional preference in early science and technology', *Folklore*, 93(ii), 151–63.

Brightwell, R. (1985) 'Is your child left-handed?', *Listener*, 7 February, pp. 10–11.

Burt, C. (1937) *The Backward Child*, London: London University Press.

Carr-Gomm, S. (1992) *Manet*, London: Studio Editions.

Coren, S. (1993) *Left Hander*, Cambridge: Cambridge University Press.

Denison, S. (1995) 'Medieval arm bones lend support to left-handers', *British Archaeology*, October: 4.

Gillett, H.G. du P. (1983) 'Left foot, right foot', *Chiropodist*, 38(5): 161–77.

Halliwell, L. (1990) *Halliwell's Film Guide*, 7th edn, London: Paladin.

Harrison, S. (1993) *Diary of Jack the Ripper*, London: BCA.

Hornsby, B. (1989) *Overcoming Dyslexia*, London: Macdonald.

de Kay, J.T. (1989) *The Natural Superiority of the Left-Hander*, New York: M. Evans.

Langford, S. (1987) *The Left Handed Book*, Glasgow: Grafton Books.

London Museum (1940) *Medieval Catalogue*, London: HMSO.

Marshall, G. (1995) 'A day in the life at Eton', *Daily Star*, 3 September.

McIlwain, J. (1994) *Cutty Sark*, Andover: Pitkin Pictorials.

McKie, R. (1984) 'Bend sinister', *Observer*, 4 November.

McMullen, R. (1975) *Mona Lisa – the Pictures and the Myth*, London: Macmillan.

Paul, D. (1990) *Living Left-handed*, London: Bloomsbury.

Paul, D. (1993) *Left Handed Helpline*, Manchester: Dextral Books.

Paul, D. (1994) *Left-Hander's Resources List*, Manchester: Dextral Books.

Porter, M. and Feger, H. (1995) 'Success is in the palm of their hands', *Sunday Express*, 13 August.

Semenov, S.A. (1964) *Prehistoric Technology*, London: Cory, McAdams & MacKay.

Smith, T. (1995) (ed.) *Complete Family Health Encyclopedia*, London: Dorling Kindersley.

Ungar, R.W. (1991) *Images of Noah the Shipbuilder*, New Brunswick, NJ: Rutgers University Press.

Trade catalogues/publicity material

Anything Left-Handed
Berol
Dextral Books
Godfrey Syrett Limited, Contract Furniture
Lloyds Bank
Parker Pens
Rowenta
Sainsbury and Sainsbury's Stationers

10

Fantastic things

MILENA VEENIS

Introduction

> The transformation of any society should be revealed by the changing
> relations of persons to objects within it.
>
> (Comaroff and Comaroff, 1990: 196)

The motion and television pictures of those exciting days when the
Berlin Wall came tumbling down are engraved in most people's
memories. They clearly portray the ecstatic atmosphere in which the
whole of Germany was immersed: long rows of Trabis waiting for
hours, sometimes even days, to cross the inter-German border; railway
stations with long queues, the impatient travellers waiting for hours
before they could get on a train which was to take them to West
Germany; East and West Germans who had never seen each other
before, crying for joy and embracing each other. On the western side of
the border we see hordes of East Germans running around in West
Berlin and other West German towns with large shopping bags, not
knowing where to turn and what to buy first. 'East Germans gorged
themselves on the symbolic goods of West Germanness ... They
flocked to the shopping centres and stores in a consumptive orgy'
(Borneman, 1992: 321).[1] It is only seven years ago, but people who have
recently visited the former GDR are amazed when they see how fast
and all-embracing the Westernization of this country has been. The
changes which have taken place in the material and consumption
structure of this former socialist country are impressive. Whereas it
used to be difficult for the average Western tourist to spend the
required amount of money in East Germany, today even the most spoilt
and exacting Westerner will be able to buy to his or her heart's content.
Shops, including (international) department stores and video-shops,
and other places of sale and consumption where the material
acquisitions from the West are displayed have sprung up everywhere.

Because Western consumer goods were highly valued in the socialist
GDR when they were not available, one would expect the inhabitants

of this country to be very happy with the material Westernization of their world. Surprisingly, however, this does not turn out to be the case. As has often been pointed out in the media, the atmosphere in the former GDR is distinctly gloomy and pessimistic, and many people are outspokenly negative about the material and consumptive changes in their country.

'Only because of the bananas ...'; with a heavy sigh the middle-aged woman who had showed me around the historical museum of Magdeburg ended her story. Although she used to show a keen interest in the history of her native town, she did not show any involvement in the Magdeburger hemispheres and the medieval ploughs displayed in the large entrance hall of the museum. During her conducted tour, she focused mainly on the most recent developments in her country: the increasing use of make-up among East German women and the rapidity with which the appearance of her native town had changed to such an extent that she no longer felt safe and at home there. 'In exchange for worthless luxury goods like bananas and make-up', ran the implicit message of her story, 'the inhabitants of the former GDR have lost too much in the reunification of the two Germanies'.

The same Western objects which used to be extremely valuable and highly desired in the old socialist days seem to have lost much of their attraction in the aftermath of German unification. Although this shift in valuation does not, of course, hold equally for all inhabitants of the former GDR, I think it is worth focusing on this change in public feelings with regard to Western material goods. Why is it that so many people joyfully celebrated the fall of the Berlin Wall by buying large amounts of Western goods? And why is it that these same people are not unanimously happy now that these goods are obtainable in every shop? This last question is usually answered with reference to the painful results and consequences of German unification in general. The inhabitants of the former GDR are then said not to be disappointed because of the material Westernization of their country as such, but because of the large-scale socio-economic drama that is taking place in the former GDR. Make-up and exotic fruits are blamed arbitrarily in place of the 'real' causes of discontent. Although this interpretation is valuable in so far as it rightly underlines the multiple reasons for the general feeling of discontent and misery in East Germany, I find it too general. It completely denies what one might call 'the form of the discontent'.

Before elaborating on this point, I will first describe the changed place and meaning of Western material goods in East Germany before, during and after the fall of the Wall. Then, I will present in greater detail the most frequently heard interpretation with regard to the complaints about the material Westernization of this country, and I will highlight its major deficiencies. After that, I will present the first outlines of an alternative interpretation, based on the assumption that, since material objects play an important role in the world in which we live, they should not be reduced to coincidental stand-ins for other things and experiences. One of the most distinct examples of this general statement is the post-war development of both Germanies, in which material goods and developments have played a very important role. As the German example makes clear, material objects are far more than just 'good to think with'. Because they are the main ingredients with which we build, develop and express our individual and collective identities, they are the proper vehicles for individual and collective dreams and fantasies about faraway realities and futures – which may come true ... one day.

Of washing powder and toasters

It is commonly known that Western consumer goods were highly desired and meaningful in the GDR before the demise of the Berlin Wall. When visiting the country, Western relatives and friends were always expected to bring their old blue jeans and other discards with them because everything from the West was considered very fashionable. People who possessed Western objects could count on a certain amount of prestige,[2] and the Christmas parcels that East Germans received from their Western relatives were always anxiously awaited because they usually contained some popular Western consumer goods, such as (cheap brands of) soap, eau de toilette, after-shave and face cream. These things were cherished all year long as precious little hoards and an enormous value was attached to them:

> for the excluded inhabitants of the GDR, Western products that the 'poor brothers and sisters in the East' received from their rich relatives became the messengers of another, sparkling product-world. The 'Westwares' not only offered ample food for daily conversations, but they represented the 'real thing', they became little relics in the subjectively experienced dreariness of the 'Eastwares'. Their possessors reaped esteem and their social status mounted.
> (Diesener and Gries, 1992: 59–60)

The high social status and the enormous value that went with possessing Western consumer goods also come to the fore in the well-known story of East German pensioners who were freely allowed to make day-trips to the Federal Republic of Germany. The elder inhabitants of East Berlin, in particular, made use of this possibility, which allowed them to do part of their shopping in the western part of the city. From their laboriously saved West German money they are said to have bought washing powder which turned out to have been produced in East Germany, but which was colourfully packaged in the western part of the country. Although this may be just hearsay, poking fun at the naïveté of East Germans, it is still significant that the joke figures in a story about what is assumed to be Western washing powder. The message is clear: Western consumer goods were considered so attractive in the GDR that people lost their minds in order to get them.

Although it is not possible, on the basis of these examples, to understand what Western consumer goods really meant or represented, why they were associated with a higher social status, or why and for whom this was (not) the case, it is obvious that these goods were highly desired and meaningful in the GDR. This of course became very clear after the opening of the Berlin Wall, when all these things were freely available and people pounced upon the sparkling material world which they had only been able to yearn for.

Most East Germans I spoke to clearly remember the overwhelming feeling that came over them when they first crossed the inter-German border and saw what life on the other side was like. The first thing which almost everybody mentions is the material abundance; the bulging shops and their colourful contents. One young man, who was at that time working in a state-owned shop where household goods were sold, told me what went through his mind when he first entered one of the large West German department stores:

> Both professionally and personally I was very curious to see what such a place would look like. So I went in. But when I stood there, in front of the rack where the toasters were displayed, I really felt sick and I left the shop. I just couldn't stand looking at it. This big rack, filled with different kinds of toasters ... whereas in our shop, we were happy when we got four toasters a month. And these were usually sold before they even arrived, because every salesman or -woman always happened to know someone who wanted or needed a toaster.

This man became sick at the sight of West German material prosperity, other people started to cry when they first entered a West German store, but the stories with which people describe their first impressions of Western material life are all coloured by indescribably strong feelings: of joy, confusion, desire, disbelief, happiness and sometimes a little bitterness as well, because in this part of the country everything that people on the other side of the border could only dream about was available. It almost sounds unbelievable that the sight of ordinary consumer goods, like toasters, evokes such strong emotions. 'One really has to have lived here to understand what it meant for us to see this abundance,' people say, when asked why they reacted so vehemently.

The *Wende* and the liquidation of the GDR

Since then, much has changed in the former GDR. It is no exaggeration
to say that the whole of the East German world has turned upside
down since the collapse of the socialist regime. Not only have
economic, political and juridical relations, conceptions and notions
changed, but also most ideological, behavioural and mental standards
and orientations are under great pressure. It is therefore not hard to
understand that the inhabitants of the former GDR are not just happy
with German unification: their lives are totally confused, and on top of
that, many people feel like 'second-class citizens'. This feeling is
connected to the way in which the unification of the two German states
occurred. Although officially the two Germanies are 'reunited', it is
clear that the western part of the country provides all the standards of
change for its former socialist neighbour. 'In the months immediately
after the opening of the Wall, Germans generally assumed that the
nation would be united ... [in] a slow process of negotiation between
the two Germanys, with consideration of proposals from both sides'
(Borneman, 1992: 293). What happened, on the contrary, was that 'the
entire corpus of law and structure from the Federal Republic was taken
over by the former citizens of the former GDR – a quick
Westintegration' (Borneman, 1992: 293). In this respect it is significant
that what was first referred to as the 'unification' of the two countries
is now publicly called 'the liquidation of the GDR' (Borneman, 1992:
314).

Partly as a consequence of the unequal power relations between the
two former countries, relations between the inhabitants of both parts of
Germany have worsened dramatically. The supposed warm inter-
German feelings that were once expressed in hopeful exclamations such
as 'Germany, the only Fatherland' and 'we are one people' are today
replaced by the mutual stereotypes of '*Jammerossi*' (lamenting East-
erner) and '*Besserwessi*' (self-opinionated Better-Westerner).[3] Comics
about the ups and downs of these fantasy figures are for sale in every
bookshop in the former GDR.

Inter-German relations suffer not only from what is felt as an
extremely unequal power balance, but also from the costs of
unification, which, in spite of Chancellor Kohl's early promises, were
very high. The inhabitants of the western part of the country question
whether unification is worth the large financial sacrifices they are
compelled to make. And the inhabitants of the former GDR feel like
second-class citizens: first, because the western part of the country
makes them feel like beggars who are living on Western expenses, and
second, apart from this humiliation, because they also pay a large
economic and social price for the transformation processes in their own

country. The extended network of social services, of which all inhabitants of the former GDR took advantage in almost all aspects of their daily life (and which, of course, was one of the reasons for the bankruptcy of the socialist GDR), has been rapidly phased out: no more free day nurseries or state-financed grocers and hairdressers. But it is not only the overall social security system which has been dismantled in order to sanitize the country: the most painful consequence of the introduction of capitalism has been the ever-growing unemployment figures. Whereas all inhabitants of the communist GDR had a job, today more than 30 per cent of the working population of the former GDR are unemployed, according to recent, unofficial estimates. This is, of course, a hard way to learn what free market principles are all about. And when one realizes that this is in a country where everybody had the right to work, where the word 'unemployed' simply did not exist for over forty years, it is understandable that the unemployed inhabitants of the former GDR feel absolutely worthless. As a result of all these confusing and painful transformations, many people feel completely at the mercy of a cruel fate over which they have no influence whatsoever. Their world has changed so rapidly and so fundamentally that they have lost track; they just sit and wait for the latest disastrous developments which are decided upon in the western part of the country.

It is not just the enormous wave of transformations, developments and novelties that brings about strong feelings of doubt and resentment; people also feel uncertain and confused about their past. West German media often suggest that 25 to 30 per cent of the inhabitants of the former GDR were unofficially working for the Stasi.[4] The whole world vies in condemning East Germany's past as morally and ethically 'wrong'. Newspapers present new Stasi scandals every day: politicians, supposed dissident writers, sportsmen and sports-women, but also ordinary people – everybody seems to have spied on neighbours, colleagues and sometimes even their own families. Apart from the painful moral and ethical sides to this part of GDR history, most people also find it difficult to cope with this ongoing stream of bad news, scandals and horrible revelations, because their whole history is being criminalized. No one seems to be interested in how people actually lived in the GDR; the only interesting question seems to be 'What side were you on and how did you relate to the regime?', and the only acceptable answer is that of the suffering martyr. The whole GDR past is reduced to terms which are decided upon by the winning Western 'brothers and sisters', who have concluded that this was the 'wrong' past of an 'illegal state' (Borneman, 1992: 303). Many East Germans have the feeling that their 'history is being rewritten and their lives are being restructured by West Germans' (Borneman, 1992: 302).

It goes without saying that when the rest of the world – the 'winners' – unanimously condemn a country's past in such vehement terms, it can have rather destructive effects on national self-esteem and self-confidence.[5]

These feelings of confusion, doubt and bitterness, which are so widespread today in the former GDR, also, of course, refer to and are fed by the rapid material changes that have taken place more recently. The same process of East German 'sales' and West German 'buying up' can be recognized in the material sphere of life. Almost no East German products are for sale any more; old shops have disappeared or are unrecognizably modernized, and the entire East German consumption and material world has changed in a very specific direction: towards the West German model. As a consequence, many people have had great difficulties in finding what to buy or where to buy it. When interviewed by a Dutch journalist, one woman remarked:

> The internationally beloved GDR cigarettes are no longer for sale ...
> The market here wanted Cabinet just like it used to be. But what
> replaced it? A new Cabinet, according to EEC-norms, because a Western
> firm has bought the Cabinet factory ... With cosmetics it went the same
> way. At a certain moment there was no Eastern cream for sale and
> nobody knew which Western cream to use. I have tried several brands.
> In fact, *I had to start all over again.*
> (Niemöller, 1991: 70–1, my italics)

The rapid Westernization of consumption in the country makes people feel uncertain. Partly as a result of this uncertainty, a wave of nostalgia washes over the former GDR: people long for the old days when life was easy and quiet and when people still had time for each other. Nowadays, so the widely heard complaint goes, everybody thinks only of himself or herself and his or her own financial and material gain. Whereas people used to discuss their family problems with their colleagues, today people do not trust each other enough to do so: since it seems that everything is allowed in the battle for work, people could use the personal problems of their colleagues to their own professional advantage.

'In the old days' ... it is said that people used to celebrate feast-days together, watch TV together, exchange services, food and goods amongst each other. Today, everything is for sale, the whole social atmosphere is becoming cold and impersonal, and money seems to make the world go round. No one is willing to help anyone else unless she or he is paid for it; no one has time for anyone other than herself or himself and her or his own personal wish fulfilment. Fully in line with this wave of 'Ostalgia' (chosen as word of the year 1993), the old material and consumption certainties under Communism are seen in a new light. Former East German beers and cigarettes are advertised with the help of mottos like 'Still number one for us' and 'East German, therefore good', while the well-known Western cigarette brand 'West' is advertised in the following way: 'West? What I don't know, I don't smoke.' Shops which exclusively sell goods produced in the eastern part of the country spring up everywhere, and there are at least three museums where one can admire consumer goods from the 'old days'. People long for the old GDR toilet paper, cheese and sausages, and some shopkeepers have consciously decided not to change or modernize their shops, since people feel at home in the old, well-known GDR atmosphere. The material changes which have flooded the country give rise to very ambivalent feelings, and many people are angry about the fact that the entire material GDR world is rapidly disappearing.

> Is everything that has defined our life now lost and worthless? One must indeed have lived here for forty years to understand what situation arises when one has saved and waited half a life-time for a Trabi, after which everything is suddenly completely ridiculed by this 'Mercedes-economy'.
>
> (Maaz, 1990: 196)

It is important to recognize that disappointment about German reunification in general, and disappointment with regard to the material and consumption changes in particular, strengthen each other. But although it is tempting to see the material and consumption transformations in the former GDR (and especially the unequal inter-German relations which are expressed in them) as an enlargement of the way German reunification in general has come about, I think it is too much to equate the two transformation processes. This would lead to the conclusion that the consumption dissension in the former GDR is just one of the many ways in which the disappointing outcomes of the transition from a socialist to a capitalist society are expressed. This would mean that the overall malaise in the former GDR has nothing to do with the material Westernization of the country as such, but that the only thing that counts is the large-scale socio-economic drama that is taking place in this former socialist country. This last conclusion in particular falls short, not only because, as I mentioned before, it completely neglects the form of the discontent, but especially because it does not relate the present material and consumption discontent to the completely different attitude towards Western consumer goods which the inhabitants of the former GDR *used* to have before the fall of the Wall. Is it coincidental that the inhabitants of the GDR attached a seemingly disproportionate meaning to Western material objects before the demise of the Berlin Wall? Or that they first celebrated their joy about the collapse of the Wall by buying Western things? Is it coincidental that the disappointment about German reunification is so explicitly attached to the things that they first bought in such large amounts?

Contrary to the line of interpretation sketched above, I think that any satisfactory explanation of the consumptive disappointment which many inhabitants of the former GDR now seem to experience should be based on the fact that these goods have always given rise to very strong emotional attitudes, first positive and later negative. Furthermore, these strong emotions can only be understood if we recognize the important role which these objects have played in daily life within the GDR. As I mentioned before, material goods are far from a neutral theme in the post-war development of both Germanies. They have always had a very specific load of meaning because they were the most visible and ideologically founded signs of the post-war partition of the country. They were not just a symbol of Western life, they were the knife that cut the two Germanies in two.

Of brand products and Christmas presents in September

After Germany lost the Second World War, the country was divided into two states, each influenced by opposing ideological spheres: the capitalist West and the socialist East. The two Germanies were each other's political, economic and ideological antipode, and although the GDR regime always tried to seclude its citizens from West German influence, the two Germanies cannot be understood as two fully separate unities; the two states must also be seen in terms of each other. They oriented themselves in relation to each other, and their respective cultural ideals were shaped and defined 'in an intimate process of mirror-imaging' (Borneman, 1992: 3–4). It is in this process of mirror-imaging that material and consumption differences have always played an important ideological, legitimizing and identificatory role.

The history of post-war recovery in West Germany reads like a miracle: within less than forty years the country which had been completely destroyed managed to develop itself into one of the leading economic world powers. Although this development would never have been possible without international financial support, it proved to be very important not only for the economic but also for the mental recovery of the country. The important role which the famous *Wirtschaftswunder* has played in the reconstruction of West German self-confidence is probably well known. But apart from that, it is interesting to note that long before the *Wirtschaftswunder* began to display its golden economic and mental fruits during the 1960s, the Allied forces recognized and made use of the enormous psychological, identificatory and symbolic potential of consumptive and material goods and welfare for the recovery of West German self-confidence.

One of the reasons why large amounts of American consumer goods were pumped into West Germany directly after the war was that in this way the Allied forces hoped to bend the injured confidence in 'Hitler, *Volk* and Fatherland' into a confidence in 'permanent consumptive growth': 'the post-war situation needed brand-products, which were not only able to remedy the material wants, but which should get the state-supporting and society-shaping mission to help the disappointed people to get over this "time without ideal", over this "spiritual–moral vacuum"' (Diesener and Gries, 1992: 58). That the material input came up to expectations, especially where it concerned identification, is clear when one listens to the life-histories of West Berliners:

> For most West Berliners, the availability of goods through the capitalist market system in the fifties had a symbolic meaning of differentiating themselves as a group from the East Germans. But only after most people could afford to purchase the goods did prosperity also become a trope which identified them and with which they identified. The significance of these two aspects of identity – demarcation from the East and prosperity – should not be underestimated. They were central to the sense of self, to the Germanness, of this generation of West Germans since the end of the war.
>
> (Borneman, 1992: 229)

As this quotation makes clear, the material and consumption boom and ongoing economic rise in the western part of Germany became one of the main identificatory tropes of West Germanness, which helped those on the Western side to differentiate themselves from their East German countrymen. Nowadays, the financial and material prosperity in the FRG is exemplary and the choosing, buying and consuming of material objects plays an important role in the West German self-image.

The inhabitants of the GDR were, of course, always aware of the booming economy, the material prosperity and the role these developments have played in the post-war formation of identity in their neighbouring country. However hard the GDR may have tried to safeguard its territory and inhabitants from reprehensible Western influences, this exclusion was never complete. Even after the Berlin Wall was erected in 1961, people were visited by their West German friends and relatives, and they received (Christmas) parcels from them. Eighty per cent of the East German population was able to watch West German TV, and some people could even – although very restrictedly – visit West Germany, in cases of 'pressing family matters'. In these ways, the inhabitants of East Germany were able to get some idea of material life in West Germany, but they were never able really to partake in its abundance. On their side of the inter-German border, material life was rather different.

When one asks people in East Germany to sketch what daily life in the GDR was like, most people come up with all kinds of material and consumption stories: about long queues in front of stores and about the fourteen years which people had to wait after applying for a car. Then there are the stories of the shopping lists which circulated among colleagues, on which everyone could write what they needed from the butcher, the baker, the grocery and the supermarket. When all consumptive needs were written down, the lists were distributed: someone was to queue at the butcher, another at the baker, etc. All this was during working time, of course, otherwise there would not have been enough time to wait until it was one's turn. An old woman told me about her bath, which had only three legs: one leg was broken off and when the woman wanted to have it repaired, she went to the municipal house agency in order to ask for a new one. She filled in all the necessary forms and waited and waited, but she never received her leg. Then there is the story of the man who wanted to start a glass shop and had the full support of the municipality because there was no glass shop in the whole city. After waiting several months, he eventually heard that he would not be granted permission to open such a shop because the city had already consumed the prescribed amount of raw materials which were needed to produce glass. Many people told me how they 'organized' their Christmas presents; one started to look for them in September, because that was the only way to be sure of getting more or less suitable presents for all members of the family. Others told of how they had eventually saved the necessary 5000 marks (average salaries were about 750 marks per month) for a colour TV and were then completely at the mercy of the shop assistant who was to inform them when the next TV would arrive. As soon as they received this news, the whole family was enlisted to spend part of the night on the pavement in front of the shop.

All these stories illustrate how strongly everyday life in the GDR was characterized by material and consumption shortages.[6] Although the situation had not always been like this, it is significant that during the last years of the GDR most people always carried a shopping bag with them because no matter where they went or what they intended to do, they always had to be prepared for the possibility that something special or rare was for sale somewhere.

It is one thing to live in a country where basic raw materials like sand and brick are hard to come by and where one knows in advance what the answer of the shop assistant will be when one asks where to look for such common things as bedclothes: 'not available'. It is another thing, however, to live with and accommodate to these constant shortages when, at the same time, the newspapers always claim and describe an opposite reality. Some headlines from July 1989 provide examples: 'GDR national economy assesses positive results for the first half year' (*Volkswacht*, 7 July 1989), 'Higher productivity and quality through new intentions' (*Volkswacht*, 13 July 1989), and 'Life gets wealthy and beautiful; better living conditions for the many' (*Volkswacht*, 18 July 1989). Whatever GDR newspaper one opened, the message was always the same: economic and material developments in the GDR were as positive as they could be, especially when it came to the successful realization of the current five-year plans.

Apart from this discrepancy with regard to the quantitative satisfaction of material and consumption needs, there was another source of tension between the official, state-proclaimed consumption and material ideals on the one hand, and everyday, genuine reality on the other. This concerned what one might call the 'qualitative' side of material care: the extent to which material circumstances in the GDR were able to satisfy other than purely quantitative material and consumption needs.

Within the socialist ideology, the material structure of society has always been ascribed a distinctly educative, mental-reformative and identificatory role. Fully in line with the economic theories of Marx, the GDR state ideology was based on the assumption that the workers in a capitalist society are alienated and estranged, not only from themselves as producers, but also from the fruits of their labour. Within a capitalist system of production the workers are deprived of their own means of production and of their own labour-force, and therefore they can only have an alienating relationship with the things they produce (Messing and van Engeldorp Gastelaars, 1986: 169). The organization and functioning of the market, where the exchange of goods in capitalist countries takes place, was taken to be the most typical example of the capitalist guiding principle that 'money breeds money'. The capitalist exchange of goods obeys only one law: goods are exchanged for money, in order to gain money. 'The goal of capitalist circulation of goods is not the individual consumption of another good, but the financial value thereof' (DDR, 1975: 963). Therefore 'it is in the very nature of capitalism to keep the masses ignorant in order to manipulate their needs for the sale of goods' (Kelm, 1971: 75). These theoretical assumptions formed the basis of a completely new economic and material organization of society in which the peasants and working classes officially owned the means of production and within which the choice between two brands of hairspray was considered 'bourgeois' and therefore reprehensible. Contrary to the market in capitalist countries, the consumptive variety in the GDR was intentionally limited: 'if possible, no product is to be produced by two different producers in the GDR' (Voskamp and Wittke, 1990: 171). This meant that often there existed only one 'brand' of a product: one kind of toilet paper, one kind of washing powder. The result was a rather homogeneous material world, where the merchandise of the state-owned shops and department stores was the same all over the country. No matter whether one entered a shop in Rostock or in Dresden: the same goods were sold everywhere. One man told me that he once saw a very special sweater somewhere. It looked far more exclusive than other sweaters so 'I immediately bought it. I was so happy to have something which I thought no one else had. But when I put it on for the first time, the whole city appeared to have bought it.'

The object world in the GDR was decided upon from above. The state not only declared which goods were to be produced in what amounts, it also fixed what was to be sold where and for what price. And apart from the fact that it was centrally decided which colour, form, size and design of goods were to be produced, these external qualities were also ascribed an important ideological function. Consumer goods were meant to visualize and represent not just a practical function; they were meant to communicate socially valued norms and ideals (see also Diesener and Gries, 1992: 59). The overall goal of socialist design was 'to incorporate an ideal, which transcended the real world of objects, viewing objects merely as a vehicle for a didactic programme. "The chief task of the designer in a socialist society is to contribute to the development of the socialist lifestyle and of the socialist character"' (Bertsch, 1990: 23). By fixing the form and looks of material objects, the state not only fixed the material world of its citizens, but it also tried to educate them, by means of a socialist object world, to be well-bred socialist people. It remains to be seen to what extent this goal was achieved and to what extent the inhabitants of the GDR identified with, and recognized themselves in, the state-ordained socialist design. Nevertheless, the ideal images of 'socialist workers, buying socialistically produced goods, by means of which they would become true socialist characters, living a socialist life, no longer running the risk of alienation from themselves' were clearly not fully in line with social-economic praxis and reality. There was a large discrepancy between the socialist ideals with regard to the material structure of society on the one hand, and economic reality on the other.

This discrepancy was recognized by everyone. Even those who actively supported the socialist ideology and who always fully identified with the GDR as their one and only fatherland realized that there were things which just 'didn't fit'. One example, told to me by someone who had always been (and still is) very loyal towards the GDR regime, dates back to the early post-war period. The Russian army had just occupied the eastern part of Germany, and the official reason given for why the Russians were to stay was that they were – as my informant said, rather ironically – 'to propagate and spread the beautiful socialist ideals, culture and way of life'. Remarkably, however, the Russians were not allowed to get in touch with the local population, and everybody knew why. It was feared that when the Russians saw the material prosperity and modernity of German life, their socialist message would be corrupted. And if the Germans, on the other hand, were to get to know the realities of the material lifestyle of these socialist heroes (a lifestyle they were to take over), nobody would ever come to believe this socialist message at all:

> Although our country was completely destroyed, it was clear to everybody that the Russian culture, their material way of life, was far less developed and worth while than ours. 'Are we to learn from them?', people asked, when they saw the newspapers which they used as curtains in front of their windows.

It is only one example of the way in which the refractory everyday material reality was markedly different from the beautiful socialist ideals.

The same tension between ideology on the one hand and economic reality on the other can be found in the sphere of production and consumption of certain categories of consumer goods. Whereas the inhabitants of the GDR were told that the market principles regulating the capitalist production and consumption of goods were reprehensible and alienating, they were at the same time producing goods which were sold on the Western market in order to earn the Western currencies which the GDR needed so desperately. But the producers were not allowed to buy these goods themselves. The same incompatibility of socialist material ideals on the one hand and economic praxis on the other finds expression in the mere existence of the so-called Intershops. These were shops where one could obtain Western consumer goods in exchange for Western currency. It would be interesting to know how the state legitimized the establishment of these material bulwarks of capitalist destruction on its own territory, but it is certainly no coincidence that many East Germans mention the existence of these shops as one of the main examples of how far socialist material and consumption ideology and the everyday material and consumption reality in the GDR had drifted apart.

These examples make clear that there was always an enormous gap between the state-proclaimed socialist ideals and norms with regard to material and consumption life in the GDR on the one hand, and the everyday material and consumption reality on the other hand. This gap characterized the quantitative material services and care which the state promised to offer, as well as the qualitative ideological and identificatory aspects of these services. I think that one of the main ways in which the inhabitants of the GDR coped with and created imaginary ways out of the omnipresent gaps and tensions between what they were supposed to see and what they actually saw was by imagining a perfect material and consumption world on the other side of the Wall. There, material and consumption life was not only considered far more beautiful and satisfying, but the Western material world was above all considered to be real, truthful, 'the real thing' (Diesener and Gries, 1992: 59).

Dreams of unattainable things: some conclusions

I have shown that material objects played a significant role in the post-war history of both Germanies: not only were they very important for the economic and mental reconstruction of West Germany, but the GDR regime bestowed an equally important, although partly opposing, ideological role upon material things. Within the GDR ideology, home-made consumer goods were used to shape and represent socialist ideology, whereas Western consumer goods were taboo. Material goods thus became the focus of several ideological and identificatory battles between and within the two German states.

As 'socialist personalities' the inhabitants of the GDR were not allowed to buy and consume Western objects. They were restricted to buying and consuming those material objects which were decided upon from above and which carried very outspoken educative and identity-shaping functions and meanings. Apart from the question of to what extent the material-ideological steerings by the state were successful, the inhabitants of the GDR have of course always been in contact with another material world: the one on the other side of the Wall (cf. Weber, 1993: 199). As mentioned before, East Germans received West German TV and (Christmas) parcels, and friends and relatives from the West always brought some things with them when they came to visit the GDR. In these ways it was always clear to the inhabitants of the GDR how important was the role played by material objects in everyday life on the other side of the Wall. It was always clear that material abundancy and goods were among the main tropes of West German identity formation.

Apart from these rather positive identificatory messages and stories with regard to material life in the West, the inhabitants of the GDR were subject to completely contradictory messages and stories surrounding this lifestyle. Because the two German states were involved in an ongoing ideological battle which was partly fought over material and consumptive topics, the GDR regime was constantly preaching the perniciousness of the capitalist system, with its vulgar, materialist, antisocial and alienating way of life (Weber, 1986: 43). In this way, the place, position and role of Western material goods within the GDR were comparable to the place, position and role of inland material goods: things were said to represent something other than they seemed to, and nothing appeared as it should have been. Taken together, these conflicting messages and meanings with regard to Western material life all contributed to make this life into a major topic in the GDR: although absent in everyday life, Western goods were always there in the republic.

The inhabitants of the GDR were caught in a rather 'schizophrenic' situation: they were forced to relate to a material world which they could never really obtain or incorporate into their own lives. They could always compare and contrast their own material lives with that of their national *alter ego*, but – unlike their Western countrymen – they were not allowed to make acquaintance with, let alone to incorporate elements of, the Western way of life into their own lives. Exactly these material instances offer a very concrete and daily example of the ways in which the GDR state tried to restrict and determine the way in which its inhabitants were supposed to see the world in which they lived and to develop their place and identity within it. By trying to fix the mental and psychological as well as the material ways in which its citizens were allowed to develop and manifest themselves, the GDR regime attempted to gain a complete hold on its citizens. Through the ideologically 'correct' fixation of the material world and consumption possibilities of its inhabitants, an attempt was made to mould the inhabitants of East Germany into ideologically correct, rather uniform, 'socialist personalities'. One can imagine the far-reaching consequences this must have had when it came to the willingness of many to identify with the GDR as a state. A vicious circle of consumption discontent and feelings of frustration has been the result within the GDR (Messing and van Engeldorp Gastelaars, 1986: 164). The East German psychologist Maaz has formulated this in the following psycho-analytical terms: 'the narcissistic offence, which formed a thousandfold part of daily life in the GDR, because material and mental desires for external values and goods could not be fulfilled ... has damaged the feeling of self-esteem of numerous GDR citizens' (1990: 69–72). However, I think that apart from a rather general discontent with regard to the GDR as a state, the simultaneous proximity and essential unattainability of Western material life have, at the same time, offered the inhabitants of the GDR an imaginary way out of this schizophrenic situation.

As I have shown above, the contradiction between the state-proclaimed messages about material life in the West and the important identificatory role which this played in everyday life in West Germany was not the only material-ideological discrepancy with which the inhabitants of the GDR were forced to cope. Apart from the very restricted way in which they were allowed to interact with their material surroundings, the inhabitants of the GDR had to live in an object world in which nothing was what it was said to be, nothing was what it was supposed to be or what it seemed to be. The ideologically desirable and the genuine everyday material reality had very little to do with each other: messages in the newspapers, official state ideology, and supplies in the shops; the difference between GDR shops where GDR things were sold, and Western things that were sold in the Intershops; official theory with regard to Western consumer goods on the one hand, and internal production of them on the other; official decrial of Western material life on the one hand, and the positive and even glamorous images of them on Western TV and in other media on the other. When we take all these examples together, it is clear that with regard to the material sphere of life things just did not 'fit' in the GDR, and the gap between the ideal and the real became ever greater.

In this world, in which not even material life was what it seemed, in which material stories conflicted with material reality, conflicted with material desires, and conflicted with other material stories; in this web of contradictory messages and meanings with regard to material life, only one thing was clear: the Western material world was essentially unattainable. People could receive parcels and goods from the West, but these things always remained strange. They belonged to another country, to another way of life; they always remained 'something from another planet' (Niemöller, 1991: 252). This certainty of the absolutely forever unattainable but simultaneously proximate world on the other side of the Wall offered the inhabitants of the GDR the perfect way out of the inextricable confusion of appearances and essences. All answers to, all alternatives for, and all flights out of a daily life characterized by tensions between what is, what appears to be, and what is supposed to be could be transported to the other side of the Wall. There, they were attached to the material goods that were such important identificatory tropes for their countrymen but that were at the same time so elusive.

Exactly because of the simultaneous proximity and unattainability of Western material life, the inhabitants of the GDR could always transport the imperfections of their own (material and consumptive) life to the other side of the Wall without being confronted with its shortcomings. Everything that did not come true, did not function properly, or was not feasible in the GDR found its imaginary solution on the other side of the Wall. Western consumer goods offered the inhabitants of the former GDR a concrete starting-point for all their fantasies about alternative possibilities, unfulfilled wishes and desires; fantasies about the way 'life could have been, if only ...': 'for many of us, everything that happened behind the invincible Wall was ... an excellent soil for paradisiacal fantasies' (Maaz, 1990: 190). Precisely because of their absence in the GDR, Western consumer goods were the perfect vehicles for collective fantasies which 'offer food to the imagination: a programme of travels through imaginary space' (Thoden van Velzen, 1992: 204).

The reason why these fantasies – which, of course, exist everywhere – were attached to material goods was that these were also the most tangible symbols of the divergent post-war developments in the two Germanies, while at the same time they were essentially unattainable.[7] They belonged to another country, to another way of life. As one woman said, these things always remained 'beyond reality. It was very strange. One imagined, but couldn't compare these imaginings with real experiences' (Niemöller, 1991: 252). And this is the quintessence of the 'fantastic capacities' which Western consumer goods had in the GDR: 'One imagined, but couldn't compare these imaginings with real experiences.' In order to dream about other realities, other identities and possibilities, dreams must be attached to essentially unattainable vehicles with which people can identify at the same time.[8] As soon as a dream is tested in reality it becomes 'vulnerable to contradiction' (McCracken, 1988: 112), and when that happens, the dream ceases to exist. I think this is exactly what happened in the former GDR. With the implantation of capitalism, the inhabitants of the GDR have not only been robbed of a former way of life, an extended web of social securities, and a society in which there existed almost no visible social-economic differences between people; they have also been robbed of one of their major means of day-dreaming. Once the unattainable fantasy goods were there, possession of them destroyed the possibility of dreaming and fantasizing about them.

It is often asked why the inhabitants of the former GDR are so discontented with the results of German unification; 'now that everything they've always dreamt about has come true, what reason is there to complain?' I think the answer to this question is hidden in the question itself: a sense of longing together is essential for a feeling of belonging. Now that East Germans can no longer long for Western consumer goods together, they feel lost in a cold world; not only because the capitalist world as such is cold, but also because they are robbed of their sense of longing together. However one may think about it, the socialist state had succeeded in making its inhabitants equal in at least one respect: except for high-ranking state officials, everybody longed for the same kinds of thing, everybody queued for oranges and bananas. Now that these things are there, everybody is able to build, cherish and pursue his or her own personal dreams, and as far as these dreams are attached to material objects, it is possible to fulfil them – that is, in principle. But because one needs money to buy things, not everybody is able to fulfil his or her dreams to the same extent. This not only means that the dreams as such are more (openly) differentiated, it also means that the extent to which people are able to realize them is differentiated as well. This is an extremely painful experience for people who used to dream the same kind of dreams with the aid of the same unattainable categories of things, and who used to complain about their unattainability together. Now that this common feeling of (be)longing has gone, people look for alternative ways of (be)longing together. One way to restore this lost experience and feeling is to romanticize about the old days, the common past, when everybody *had to be* satisfied with the same cheese, sausages and toilet paper.

Notes

1 Also, see Korff (1990a, 1990b) for interesting descriptions of this 'consumptive orgy'.
2 See Borneman (1992), Diesener and Gries (1992) and Niemöller (1991).
3 These terms were already used before November 1989, but 'they are used much more frequently and have become more pejorative since then' (Borneman, 1992: 306).
4 The *Staatssicherheitdienst*, or State Security Service, was informed about the most private affairs of the East German people because elements of the population worked for it as undercover informants.
5 For those who witnessed the Second World War, it is the second time that they have been subject to such a large-scale, partly external condemnation of their past; cf. Veenis (1993, 1995), with respect to a German community of post-war immigrants in Argentina.
6 See Niethammer, who, when he interviewed East Germans (one year before the *Wende*), was surprised to notice that 'the criticisms about consumption care became a dominant theme of almost every interview ... they were often concentrated on the supply of consumer goods ... the criticisms about consumption care seemed to be an officially licensed valve ... [this] reduction of everything in life to the material had become a "lingua franca" in the GDR, into which all emotions had to be translated' (1991: 39).
7 The role of material goods in recent German history is in fact a very clear example of Daniel Miller's (1987) theory with regard to the role of the material in daily life. Miller's theory is based on the assumption that material objects not only represent cultural identities and mental preoccupations – the (neo-)structuralist point of view – but are the most concrete way in which we learn to understand the world in which we live and with the aid of which we learn to see and develop our place in it.
   Also see Campbell (1987), who asserts that material objects are always the perfect starting-points for dreams and unrealistic desires.
8 Also see the unpublished paper of van de Port (1993), who asserts that collective fantasies are always spun out of a mixture of 'strange' and

'familiar' elements. Only in this way it is possible (thus van de Port) to identify with something, while at the same time not running the risk of being confronted with the more painful, or (as I assert) more contradictory, sides of the things which people secretly identify with and/or dream about.

Bibliography

Bertsch, G.C. (1990) 'Foreword', in G.C. Bertsch, E. Hedler and M. Dietz, *SED. Schönes einheits Design*, Cologne: Benedikt Taschenbuch Verlag.

Borneman, J. (1992) *Belonging in the Two Berlins: Kin, State, Nation*, Cambridge: Cambridge University Press.

Campbell, C. (1987) *The Romantic Ethic and the Spirit of Modern Consumerism*, Oxford: Blackwell.

Comaroff, J. and Comaroff, J.L. (1990) 'Goodly beasts, beastly goods: cattle and commodities in a South-African context', *American Ethnologist*, 17(2), 195–217.

DDR (1975) *DDR Handbuch*, Bonn: Bundesministerium für innerdeutschen Beziehungen.

Diesener, G. and Gries, R. (1992) ' "Chic zum Geburtstag unserer Republik". Zwei Projekte zur Produkt- und Politikpropaganda im Deutsch-Deutschen Vergleich', *Geschichtswerkstatt*, 25, 56–69.

Kelm, M. (1971) *Produktgestaltung im Sozialismus*, Berlin: Rowohlt.

Korff, G. (1990a) 'S-Bahn-Ethnologie', *Österreichische Zeitschrift für Volkskunde*, 93(1), 5–27.

Korff, G. (1990b) 'Rote Fahnen und Bananen. Notizen zur politischen Symbolik im Prozess der Vereinigung von DDR und BRD', *Schweizerisches Archiv für Volkskunde*, 86 (3–4), 130–61.

Maaz, H.-J. (1990) *Psychogram van Oost-Duitsland*. Amsterdam: Uitgeverspers.

McCracken, G. (1988) *Culture and Consumption: New Approaches to the Symbolic Character of Consumer Goods and Activities*, Bloomington: Indiana University Press.

Messing, M. and van Engeldorp Gastelaars, Ph. (1986) 'Arbeidssatisfactie en maatschappelijke Orde', in Ph. van Engeldorp Gastelaars (ed.), *De DDR. Het onbekende Duitsland*, Delft: Eburon.

Miller, D. (1987) *Material Culture and Mass Consumption*, Oxford: Blackwell.

Niemöller, J. (1991) *Over de muur. Oostduitse levensverhalen*, Amsterdam: Bert Bakker.

Niethammer, L. (1991) 'Glasnost privat 1987', in L. Niethammer, A. von Plato and D. Wierling, *Die volkseigene Erfahrung: Eine Archäologie des Lebens in der Industrieprovinz der DDR*, Berlin: Rowohlt.

Port, M. van de (1993) 'Over modder, over zigeuners, oftewel, over de mens en de wereld zoals die nu eenmaal is', unpublished paper.

Thoden van Velzen, H.U.E. (1992) 'On power and imagination: religious regimes and collective fantasies', in M. Bax, P. Kloos and A. Koster (eds),

Faith and Polity: Essays on Religion and Politics, Amsterdam: VU University Press.

Veenis, M. (1993) 'Dierbare herinneringen die rondspoken. Het verleden in een Duits dorp in Argentinië', *Etnofoor*, 6(1), 45–83.

Veenis, M. (1995) *Kartoffeln, Kuchen und Asado: Over de verborgen keuken van Duitsers in Argentinië*, Amsterdam: Spinhuis.

Volkswacht. Organ der Bezirksleitung Gera der Sozialistischen Einheitspartei Deutschlands.

Voskamp, U. and Wittke, V. (1990) 'Fordismus in einem Land: Das Produktionsmodell der DDR', *SOWI*, 19(3), 170–81.

Weber, H. (1986) 'De geschiedenis van de DDR', in Ph. van Engeldorp Gastelaars (ed.), *De DDR. Het onbekende Duitsland*, Delft: Eburon.

Weber, H. (1993) 'Die Geschichte der DDR. Versuch einer vorläufigen Bilanz', *Zeitschrift für Geschichtswissenschaft*, 41(3), 195–204.

11

The work of art as gift and commodity

ANDREW WERNICK

Introduction

The romantic esteem of high art as the sacred repository of the highest values has been confronted in our century by a contrary view which emphasizes the entanglement of the artwork in commerce, ideology and status competition, the consequent hollowness of any program of *l'art pour l'art*, and, at the iconoclastic limit, the need – in service to those same values – to make war on the auratic object itself, together with the cultic setting in which its aura is preserved, presented and received. A parallel line of thinking, running through French anthropology from Mauss (1967) to Bataille (1988–91), but also stemming from Veblen's (1967) reflections on the transformed consumption style of industrial capitalism's 'leisure class', has highlighted a wider change in the process of circulation as such. Here the focus is on the way in which the market, with its competitive trade in equivalents, has undermined symbolic exchange – epitomized in gift and sacrifice – as the once primary mode of circulating and expending accumulated wealth.

Baudrillard's early work on 'the political economy of the sign' (1981) brought these two streams together in a vision of late capitalism, wherein both the production and consumption of sumptuary excess and the money-mediated system of economic exchange had been subsumed into a still more generalized and denatured system of 'sign-exchange'. In the logic of such an economy the artwork plays a special role as the virtual incarnation of differential prestige value, especially where it takes the form, as with painting, of a movable, transferable and hence exchangeable artefact. In the art auction, he notes, 'the decisive action is one of a simultaneous double reduction – that of exchange value (money) and of symbolic value (the painting as an *oeuvre*) – and of their transformation into sign value (the signed, appraised painting as a luxury value and rare object)' (1981: 112). In the purchase that results, 'good investment value' just as much as 'love of art' functions as a 'reference-alibi' for the conversion of money into the competitive and differential social prestige which ownership, particularly of a celebrated masterpiece, can confer. The same can be said of the auction itself. As an upscale wagering session it stages an 'aristocratic parity' between bidders – reproducing a phantom aristocratism that haunts the old nobility's considerably more calculating and instrumental successor class. No less than the absolutization of aesthetic value, the auction mystifies the character of the transaction. Yet its ritual mode of prestigious wagering is no less necessary as a guarantor – and generator – of the socially supported worth of the sign-exchange-value which the painting becomes. Of course, artworks are not always privately owned. They can be taken out of circulation by being 'nationalized' and placed in public institutions like museums for conservation and display. But this by no means severs the reductive link between the aesthetic capitalization of art and the functioning of its market. Museum collections serve as a kind of gold reserve 'for the functioning of the sign-exchange of paintings' (1981: 120–21). Museums themselves are 'an agency guaranteeing the universality of painting and so also the aesthetic enjoyment of all others'. In the cultural economy of art-objects, then, museums 'play the role of banks'.

It is with these considerations in mind that I would like to offer some reflections on the provenance and current status of one particular painting: *The Adoration of the Magi* by Sir Peter Paul Rubens (as he was when he painted it in 1634), which now hangs over the east altar in King's College Chapel, Cambridge.

The work came to Cambridge after it had been sold by the trustees of the Duke of Westminster in 1959 for the then unheard-of price of £275,000. At the time this was a newsworthy event, dramatizing the escalating prices of artworks during the post-war boom and establishing the painting itself, for a celebrated moment, as the most valuable in the world. The record price reflected the vagaries of rarity – this was the last Rubens altarpiece that would be likely ever to come on to the market – and of timing, with the post-war speculative boom in paintings at its peak. The painting itself, however, had never been regarded as a particularly important work. That arbiter of eighteenth-century British taste Sir Joshua Reynolds, first President of the Royal Academy, dismissed it as 'a slight work, awkwardly composed' (Dillon, 1988: 176). Judged inferior to several other treatments by Rubens of the Adoration (notably the Antwerp Town Hall painting now in the Prado, and the altarpiece for St Martin's Abbey in Tournai, which went to the Musées Royaux in Brussels), it has rarely been reproduced or commented upon in art historical treatments of Rubens or the Baroque.

One might anticipate that this estimation will change. The publicity attending the sale, combined with the painting's subsequent relocation, certainly enhanced the painting's relative sign-value in the status system of old masters. If King's were ever forced to sell, the price would be astronomical.

So far, we may say, with Baudrillard. But the painting in question, sited where and as it is, has two singular features in relation to the schema he proposes. First, after being auctioned off it was transferred neither to another private collector nor to a public museum, but to a place of religious worship. Originally designed as an altarpiece for the White Sisters of the convent in Louvain, and after a long sojourn (1806–1959) in the Grosvenor family and the Duchy of Westminster, the *Adoration* was returned to the altar. Not the same altar, but an altar none the less: the place of cultic honour in a Christian church, and backdrop to its most sacred rite. To be sure, churches are public buildings and King's College Chapel, that soaring masterpiece of perpendicular gothic, is particularly suitable for display. In some continuity, then, with the national museums Baudrillard mentions, the chapel serves in part as a bank to stockpile and assure aesthetic value. At the same time, though, it functions daily, as it has for centuries, as a church. And in this functioning the painting is neither incidental nor merely decorative. It depicts a theologically charged biblical episode (a nativity scene based loosely on Matthew 2: 1–2)[1] and, in its placement over the altar, it is assigned a sacred role in the iconic representation of the very deity whose sacrifice and resurrection are symbolically re-enacted upon it.

Second, and again in a displaced version of the initial deposition in the Convent church at Louvain, the painting comes to its current owner not as a purchase but as a gift. The intermediary between King's College and the House of Westminster was a property speculator and philanthropist, Major Allnatt.[2] In a gesture which only added to the publicity surrounding the transfer, the worthy major bought the painting in order to prevent its purchase overseas – which then meant the United States – and to ensure its appropriate availability as a national treasure. Appropriate, given the provenance of the painting, meant a church; and, he resolved, the most appropriate church, which would have to be a masterpiece in itself, was that attaching to King's College.

Gifts come with a charge. A religious icon – here, as we shall see, at the centre of several cults – is not reducible to its exhibition value. I introduce these complications not so much to refute an argument that is admittedly abstract and revels in the truth-value of its exaggerations as to extend it in the light of precisely the kinds of complication that the concrete case entails. At the same time, a consideration of them will immediately lead us to abandon a key simplifying assumption not only in Baudrillard's own argument but in the whole discourse about site and provenance which traverses the language of connoisseurship and art history. This is that the status of the art-object at any particular point along the chain of transactions through which it circulates is (for however long or short a time) fixed and univocal. If the artwork can belong, in its current time and place, to a multiplicity of modes of circulation and appropriation, then not only will any simple notion of provenance have to be rethought, but the more extravagant models of art's symbolic reduction by markets for money and status will have to be qualified, so as to take into account the tensions, distortions, ambivalences and ambiguities that a complex localization entails.

However, what makes the King's College Rubens particularly interesting as a case of the complex circulation in which the commodified artwork is caught is the thematic content of the painting itself. The Magi adore the infant Jesus with gifts, most prominently the cup of gold which the red-cloaked figure in the lower left foreground rises to present. From above, through angels on the left and Mary in the centre, an unseen Eminence gives his only Son to Man – a gift for a gift. Conservatively framed as it is in Counter-Reformation pedagogics concerning the mystery of the Eucharist, the sacramental role of the Church, and the divine mandate of kings, the painting bespeaks, in fact, an entire pre-capitalist allegorization of the gift, including, in classically self-referential terms, the gift of the painting itself. What happens, we may ask, when we play this allegory off against the network of gift and non-gift relations in which the painting, through all its peregrinations, has come to be embedded? That is, when not only do we decode the painting in terms of contemporary concepts and realities of value and exchange, but when the meaning that can be released from the painting as an icon is brought to bear on the nexus that has come to frame it as the kind of object it is?

The allegory of the gift

The fact that the King's College *Adoration*, like many other Renaissance and Baroque paintings on that theme, was intended as an altarpiece warrants our seeing in it not just a scene of joyful Nativity but a representation of the sacrificial mystery at the heart of medieval and Counter-Reformation Christianity. The newborn babe rising radiantly over the altar amidst the ceremonials of the Mass visibly reminds the faithful that His body and blood are really present in the sacramental bread and wine.[3] Within the picture frame itself the cruciform beams of the stable show a birth shadowed by the Cross, hence a sacrificial birth, God's supreme gift as a sacrifice both to and of Himself. The magic of the Catholic Mass, the picture tells us, is continually to repeat the sacrifice and resurrection lived by the incarnate God. Finally, and if we take the ambiguously attired Magi to represent spiritual rather than temporal powers (in the slide from the biblical 'wise men' to the later tradition that they were 'kings' there is room for this play), the whole first-order scene can be read as a representation not just of the inner truth of the Eucharist but of its ceremonial motion. Priests, with incense, holy oil and communion cup, abase themselves before a manger/table which presents the living Christ. In the hierarchical analogy between sacred and secular orders, they themselves play the earthly part of angels. Through the grace of the priestly sacrament – an indispensable mediation – the divine grace is distributed to all.

The Eucharistic meaning of the painting, however, does not exhaust its second-order thematics. To go further we must take into account the relation between this meaning and that of the Nativity which evokes it. As well – on the figurative plane of the picture – we must consider the relation between the giving, self-sacrificing God, whose action fills the top half of the frame, and the donating and adoring Magi/kings, who gesture from below. Viewed thus, in the fullness of its composition, what the painting depicts is a symbolic exchange between humanity and the divine, a cosmic juncture between two gifts. On the one side is God's gift of Jesus – a human infant who is born Lord of Lords and whose destiny, precisely as a gift, is to be redemptively sacrificed on the altar of sinful humanity. On the other side are the three gifts (to which a later tradition attached three kings) of gold, frankincense and myrrh, which their regal/priestly bearers 'from the East' offer up in response. But there is an asymmetry. Adoration is itself a rite of kingship deriving from the ancient empires of the near East. In offering up gifts to the infant, the Magi invest him with kingly attributes. The paradox of the lowly birth implies that the child in the manger is as elevated above the earthly kings as they themselves are over a poverty that finds company with cattle. Unlike the divine gift, then, these gifts are tribute. In the very gesture of offering them, the donors ritually acknowledge the suzerainty of the donee.

After Justinian's sixth-century mosaics at Ravenna and Bethlehem gave the Magi names and a Persian pedigree (Roberts, 1995: 12), the tableau acquired an imperial cast. The Magi's gifts ratified the obeisance of the ancient empires east of Rome to a Christendom centred on its western seat. The European mandate, as it became after the Germanic invasions, had a long history. Revived during the Crusades, it was given new meaning and ferocity during the age of discovery and the conquistadors when the Spanish crown (which commissioned the painting through its Flemish regents) extended the range of the subject peoples it covered. Rubens certainly did not ward off such a reading. In the King's College *Adoration*, as in others, he followed tradition in giving the Magi servants in 'eastern' garb, and in making Balthasar exotically black.[4] But the foregrounded Melchior is ethnically indeterminate, even European in features, so that if the kings' adoration can be read as a colonizing, orientalist move, Rubens has also allowed for a more general, that is transnational, significance for the occasion of their gifts. The homage they pay to the incarnate God is owed by all monarchs, and through them by all accumulators of power, wealth and glory.

Putting regional particularity to one side, then, the gifts are simply the gifts of kings. They represent and embody, through the preciousness of their substance, the paramount power and prestige of the givers. But how? While gold, frankincense and myrrh are a delight to the senses, it is not this quality *per se* which makes them suitable for the role. In being sensorily consumed, two would disappear while the third would become a bauble. Their value, or rather their aptness to stand in as a persuasive token of it, stems rather from their rarity, and from the labour – disproportionate to the material benefits of use – that must be spent to obtain them. The unguent, fragrance and purified yellow metal are stores of luxury convertible into the status which their ritual mobilization confers. The Magi's gifts, in short, represent wealth in its most useless, and for that reason also its most valuable, prized, and symbolically powerful, form.

The powers of the world distinguish their power precisely by their capacity to accumulate, display and give away such wealth, a wealth that itself signifies nothing so much as useless expenditure and excess beyond necessity. But rank and glory are differential and invidious. The prospect, then, can only be one of rivalry and conflict without end. Each presentation of surplus wealth – among dynastic states as between wealthy families within them – tests the existing hierarchy of social standing. By challenging a response it risks an escalating series of moves and counter-moves. The world of gift and symbolic exchange is one of violence and war. It is just here, though, that Christianity shows its sublimely pacific face. For, in the allegory of the painting, the agonic disposal of surplus wealth culminates in the offering made by the lords of the earth to the Lord of Lords.[5]

Indeed, the troubled passage of wealth between powers not only culminates here, but comes to a complete rest. First at the manger, but eternally ever after, the kings' gifts – the most precious possessions which the most powerful have to offer – encounter a counter-gift which is self-sufficient and cannot be topped. In the face of God's gift of Jesus, and through him of remission from sin and entry into paradise, those of mere kings can offer no challenge. In the supplicatory gestures with which they are tendered in Rubens's depiction – bended knee, hands outstretched – the provocation of the luxury gifts is thus transmuted into abjection. It is a reversal founded on the acknowledgement that no return could ever suffice, let alone act as a challenge to the divine other to give more. In short, the violence of symbolic exchange, which waxes with the growth of a glory-seeking concentration of social and political power, is stemmed by Christian order. Nor is this just a frustrated impasse, the aporetic halting of the cycle by an eternally unbridgeable status gap. In the new dispensation, the cycle of competitive expenditure has been broken once and for all by the irruption of a gift *sans pareil*, a gift which establishes the incarnate, self-sacrificing divinity at the apex of gift-giving, as the proper and final destination for the whole surplus-generating movement.

For the Counter-Reformation monarchy of seventeenth-century Spain the practical consequences of this mythic scenario were clear: the greatest glory of kings, and the ultimate destination of their munificent largesse, was to serve Christ and honour His Holy Mother by materially endowing the Church. From this angle, of course, the very painting which conveys the message can be thematized within its frame. It was commissioned from Rubens by representatives of the Spanish crown in Flanders,[6] for donation to the Convent of Louvain. It was itself, then, from the project's initiation to the painting's placement over the convent church's altar, a gift of kings in just the exalted and ultimate sense depicted.

At the same time, in the substitutions at Louvain, what his Sacred Majesty actually donates is not gold, frankincense or myrrh but a painting. We may read in this no more than an extension of the category of donatable luxury and excess to cover the 'treasures' of Art. In the early colonial period, movable artefacts, ancient and modern, were already drifting into imperial centres as cosmopolitan and aesthetic trophies of war and commercial contact. The rise of a fully organized art market by the end of the eighteenth century (the *Adoration* was first sold, to the Marquis of Lansdowne, in 1783) testified to the eagerness of new wealth, above all in London, to acquire status through such collection (Reitlinger, 1961: 3–26). But we may also see in the implicit identification of the painting with the depicted kingly gifts a covert ennobling of painting itself. Paul Douro (1996) has traced a similar theme in the work of LeBrun and fellow academicians in the ceiling paintings at Versailles. Elevating the prestige of painting, backed by the wealth the best could command, facilitated the upward mobility of a painterly elite. Tropes concerning the truth and sublimity of painting accompanied efforts to emancipate it from the tag of craft and decoration and place it within the 'noble arts'. This ran parallel with efforts to emancipate painters themselves from the monopoly and middling status of the guilds. Like his French counterparts, Rubens was able to move up and out of the guild system through royal and aristocratic patronage. Practically speaking, the ennoblement of painting and painting as the king's gift went hand in hand.

In the case of the *Adoration* the elevation of painting is firmly linked to a Christian symbology. However, if the painting *per se*, and not just its depiction of the Holy Child, is taken as emblematic of the real presence religiously conjured over the altar, we may also see here a hint of a less orthodox elevation. To identify the art of painting with the child implies the pagan apotheosis of human creativity ('genius') as the essence not only of Art but of divinity itself; to which extent the iconoclasts who saw idolatry in the Council of Trent's ecclesiastical embrace of visual and theatrical culture were not incorrect. Either way, though, to represent painting as a suitable substitute for, or instantiation of, what the Magi offer Jesus is not only to elevate Art as the quintessence of luxury and sign-value. It is to predicate for art a transcendental framework. Within that framework the deity who gives himself on the altar is both the ultimate source of all artistic value and the proper destination of art as a gift. And this is so whether that art is given through another giver, as her or his gift, or by artists themselves in the very process of creation. Through the self-referring optic of Rubens's painting, all this is to say, art is a gift whose highest vocation, as the embodiment of divine striving within Man, is to be offered up, in a final homecoming, to God.

The journey of the *Adoration*

Rubens's *Adoration* was a royal gift to the Soeurs Blancs. But Rubens himself painted it for money. His usual commission for such a piece (which according to one tradition took him only weeks to complete) was 3000 to 4000 florins (Lescourret, 1993: 77).[7]

Besides his prodigious talents as a painter, we might observe, Rubens distinguished himself as a pioneer in the art of making money from it. Biographers have noted the link between this and his drive to resolve an anomalous social situation. Born to an exiled magistrate from an upwardly mobile Antwerp family whose (transitory) Calvinist and anti-Spanish sympathies led to rebellion, and then brought up after his father's death by an equally ambitious mother who secured him a classical education followed by admission to a noble household, Rubens was educated with aspirations and a class identity above his material station. This gave him the connections and bearing for diplomatic missions.[8] With only a meagre inheritance, however, he was faced with the task of closing the gap between what he might earn through his artistic talents and the cost of reaching and maintaining the social standing to which he aspired. An aspect of that aspiration was the need to raise the status of painter beyond artisan. But that would have been empty without ways to make art-making a route to wealth. On the basis of the fame he had achieved in Italy (1600–8), when he returned to Antwerp he was able to talk up family connections into royal and aristocratic commissions from which (while retaining tax-free membership in the Guild of St Luke) he began to make his fortune. Just as important to his financial success was the entrepreneurial management he brought to his art. More systematically than any before, Rubens organized his workshop along factory lines. He introduced a specialized division of labour, and hired a handpicked roster of younger talents to fill in the details, and sometimes more (though never the final touches), of his initial designs. Meticulous records were kept, and a regular scale of prices was established, with the cost of a painting varying according to its type, size, and degree of authorship by the master.

Nor did he neglect the marketing side. He personally supervised the sales as well as the production side of his business. The magnificent set of studios attached to his palatial Antwerp residence was designed to serve as a showroom. Through the princely style of both his art and his life, Rubens cultivated the promotional value of his own name so that his signature could serve as a top-quality trademark for his factory's productions. He was also assiduous in obtaining and enforcing royal patents to protect copyright in his published engravings. Here indeed, as illustrator, his relation to the market was similar to that of writers and composers, whose income derives from making a reproducible model that can earn rent. In the absence of generally recognized rules of copyright, Rubens's success in this regard was anticipatory and singular. Finally, as Jeffrey Muller has shown (1989), Rubens was not just a major producer of art but also a collector. He was a participant therefore in the growth of a secondary market for artworks as collectibles – i.e., for that special kind of consumer good, of which 'great paintings' and antique artefacts were the prototype, which is both for immediate enjoyment and display and also a store of value and speculative investment.

None of this is to make a reductive point about commercial motivation. It is simply to note that the elevation of painting as a noble art was ideologically entangled with the process wherein, even at the high and luxury end, the making of artefacts was being transformed from petty-commodity production to a fully capitalist mode. The consequence to be emphasized here concerns the nature of the object produced. Rubens's painting may have been a gift – from king to Church, from artist to world – but it also came into the world as a commodity, indeed, a commodity in a double sense. What was purchased and donated to the convent was both an icon to possess and (spiritually) enjoy, and a signed Rubens for which there was, increasingly, a resale market. To this we might add that the painting was a commodity in a more archaic sense as well. Like ancient pottery, but unlike architecture or large-scale statuary, it was light and portable. This facilitated the capacity of paintings to circulate commercially, while ensuring at the same time that commercial circulation would entail re-siting. The art-object as movable property has no permanent home. It is a nomadic commodity. Overall, then, for Rubens to produce the painting and let it go – under whatever circumstances – was already to launch it, physically and commercially, into an unpredictable circulation. And once on its way, its transactional status as a gift could never be more than a starting-point in a process of exchange that exceeded that of the solely symbolic exchange depicted on the canvas.

In this instance, the *Adoration* remained at Louvain for more than a century until receding Spanish power and waning religious enthusiasm brought the convent into difficult times. It came onto the market in 1783 through a sequestration sale of convent property at Brussels. Thence the painting migrated to England. The Marquis of Lansdowne, the first buyer, sold it to Lord Grosvenor in 1806 for £800 (Reitlinger, 1961: 442). For the next century and a half the painting remained a family heirloom in the private collection of the Dukes of Westminster. In 1959, however, death duties and the escalating costs of maintaining stately homes led once more to its being put up for sale. Following Major Allnatt's purchase and donation the painting was moved to Cambridge. Nine years later, after debating whether to accept the gift, and then how to display it, and after spending a further £161,000 modifying the chapel to accommodate it,[9] the College Fellows finally mounted the *Adoration* in the place prepared over the high altar.

Abstractly considered, the painting's journey has taken it through two kinds of transformation. Between owners it has alternately circulated as purchase and gift, in either case becoming, in transit, an abstract but volatile mix of symbolic, semiotic and commercial value. In addition, with each change of owner, and with each change of site, the painting has entered into a new configuration of iconicity, possession and display. As a Westminster heirloom in the duke's private gallery it was evidently embedded in a different nexus of relations and meanings from that as an altarpiece at Louvain, or as the famous painting it now is in Cambridge. There is a generality to this. In the rhythm of its transfers and stations, the painting's metamorphoses with respect to its status as an object illustrate what happens to all classical (i.e., 'auratic') art-objects once they begin to circulate on the wings of commodity-hood. But what is striking about the particular circulation of the Louvain/Westminster/Cambridge *Adoration* is that the metamorphoses really do seem to have taken the painting round a circle. From being a gift at the altar the *Adoration* moved first, through a forced sale, into the circuit of private family property, and then, after another sell-off, to being once more a gift in a church.

In order to judge how really circular this 'circle' is, we must consider not only the relation and difference between the painting at its (current) point of arrival and at its initial liturgical site, but also those between the motion that bore it away and the one that has brought it back. If there had been a full reversal, the waywardness of the artwork as commodity would have been recuperated by the dynamics of the gift, and the painting's own allegory of art's sacred destination would have been triumphantly realized (again). As we may suspect, though, something more complex has occurred.

Take first the changes of status of the painting entailed by its first movement, from Louvain to Westminster. In the sequence of transactions which brought the painting to its new home, the icon with cult value first transmutes, through money, into a tradable token of differential prestige (Baudrillard's 'pure sign-value'). What had been an altarpiece with liturgical significance is then reframed, in a private collection, as 'art'. Benjamin, in his account of the declining aura of artworks, mentions a midway case between cult and exhibition value, in which the cult of Art supersedes that of religion. *En route* to becoming a tourist attraction, the work of art passes from being organic to rituals surrounding the sacred to becoming the sacred centre of its own cult. In being secularized for profane display, the *Adoration* was certainly transformed in that direction. At the same time, in becoming a private possession, the painting's participation in the cult of Art was severely curtailed. The exhibition value that derived from, and contributed to, the painting's transferred use as 'great art' was itself privately appropriated. In the Lansdowne and then the Westminster household the painting became an expression of aristocratic splendour and an aid in the formation of a refined taste. In this regard, we might say, the cult value of the painting was not just displaced, but sharply diminished. In moving directly from church to household it bypassed the stage of public exhibition, and status as great art, to become a semiotic prop in a theatre of intra-class prestige.

Within this same movement, the painting's symbolic status as a gift was also dissolved. This occurred precisely at the point of sale in Brussels. What was held in trust by a specific church for the Church as a whole was suddenly let go. Released from obligation, it thus became what it had potentially been all along: an alienable commodity. In this, the painting's two values, in exchange and for use, split apart. The one was traded for the other – though of course what Lord Lansdowne paid for included its (perhaps profitable) reconversion into cash. Recomposed as family property in the Lansdowne and then the Grosvenor estates, the painting became once more a gift, an inherited hand-me-down. But, as it was the product of a mere purchase, the duty to retain the gift became more local and contingent. Moreover, while the fortunes of the Baroque fluctuated, the resale market for old paintings steadily developed. The prospect always remained, then, that this succession of 'internal' gifts might be liquidated, and its investment value realized, any time that financial circumstances (or the exigencies of developing an art collection, as in the case of Lord Lansdowne) forced the issue.

In the first movement, then, the painting undergoes a double reduction in its symbolic status. The religious icon becomes a sign, the gift becomes a commodity. But what in these terms are we to say about the second movement? How are we to regard its apparent reversal of the first?

The transactions which brought the Rubens to Cambridge, to a church and to a high altar certainly resumed what had formerly been the painting's fixed and intrinsic relation to religious practice. But there was a difference. The painting's migration from Westminster to Cambridge also enhanced the painting's exhibition value by springing it from a private collection to a very public place. The Louvain *Adoration* had its visitors, including Joshua Reynolds, but these were few in relation to congregants and nuns. In its new location the reverse was true. With respect to its iconicity, then, the effects of relocation were contradictory. They were to send the painting simultaneously from the middle position in Benjamin's schema – as revered art-object – to both ends of the spectrum between cult and exhibition.

A similar paradox attends the other aspect of reversal, in which the painting passed to King's College as a gift. This was a gift in the grand style. When viewed in relation to the whole provenance of the painting, moreover, its significance as such was more than 'local'. By returning the painting to a church the gesture responded to the call of its initial destination. It thus repaired the profanation of the painting's exile, and the gift's abeyance, as mere private property. At the same time, it both undershot and overshot the original donation. Conducted with a minimum of ostentation and reflected glory, this second gift had no aspect of patronage or tribute. The fact that it was directed towards a church at all, moreover, was secondary to its stated meaning. For beyond the chapel, beyond even the church as such, there was another intended recipient. Through the efforts of Major Allnatt (and, in the chapel restoration, other contributors), the painting was presented as a gift to the nation. In this curious case of quasi-nationalization, ownership was vested in an autonomous, publicly subsidized, ruling-class institution. As a result, the Fellows of King's College became stewards for the painting (as they already were for the chapel) as an aspect of preserving what has come to be called 'heritage'.

Through the Westminster *Adoration*'s passage into the public domain, the movement of private appropriation marking the middle stages of its circulation might seem to be annulled. In an age of mass travel, the public accessibility of art makes it accessible everywhere. But geography is a powerful emblem. The Rubens was purchased to prevent its sale overseas. When the painting passed into private hands in 1783 it crossed the Channel. With the 1959 sale and donation it was determined that it should stay. What had been an act of individual appropriation was thus generalized to the national level. To be sure, Rubens had a strong British connection. In the latter part of James I's reign he was an important intermediary between Spain and its Catholic continental allies and the British crown. He visited and painted commissions in England many times in the 1620s, including the stunning ceilings of the Guildhall with their encomium to James I. Both this and diplomatic service to the Stuart court earned him a knighthood. Nevertheless, for its first hundred and fifty years the *Adoration* had been housed in a Flemish church. It was only drawn from Louvain and Brussels by the eclipsing rise of English wealth. Now, with a similar rise of American (and, increasingly, Japanese) economic power, an English peer had lost his own power to hold it. With Britain in the place of Flanders, Allnatt's purchase and gift aimed to prevent a repeat.

In context, then, the second gift of the Rubens was quite unlike the first. Whereas the original gift projected the munificent piety of a crusading Catholic monarchy, the second was a defensive measure to protect the store of art treasures held 'in the nation'. In the transaction of 1959 the *Adoration* became a minor stake in the game of maintaining Britain's sense of identity as a great power, against the background of its steep post-1945 imperial decline.

Here, in fact, the second point about the ambiguity of the painting's restored status converges with the first. It was not enough for the Rubens to be 'saved'. It had also to be exhibited as a national treasure. As already one of the most architecturally renowned – and visited – churches in England, King's College Chapel was ideal as a site for its appropriate exposure. From Christmas carols on television to the visiting hordes of summer, the chapel is on permanent show. Not only, then, was the gift to King's not a straightforward return of a religious painting to its (or a) sacred home. Because of the kind of gift it was, because of the gift's national/political character, it secured a place for the work guaranteed to enhance its exhibition value just as much as its cult value. The transfer to Cambridge ensured, indeed, that these two functions and values of the painting would, in some fashion, collide.

The Rubens in the Chapel

As a nationally prominent, and beautiful, church, the Chapel of King's College eminently met the desiderata of the *Adoration*'s second benefactor. In these and other ways too, the painting's new site also provided lines of continuity with the gesture which had initiated its journey at Louvain. What started off as a royal gift was received back by an institution which was founded by a monarch and named after royalty as such. King's College, a sister foundation of Eton, was established by Henry VI to 'support poor scholars'. Work on the chapel was begun, to the King's personal specifications, in 1446. It was completed under Henry VIII some one hundred years later (Willis, 1886: 465–484; Saltmarsh, 1964: 1–2). Tudor heraldic devices were woven into the doorways, oak panelling and ribbed masonry. 'Our royal founder', as he is still piously referred to in some circles, continues to be remembered with gratitude at the annual service to mark 'Founder's Obit'. On this arcane occasion a commoner and an Old Etonian undergraduate present to the altar a white lily and a white rose. Of course, the chapel is Anglican, not Catholic. But by the same token, in perpetuating the archaic and residual cult of monarchy, royalty can be religiously acknowledged both as founder of the shrine and as defender of its faith. Here too, for all the difference, and even enmity, between the houses of Tudor and Hapsburg/Castille, there is a clear continuity between the painting's incarnations in Cambridge and Louvain.

The chapel was also a suitable locale by virtue of its function as an aesthetic shrine. The same could be said, more or less, about all churches, indeed all traditional places of worship, from temples and pagodas to cathedrals and mosques. Even amidst the fervour of revivals, the art lavished on such buildings has steadily come to be appreciated, with wonder, as precisely that. What has distinguished King's College Chapel in that regard is not just the perfection of its architecture – its palpable sublimity, its well-nigh unsurpassable integration of form and meaning, the engineering miracle of its glass-filled walls and mighty but delicate fan-vaulting – but the culture of art worship that grew up around it, especially within the college itself. Through the choir this extended to music, and indeed, in the august and often spectacular round of rituals and events that fill the chapel's calendar, to the theatrical as well. From Sir Christopher Wren gazing in wonder at the ceiling, to the non-believing aesthetes of the 1920s, and later, who attended Evensong to elevate their senses, to the devoted, even pedantic, researches of post-war College Fellows into the chapel's architectural history, the late Gothic church on King's Parade has long been a special place for cultivating piety towards the Beautiful. No doubt in the sentiments of acolytes and congregants the religious and aesthetic interests seamlessly merge. If 'I am the Way', and if the Beautiful is the Good and the True, then the God of Christianity can blur with the romantic sublime.

Altogether, in its new location, the painting's cult value was reasserted. To be sure, the cultic elements that had attended the *Adoration* in the convent were mixed in different ratios. The recuperated value of the painting as a religious (and royal) icon gave cover, in the chapel, for the even more considerable enhancement of its cult value as Art. But they were the same elements. Indeed, if we recall the pagan theme in Rubens's *oeuvre*, his Baroque tendency to glorify Art in the very act of using it to glorify Christ and king, we may say that the chapel cult at the college made it even more apt than the Louvain convent to house his celebration of the gift.

Nevertheless, as the years of debate and discussion prior to the picture's actual mounting over the chapel altar attest, the fit between (newly received) symbol and (old) setting was not perfect. The gift proved hard to assimilate.

There was, to begin with, the question of visual fit. If hung in the chapel, where was it to go? It may be functionally right, said some, to place it, as before, over the high altar. But the box-like verticality of the painting, taller than it is wide, might mar the proportions of the east wall, undercut its perpendicular motion, and distract attention from the glory of the late medieval stained glass.[10] The solution devised to meet this objection was expensive, almost as expensive as the painting itself. Boosted by a further gift from Major Allnatt (through the Chase Foundation), the college elected to lower the slate floor, which in the eighteenth century had been raised in ascending steps down the nave, back to its earlier level. The actual painting was given a plain frame, and black shutters were placed on either side (an idea of Fellow and Fitzwilliam Museum Director Michael Jaffé) to compensate for its shape. This eased the visual entry of the picture into its place beneath the east window. There was no way, though, except through a tolerant eclecticism, to mitigate the still remaining stylistic clash. This was made easier, perhaps, by the fact that in the previous century, preceding a fad for the neo-Gothic, a Rubens tapestry had been draped high on the wall. But there was no disguising the gulf between the round, energetic forms of the painting and the austere, tapering lines of the chapel's limestone and glass.

In his will, Henry VI had left instructions that the chapel and other college buildings 'procede in large fourme clene and substancial, settyng a parte superfluite of too gret curious werkes of entaille and besy moldyng' (Roberts, 1927: 42). Presumably what he wished to avoid for his monument was the exuberant decorative flourish that already characterized Italian church building in the quattrocento.

Ranged beside William Caxton's similar espousal of English as it is plainly spoken, the king's aesthetic preference can be regarded as the emerging expression of a national (and anti-Continental) vernacular. But such an attitude, a prejudice for the plain and unadorned, also resonated with the stirrings of a proto-Protestant religiosity, a spirit which was as allergic to the allegory and ornament associated with the gathering European enthusiasm for painting as it was to the deceptive artifices of rhetoric or the obscure logic-chopping of Scholastic philosophy. In contrast, at the apex of the alliance between Catholic absolutism and the Counter-Reformation Church, Rubens's career was borne aloft by a full-fledged espousal, and northwards migration, of the Italianate flourish and iconicity repudiated by Henry VI.

The stylistic anomaly, then, was indexed to a religious difference. That same difference indeed was made explicit in the allegorical content of Rubens's picture. In the early modern fault-line between Protestant and Catholic, what could be more contentious than the doctrinal meaning of the Mass? The chapel's liturgy, with its retained medieval traces, was High Church enough to make a bridge towards the transubstantiation hinted at in the painting. In the Anglican compromise, in any case, the question of commemoration versus real presence was fudged, along with much else. But the presence of the Rubens over the altar does accent the second interpretation over the first, just as it more generally emphasizes a spirit of clerical-monarchical reaction which the college, in its modern drift towards progressivism, could not but find alien. L.P. Wilkinson (1980) has documented the college's determined shift, since the late nineteenth century, from being a cosy sinecure for eccentric and antiquarian Etonians to becoming a meritocratic and fiercely competitive forcing house, eminent in such non-traditional domains as economics and natural science. In the past thirty years the college, regularly at the top in the Cambridge league table of tripos results, terminated altogether its bias towards public school admissions, and was (with Clare and Churchill) among the first, in 1972, to admit women. During the 1960s, when the painting was being digested, the contradictions entailed by this transformation were at their height, amplified by the more general cultural tensions of the times. The split between devotion to the chapel and to the enlightened intellect championed by the college would have been more severe but for the ongoing compromise according to which the aesthetic power of the chapel broadened support among the college's seculars, while the theology and social message associated with the chapel as a religious institution tacked to the left.

The consequences of this situation for the cult value of the Rubens in its Cambridge location have been twofold. On the one hand, as traditional Catholicity has drained from the chapel, the anomaly of the painting's doctrinal meaning has only increased. On the other hand, because of the decreased salience and energy of organized religion, particularly in the Anglican church, and especially in matters of doctrine, this has ceased to matter. Moreover, what is true of the painting's function in religious ritual is truer still for its place in the (local) cult of monarchy. If life has ebbed from organized religion, it has altogether evaporated from the latter. Thus the fact that the painting, as a gift of kings, found its way back to a site that was also a gift of kings loses its point. In the end, Rubens's monarchism ceases to offend. Already in 1959 it was on the way to becoming a merely historical feature, if noticed at all. The painting itself, meanwhile, was positioned to become, through all the contradictory determinations of its symbolic value, ever more exclusively radiant as great Art, a wonderful offering at a shrine to the aesthetic.

That this was all to the greater glory (and cultural capital) of King's College corporately need hardly be said. But what of the other incarnation of the painting, of the commodity object that even as gift and icon it never ceased to be?

Baudrillard's essay on the art auction argued that the trend was for both symbolic and economic-exchange-value to be subsumed in a general system of sign exchange. If the Rubens in the chapel was just resting, between agonic transactions, as a tradable store of differential prestige, he would be right. However, and leaving aside the ambiguities surrounding its renewed cult value, the commodity character of the painting cannot be so simply dismissed. This character does not depend solely on its commercial disposability, its reconvertibility into money – though this does shape the artwork's trajectory through time and space, and imparts a transitoriness to its relational field which Baudrillard ignores. In its Cambridge setting, the commodity character of the painting is also a constant. It resides in the painting's daily function as a cultural asset which contributes, within the wider chapel, college, and city ensemble, not simply to its own rentability but to the production and distribution of other commodities. The indirectness of the painting's commodity form in this respect should be stressed. No doubt the pound or two which visitors to the chapel are now charged at the door indicates the income-earning capacity of what they have travelled to see. But this hardly begins to cover maintenance costs, and what matters much more, commercially speaking, is the secondary effects. Some are internal. The chapel is a performance venue for live as well as recorded music, most notably by its world-famous choir. In a small way, the painting enhances the setting for such events, including Christmas Eve, to which its iconography directly pertains. It thus contributes, as a promotional sign for Christmas, the chapel and its choir, to marketing the increasing flow of musical product emanating from the chapel itself. More significantly, the chapel and its paintings are, nationally and internationally, a major tourist draw. Of the countless visitors to Cambridge every year, over half a million file in to see the building's interior. Tourism is a major economic contributor to the region, with spill-over demand not only for hotels, restaurants, pubs, tea shops and gift stores, but also via the multiplier effect generated for others by small-business profits and service-worker wages.

The exhibition value of the painting, however, as of the chapel, the college and Cambridge as a whole, is a mixed blessing for those who live and work there. Tourists clutter and distract. In catering for visitors, the city centre round the market (which has become a pedestrian precinct to ward off the chaos of traffic) has become decreasingly served by retail outlets catering for daily needs. The college is a residence as well as would-be 'temple of the intellect' (in Noel Annan's phrase). In view of the masses that descend, King's, like other colleges, closes its doors entirely to 'non-members' during the summer months. Admission to chapel services, and access between times, is through the south door, rather than through the college grounds. When it was reluctantly decided to introduce a small charge (between services), this was as much to regulate the traffic as to cash in on the trade.

The protection sought, though, is not just a matter of peace and quiet. Even in its attenuating form as art shrine the painting holds, for those within, a cultic place. Benjamin noted that 'Today the cult value would seem to demand that the work of art remain hidden' (1969: 225). The pressure of visitors emphasizes the chapel's function as show-piece, and unchecked would overwhelm its inner life. The same is true, indeed, of its role as performance and recording venue. At the limit, one could imagine a reversal in which the building, the painting, and the religio-aesthetic practices and traditions clinging to them become mere instruments as sources of mystique for the commercial production they help stimulate. Cambridge could go the way of Heidelberg, or Venice. Overall, then, the contradictions surrounding the symbolism of the painting, relative to the religious, royal and aesthetic circuits of worship in which it is placed, are overtaken by a larger one. This is between the painting's simultaneously enhanced cult and exhibition values in its new location. And this contradiction in turn instantiates an even more fundamental one between the artwork's two statuses as symbol (*qua* gift and icon) and commodity.

But this is not the end of the story. The cult value of the painting as Art – which tacitly rises to the fore even in its place over the altar – passes over into its exhibition value as tourist attraction, while both merge into the once-removed, but equally reverential category of heritage. Heritage is to collectivities what inheritance is to individuals, but with the qualification that in a throw-away culture it becomes the object of policy in a formal effort to preserve not just the best of the past but traces of pastness as such. The 1959 gift of the painting to the chapel was itself already a gift in this sense, and not just a gift in support of all that it was customary to worship there. The contradiction of the *Adoration*'s dual character as symbol and commodity, as cult object and as object for display, is reproduced as the clash of crowds and care within the gift of 'heritage' itself. So too is the mitigation of this contradiction through the subsumption of art into that category, with distancing, even quotational, effects with regard to the specific (and 'preferred') meaning of any particular work.

This then – at least today – is the terminus of the work of art along its journey as divine gift: not in returning to God, not in stilling the waters of symbolic exchange, nor, at the same time, in being simply reduced to sign-value, in a meaningless oscillation between private and public collector. The gift of art terminates rather in a social pact (usually but not always managed by the state) to preserve the past for public inspection and display, a move which, in a commodified culture, simultaneously converts it into a 'free' input for the service and merchandise production symbiotic with it. Thus the second gift only fulfils the promise of the first ironically, while Rubens's allegory of the gift's destination is countermanded by forms of exchange, and consequent modes of being as an object, which he excluded from the painting but to which, from the outset, it was bound.

Notes

Help by Jan Campbell-Luxton and Heather Jon Maroney in finding and obtaining materials is gratefully acknowledged, as too is the stimulus of Sarah Clift, who introduced me to the question of 'heritage', and of Jonathan Bordo, who has led me to think about early modern painting, and much else.

1 Rubens follows traditional nativity scenes in conflating elements drawn indifferently from Matthew and Luke. Matthew has 'wise men' visiting Mary, Joseph and the Child in Bethlehem where they live; Luke has the Holy Family obeying the census call in the outbuildings of an inn, and visited by shepherds. For a recent discussion, which argues that the Magi were political-cum-religious emissaries from the Zoroastrian high priest-hood, see Roberts (1995: 5–10).
2 I am following the account given in Wilkinson (1980: 130–1).
3 For a discussion of Eucharistic representation in relation to the 'witness' function in early modern painting see Bordo (1996).
4 Roberts (1995: 106) cites the Venerable Bede as follows: 'The Magi were the ones who gave gifts to the Lord. The first is said to have been Melchior, an old man with white hair and a long beard ... who offered

gold to the Lord as to a king. The second, Gaspar by name, young and beardless and ruddy complexioned ... honoured him as God by his gift of incense, an oblation worthy of divinity. The third, black-skinned and heavily bearded, named Balthasar ... by his gift of myrrh testified to the Son of Man who was to die.'

5 For an alternative – and emphatically non-sacrificial – reading of the Crucifixion in relation to the staying of anthropologically understood originary violence, see Girard (1987: 180–224).

6 The Spanish king was Philip IV. In 1631 he had knighted Rubens for services rendered, after the artist had petitioned for the same honour which had been accorded to Titian.

7 Not that Rubens always painted for money. Lescourret (1993: 216) recounts that in gratitude to Fabrice Valguarnera, who cured Rubens of chronic and painful gout, he offered to paint the doctor a work 'in my own hand ... to serve whatever is your taste'. In the same letter he alternatively offers to finish off an *Adoration* he has in his studio, which will 'serve for the altar of some private chapel or could decorate the fire place in a big room'. This *Adoration* is now in the Hermitage Museum, St Petersburg.

8 Rubens's father had served as lawyer and diplomatic adviser to the independentist William of Orange. His own missions were for Spain. In later years he mediated between the courts of Philip IV of Spain and Charles I, helping to secure the treaty of 1630. It was these services as much as his artistic ones which secured him his British knighthood – though the Spanish, and Catholic, connection proved ruinous to Charles I himself.

9 According to Wilkinson (1980: 130–1), the modifications (following a 1965 plan prepared by Sir Martyn Beckett) included stripping the woodwork, 'not only Detmar Blow's work but the fine seventeenth century panelling of Cornelius Austin on the side walls' beyond the stalls, so that the painting would be set against stark limestone. As well, the altar itself was shortened, 'with a new frontal by Joyce Conway Evans'. The largest project, however, involved levelling the sanctuary floor (gradations had been introduced by James Essex in 1774) and 'reconstituting its black and white marble patterning'. The whole undertaking was combined with a general refurbishment of the chapel's interior.

10 Until 1964 the painting was placed, for viewing and comment, to the right of the choir screen. Then, as a visual experiment, it was placed on the existing altar. Given the height of the painting, it almost touched the lower edge of the east windows. Worries were expressed about blurring between them, and also about the diminished impact of the painting under the dazzling wall of stained glass (Wilkinson, 1980: 130).

Bibliography

Bataille, G. (1988–91) *The Accursed Share: An Essay on General Exchange*, 3 vols, New York: Zone Books.

Baudrillard, J. (1981) *Towards a Critique of the Political Economy of the Sign*, St Louis, MI: Telos Press.

Benjamin, W. (1969) *Illuminations*, New York: Schocken Books.

Bordo, J. (1996) 'The witness in the errings of modern art', in P. Douro (ed.), *The Rhetoric of the Frame*, Cambridge: Cambridge University Press.

Dillon, E. (1988), *Rubens*, London: Methuen.

Douro, P. (1996) (ed.) *The Rhetoric of the Frame*, Cambridge: Cambridge University Press.

Girard, R. (1987) *Things Hidden Since the Foundation of the World*, Stanford, CA: Stanford University Press.

Lescourret, M.-P. (1993) *Rubens: A Double Life*, London: Allison and Busby.

Mauss, M. (1967) *The Gift: Forms and Functions of Exchange in Archaic Societies*, New York: Norton.

Muller, J. (1989) *Rubens: The Artist as Collector*, Princeton, NJ: Princeton University Press.

Roberts, P. (1995) *Journey of the Magi: In Search of the Birth of Jesus*, Toronto: Stoddard.

Roberts, S.G. (1927) *The Charm of Cambridge*, London: A. & C. Black.

Reitlinger, G. (1961) *The Economics of Taste: The Rise and Fall of the Art Market, 1760–1960*, New York, Chicago and San Francisco: Holt, Rinehart and Winston.

Saltmarsh, J. (1964) *King's College and Its Chapel*, Cambridge: Jarrold & Sons for King's College.

Veblen, T. (1967) *The Theory of the Leisure Class*, New York: Viking.

Wilkinson, L.P. (1980) *A Century of King's*, Cambridge: King's College.

Willis, R. (1886) *The Architectural History of the University of Cambridge and of the Colleges of Cambridge and Eton*, Vol. I, Cambridge: Cambridge University Press.

12

The People's Show Festival 1994: a survey

JANINE ROMINA LOVATT

Introduction

People's Shows are exhibitions of collections belonging to local people and displayed in public places. The concept is not a new one, but it was brought to prominence by the People's Show in 1990 at Walsall Museum and Art Gallery. The runaway success of this project prompted Walsall to undertake the same venture in 1992, but this time it was one of fourteen venues in the United Kingdom. The year 1994 saw the phenomenon blossom, with over forty venues taking part in a nationwide People's Show Festival. It had a logo, and a communal title, poster and leaflet (though several venues did not use any or all of these).

Despite the proliferation of People's Shows in the 1990s, there is still much confusion and misunderstanding concerning the absolute nature of the concept. Many curators have said to me that they have done this sort of exhibition before, and some have, but most describe museum exhibitions where private collections have augmented their own to form the display. Alternatively, exhibitions have utilized collections belonging to a group of people who are members of, for example, a stamp collectors' club. The difference, I would venture, between these and a People's Show is that whilst the former are drawing upon items from collectors as content, a People's Show draws upon the collector and his or her collection: a People's Show is a glorification of the collector and his or her passion as well as of what he or she collects. Through this glorification, the valuable role which the collector plays in the preservation and making of history becomes more clearly recognized.

This chapter, which is part of a wider study, looks at what actually happened in 1994 when People's Shows dominated the exhibition programmes of museums throughout the United Kingdom. I shall consider reasons why collectors and venues wanted to take part in the project, and then collate information about the People's Shows themselves, and the search for collections. I shall next look at the impact People's Shows have had on venues, collectors, and, where possible, the people who saw the exhibitions. The possible future of People's Shows, as both a practical exhibition and a concept, is also discussed. The conclusion gives an overview of the way in which I feel the concept of the People's Show should go, based on the information I have collected.

This study of the People's Show Festival 1994 was carried out through the distribution of questionnaires. Thirty-nine museum venues that were involved in mounting People's Shows in 1994 were contacted. All of these were sent Questionnaire A; the return rate for the questionnaire was 100 per cent (Appendix I). As a result of this response, 282 collectors, representing twenty-four of the thirty-nine venues, were also sent questionnaires (Questionnaire B); this brought in 201, or 71 per cent, replies. Each reply was allotted its own number against which quotations are referenced in this text. (The text of collectors' Questionnaire B, the analysis of the replies by age and gender, and their collections categorized into types are presented in Appendix II. The complete lists of all the collections exhibited at all the venues are given in Appendix III.)

Although this survey started out as a straightforward collection of data about the 1994 People's Show Festival, stemming from my involvement in the Leicestershire exhibition, it is now far more than that. The voices of the collectors and museum professionals pass judgement on the phenomenon and its future, and I have joined my voice to theirs. The People's Show has a place in a journey which, I feel, many museums are undertaking in the 1990s; a journey into the territory of the user-friendly, customer-tailored services which are surrounding them, and with which they must compete. Public access is seen as more important today than ever before. History belongs to the people, and they are entitled to have a say in what is done with it, and how it is presented.

The motivations of the museum and of the collector

The motivations of both venues and collectors for taking on a People's Show are diverse. This section looks in detail at their reasons and motives and, in so doing, helps to ascertain the cause of the People's Show phenomenon which led to such a widespread festival in 1994 (and tries to go beyond the 'let's put on a show' explanation). Table 12.1 sets out the motivations of the museums involved, their reasons for holding a People's Show, and their expectations.

Table 12.1   *Reasons and expectations for hosting a People's Show*

Response	Frequency	%
Strengthen links within community, encourage involvement	22	56
Democratize museum	11	28
Raise profile of museum	10	27
Broaden appeal, bring in different audiences	9	23
Explore areas of collecting within local community	5	13
Past People's Show very popular with staff and community	4	10
Increase visitor figures	4	10
Stimulate popular interest	4	10
Take part in national event	4	10
Interesting concept/good idea	3	8
Enthusiasm of staff	2	5
Sounded fun	2	5
Encouragement from Area Museum Council	1	3
As a contrast to other parts of exhibition programme	1	3
Total surveyed	39	

The most popular reasons venues gave for taking part in the People's Show Festival were that they felt it would involve local people and increase accessibility by giving their museum a more popular image. Yvonne Cresswell of Manx National Heritage (not part of the 1994 festival) wanted 'a community event that would involve local people staging their own exhibition at the museum'. Harriet Purkis, then at the Museum of St Albans (not part of the 1994 festival) felt that the People's Show was 'alive and kicking'. The City Museum, Lancaster, said they participated in the festival in order 'to endorse the tenet we hold that this is their museum and they are as much a part of the "district's history" as our collections'. Bewdley Museum also stressed this point. Kingston felt this sentiment important too, stating in its introductory panel:

> The People's Show is about showing the things that local people care about and collect. It's about saying 'this is your Museum and Art Gallery, what are you interested in?' In showing the things that local people collect, the People's Show turns the accepted norms for a museum and art gallery on their heads. No longer is it a place of 'dusty, precious items' only accessible, in a lot of people's eyes, to a select few, but it becomes a space for everyone to participate in.

Jenny Costigan, Assistant Director (Services) of West Midlands Area Museum Service, was worried about the way in which the People's Show was being promoted as improving links with the community, when the mechanisms weren't in place to carry through the proposed ideas.

Table 12.2 *Visitor figures*

Response	Frequency	%
Increase	8	21
Status quo (+/− 10%)	6	15
Decrease	9	23
Unknown	16	41
Total surveyed	39	

I have strong reservations concerning the process used in some museums to arrive at the exhibition ... Some of the museums taking part this time appear to have begun the process of consultation with insufficient preparation as to how they intend building on and extending the relationships made and then find themselves having to deal with the mismatch of expectation which results ... more worrying is that they regard it as a one-off activity which is seen as finite and not intended to affect their future curatorial practice.

(Costigan, 1994)

Another reason given for putting on a People's Show was a hoped-for effect on visitor figures. However, the idea that visitor figures will automatically be raised by putting on a People's Show is a misconception, as Table 12.2 shows. Fourteen of the thirty-nine venues saw relative stability or an increase in their visitor figures during the period of the People's Show compared with an equivalent time span in the previous year. Susan Ashworth of City Museum, Lancaster, said that their People's Show was 'fast becoming the "best" attended exhibition we have had since I have been at the museum (i.e. since 1987)' (Ashworth, 1994). However, nine venues saw a decrease in their visitor figures. At Leicestershire, the decrease in visitor figures was attributed to the closure, in summer 1994, of most of the museum and art gallery for refurbishment. Chertsey, Churchill and Salisbury were all concerned by their low visitor figures, though of the three only Salisbury actually saw a substantial decrease (of 22 per cent). Chertsey admitted that it 'did not have as much time as [I] would have liked to have advertised it. I had hoped for many more visitors.'

Collectors often shared their reasons for taking part in a People's Show with those of the venues. When we compare the results of Table 12.1 to those of Table 12.3, which shows some of the motivations for participating in the festival, we can see many similarities and parallels.

By far the most popular reasons why collectors took part in a People's Show were for the enjoyment, for the interest of others, and to teach and show knowledge. A collector commented 'I felt it more worthwhile collecting things if people could appreciate or at least look

Table 12.3 *Reasons why collectors wanted to take part in the People's Show*

Response	Frequency	%
For enjoyment and interest of others	75	37
To teach and share knowledge	62	31
General personal aspirations (not listed elsewhere)	38	19
To support museum	26	13
Asked to by museum, family, friend	23	11
Personal pride	22	11
Thought exhibition was good idea	16	8
To meet other collectors/see other collections	13	6
Encourage others to collect	10	5
To add to own collection through contacts made	5	2
Enthusiasm of museum staff	3	1
Total surveyed	201	

at the items, not just me' (230 – numbers following quotations relate to anonymous participating collectors). Sue McAlpine of Gunnersby Park Museum said that the collectors in her People's Show 1995 'all seem keen that their interests are passed to a wider public'. The visitor book from Walsall's People's Show indicates that people appreciated seeing what people collect, leaving comments such as 'I liked the exhibition, it was interesting to see what people collected' and 'Endlessly fascinating. This shows the extra-ordinariness of so-called ordinary people!' The idea of collectors wishing to share their collections with others can be linked with the museums' wish to be more relevant to all areas of the local community and to broaden their horizons. Most museums followed Walsall's lead of addressing the wish for contacts between collectors themselves and the public by organizing 'Meet the Collectors' days. Walsall actively tried to help collectors to make links by creating a contact service for the duration of the exhibition, via postcards.

Collectors had many other reasons, often very personal, for wishing to take part in People's Shows. Some felt that it gave them 'an aim: [my] collection was just lying around [the] house and [this] made me do something with it' (18). Others wished 'to provide another dimension to the items already chosen – to show that not all collectables are expensive' (53). A lady in Walsall submitted the Coca-Cola collection of her deceased daughter: 'Angie's collection meant everything to her ... She would love to know it is now being exhibited!' (Walsall Museum and Art Gallery: label). Pride was an important factor for many who participated, as they often felt that they had somehow 'really made it' (Paul Hill and Tracey Mardles, interview, 1994). They felt that when their collections were on display they were improved.

Others wanted to support their local museum, many being keen visitors. Of the surveyed collectors, 11 per cent found out about the People's Show from a visit to the museum, whilst 10 per cent were contacted by museums and 9 per cent had a contact within it: for example, they were members of a Friends' organization, on a mailing list or related to staff. As one participant put it, 'as a friend of the Museum, I imagined that I had a duty to support what seemed to be a worthwhile initiative' (131). Visitors and collectors alike seemed to think that the People's Show was a good idea: '[I] thought a People's collection, ordinary people's choices, not antiques or costly articles, was an excellent concept' (13); 'The People's Show was particularly enlightening – what a good idea!' (Bangor Museum and Art Gallery: visitor book).

The People's Show collectors

In order for an exhibition to be seen by the public, some form of publicity must be employed. This may be as simple as word of mouth, or as local as a parish magazine, but it is essential that it happens. Publicity for a People's Show occurs in two stages, the first in order to find exhibits (in this case collections), the second to find an audience.

People's Show venues used many tactics to find collectors, including the press and other media, leaflet and poster distribution, contacts within the local community and word of mouth. A popular way of advertising for collectors (apart from the obligatory press release) was on the distributed application forms. Salisbury's leaflet is a typical example:

Are you a collector?
Would you like to show your collection in your Museum?
You may be just the person Salisbury Museum is looking for.
Whatever your age, whatever you collect – from garden gnomes to matchbox tops – The People's Show is your show.

Many museums felt that Walsall's initial advice on how to put on a People's Show was extremely useful. Kingston Museum said that 'although every museum situation is different, it was a very useful guide'. Some venues, like the Grosvenor Museum, used publicity stunts. Their 'Invasion of the Daleks!' was a pre-exhibition stunt which used part of a collection of a member of staff to encourage members of the public to submit their collections.

The 201 surveyed collectors were asked how they had initially heard about the People's Show in their area. Table 12.4 is a collation of their responses. It is very clear from these statistics that the press is by far the most effective way of reaching a target audience, with leaflet

Table 12.4	*Finding out about the People's Show*

Response	Frequency	%
Press: local, national, free	110	55
Leaflets: distributed outside museum*	28	14
Visit to museum	23	11
Contacted by museum/museum representative	20	10
Friend/family	19	9
Contact within museum, incl. Friends' organization	18	9
Media: TV, radio	13	6
Previous exhibition	4	2
Total surveyed	201	

* These leaflets were picked up in the following places: holiday camp; library; cafeteria; front door; theatre; council offices; bus; local societies.

distribution also being fairly effective. Museums left leaflets in such places as doctors' and dentists' waiting rooms, tourist information centres, public halls and leisure centres as well. Whilst much care was taken that collectors should be found, some felt that there was a lack of, or poor, publicity carried out by some venues. One collector said 'there wasn't much publicity that they were looking for collections' (154).

The selection process, through which the museum chose collections for display, was very important. Table 12.5 shows the role that different criteria played in the selection process at the various host venues of the People's Show Festival 1994. District, age, and sex were by far the most common criteria noted by museums, many using those three in tandem. In the guiding literature sent out by Walsall to prospective venues for the 1994 festival, district, age and sex were listed as being important criteria. However, many venues had very individual stated perspectives on the way in which they would select a collection. For example, Lancaster Museum said that collectors 'had to volunteer collections for lending – we did not "target" collectors themselves'.

Part of the selection process for many museums was the interview. It was at this stage that museum staff and collectors could judge whether they would be able to work together, an essential factor in the working life of any exhibition. It was also a chance for the museum to judge the collections, or parts thereof. Grosvenor Museum said 'When I interviewed each collector I assessed whether they really wanted to take part and whether they would be reliable and co-operative. For me, this was the important criterion.' In its guidance literature, Walsall suggested that museums should interview collectors prior to selection. At Leicestershire, where interviews took place after selection, it was

Table 12.5 *Selection criteria*

Response	Frequency	%
District	24	62
Age of collector	20	51
Sex of collector	12	31
No criteria used	5	13
All selected regardless	3	8
Variety of collections	3	8
Space limitations	2	5
Co-operative collectors	1	3
Collector's need to take part	1	3
Collections displayed elsewhere for profit	1	3
Not an anonymous collector	1	3
Total surveyed	39	

Venues only asked specific questions with regard to district, age and sex.

later felt that some collections and collectors might not have been selected if interviews prior to selection had taken place. It was also felt that where no interviewing takes place before selection it is perhaps advisable to have a 'get-out' clause in the acceptance letter.

Of the thirty-nine participating venues, twenty-seven did interview as part of the selection process, whilst three stated that they only interviewed some collectors. All the venues surveyed, except one, had labels about the collectors forming part of their display, so a dialogue with collectors by way of an informal interview or questionnaire must have taken place. Interviews varied from venue to venue, and from interview to interview. For example, one interview at Rhondda lasted only five minutes, whilst one at Walsall lasted three hours. Questions asked by museums related to 'housekeeping' duties such as insurance valuations and information about the collections themselves. Some venues used a set of prescribed questions, often copied from those given out by Walsall in its guidance pack, while others formulated questionnaires. These methods are very useful, as they ensure that there can be some sort of structure to labels. If there is more than one interviewer, a predetermined list of questions means that everyone gets similar types of information from their interviewees. Interviews generally provided the basis for decisions at the selection stage of a People's Show, and also gave an opportunity for collectors and staff to inform each other of things which each felt the other should know. In the case of the collector this might have meant special display requirements or handling instructions. For the staff it might have meant questions of publicity and insurance.

Once the selection process had been completed, the task of notifying those collectors who had been selected, and those who had not, needed to be carried out. Time was a big consideration in whether collectors were notified face-to-face, or by telephone or letter. By far the greatest number of venues (twenty-three out of thirty-nine) used a letter for notification purposes. Only Hereford used the face-to-face method, whilst Harborough, Kingston, Lancaster and Chertsey chose the telephone (though Lancaster and Chertsey did have to resort to using the letter method in a few cases). Springburn and Clotworthy used a combination of face-to-face and telephone. Both Lancaster and Newcastle pointed out that non-selected collectors were invited to openings, though this happened at many other venues too.

The response to the call for collectors varied from People's Show to People's Show. There was a significant discrepancy between collectors/collections submitting and collectors/collections being accepted, and as Table 12.6 suggests, the 28 per cent of venues that selected all collections submitted did so where a smaller number of applications were received. Leeds is the main exception to this rule, though its accepted collections were fairly equally distributed between four museums in the city. Table 12.6 also shows how 82 per cent of venues selected more than 50 per cent of collections submitted, while 38 per cent of venues showed more than one collection belonging to a single collector in their People's Show.

Table 12.6 *Differential percentage of collections and collectors selected by museums from those entered*

	Frequency	
Percentage accepted	*Collections*	*Collectors*
0–50	7	5
51–60	7	6
61–70	3	4
71–80	4	4
81–90	5	8
91–99	4	3
100	6*	6*
Total surveyed	39	39

* The four museums at Leeds are here counted as one.

Many different types of collection have been formed by individuals operating within society, and People's Shows have seen many of these. Table 12.7 is a breakdown of the types of collection displayed at the thirty-nine People's Show venues in 1994.

Table 12.7 *Summary of collections displayed at all thirty-nine venues of the People's Show Festival 1994*

Categorized collections*	Frequency
Domestic life	169
The natural world	146
Miscellaneous	133
Themed collections	97
Toys and games	73
Transport and travel	73
Fashion	60
Packaging	50
Badges/medals/patches	44
Ceramics	42
Smoking	38
Stationery	29
Technology	21
Militaria (not badges)	19
Bottles	17
Photography	16
Alcohol	16
Stamps	16
Jewellery	14
Money	14
Agriculture/farming/hunting	13
The dairy	12
Football	11
Books	11
Building/joinery	11
Art	10
Glass	8
Comics	8
Theatre/dance	7
Calling cards, etc.	5
Lighting (not transport)	5
Film	3
Measures	3
Medicine	3
Total	1178

* Categories, and a collection's place in them, are purely subjective, but follow what is becoming broad analytical practice in collecting studies.

Every exhibition must be publicized, but where collectors' personalities are involved, you can't please everyone. Rory O'Connell of the Museum of London spoke of how many of their collectors wanted, as is their right, to remain anonymous. He also told how the bendy toy collection was popular with the press, and this did not please some of the other collectors, each of whom naturally felt their collection was the most special.

The People's Show was generally publicized as being a rare opportunity to see what people 'like you or me' do behind closed doors.

> Museums display collections all the time – but who decides what is worthwhile collecting and displaying? Now, the things people in Runnymede collect behind closed doors, are out in the open. Can you resist going to have a look?!
>
> (Chertsey: press release, 15 July 1994)

It was also portrayed as a celebration of collecting, and of personalities: 'Carry on collecting! will be a celebration of Londoner's collections' (London: press release). Many venues expected, and got, above average publicity for their exhibitions. However, this was not, by any means, always the case. Eve Finney, Churchill House Museum and Art Gallery, felt that perhaps, in certain areas, the media were getting bored with the whole concept of the People's Show. Amanda Devonshire at Chertsey Museum said, 'I don't think we did enough to publicise it, mainly because of too many other areas of the job to concentrate on' (Devonshire, 1994). Certainly, some collectors felt that the publicity for their exhibitions was short-changed.

> publicising the People's Show was very poor ... the only poster I saw was on the drum outside the museum and though there was a big spread in the Mercury it was I who wrote to the 'Talkback' programme and suggested that they broadcast live from the exhibition.
>
> (Norman Rochester, collector)

> I did feel that the exhibition needed more publicity in the local press, as the attendance was very disappointing. (150)

However, Bradford certainly had excellent press coverage, because the exhibition was sponsored by their regional newspaper, the *Telegraph and Argus*. The newspaper produced 'The Telegraph and Argus Souvenir Programme. For our Collections of Collections at Cartwright Hall, Bradford'. This was a twelve-page supplement with photographs and pictures of the collectors in the exhibition, and a plan of the gallery and positions of collectors in it. This was distributed with the *Telegraph and Argus* and was also used as a free guide in the museum for the People's Show.

Design

The design of any exhibition is always a considered one, dependent upon staff/volunteer ability, budget and space. With the People's Show, design considerations such as how items would be displayed were often left to the last moment, due to opportunity rather than necessity. Objects from collections were not, generally, brought into museums until just before a gallery was ready to be redisplayed.

Almost everybody and anybody designs the look of a People's Show. At Leicestershire, although a designer was involved, the final display of collections was a joint effort between student placements and staff. At the Museum of London, Kingston Heritage Centre and Churchill House Museum, collectors displayed their own collections, with the help and advice (where required) of venue staff. At venues where museum designers were involved there was generally close collaboration throughout the stages of the creation of the exhibition. Walsall said of meetings with designers that there were 'Lots – endless meetings – About five design meetings. The final details of design were worked out whilst the exhibition was going up.'

Availability and size of space were a constraint in most, if not all, venues. Once collections were selected they usually had to be reduced by a further selection process made by either the venue or the collector. Such selections were not always deemed successful: 'I felt it was a pity to include several kitsch plastic examples [of fans] at the expense of some of the older, more beautiful ones (which admittedly were larger)' (183). It is for this reason that certain museums, like the Museum of Richmond, tried to make special provision:

> To ensure that the key elements of your collection are not omitted could you identify any of the items within your collection that have special interest (i.e. the oldest, your favourite, the rarest etc.). We will try to display as many as possible.
>
> (letter to participating collectors, 7 April 1994)

At Kingston, where collectors generally arranged their own collections, the organizer was very specific about how much space was available to each collector. The amount of space available, however, was linked not just to availability, but also to the style a venue wished to create for their People's Show. For example, Kingston did not want the gallery to be cluttered like Walsall's, as they felt that there was too much to take in at once.

A spartan exhibition meant that only a few collections of a reduced size could be shown in a large space, just as a cluttered exhibition meant that a large number of collections of a reduced size could be packed into a given space. The display desires of the collector were just as diverse as those of the venues. One collector expressed a wish for 'more room ... as it did appear a bit cramped and a mish mash' (240). Wanting more of their collection on display was a common theme in collectors' comments, and in the observations of People's Show organizers. As one collector put it, '[it] would have been nice to have [the] whole collection on display. But perhaps that's being a little greedy!!!' (51). Where a cluttered approach was not taken, collectors often perceived it as unfair when, on arriving at the venue to view the finished exhibition, there appeared to be more space than they were originally told.

Table 12.8 shows how collectors participating in People's Shows felt about the way in which their collections were displayed. Sixty-nine per cent of surveyed collectors were pleased with the way in which their collections were displayed; they felt their collections were 'safe' (37) and 'not overcrowded' (39), and that the 'items looked so much better – properly displayed' (108). A collector commented, 'It was as though the person setting it up liked the collection and enjoyed doing it' (225). However, with regard to a collection's display in relation to its designer, common comments voiced across the board were that the collectors were pleased with the display because they had done it themselves, or their opinion was asked. One collector said, 'I asked to display them myself, the curator agreed ... museum staff [were] most helpful' (14). Where collectors at venues were not happy with displays, it was generally politic either to compromise or simply to follow their lead. 'I was disappointed with the display at first ... I had a word ... She displayed them much better for all to see' (161). Despite their number of collectors, certain venues did allow those collectors to display, or help with the display of, their collections. However, due to staff and time shortages, and museum policies, this was not by any means the general case. Many collectors do realize the limitations which mean that they may not be able to display their own collection: 'I think I would like to have arranged the prams myself, but I realise that it is not possible to have 50 people all arranging their collections at the same time' (280).

Certain collectors felt that not enough care was taken in the display and siting of collections. Collectors commented that 'care had not been taken that they were facing the right way' (100) and that 'an egg cup collector was not happy that the beauty of her best and favourite egg cup had been lost by being placed at the back of all the others in the glass case' (Norman Rochester).

Where more than one site was used for a People's Show, certain ones, often deemed as having a higher profile than another, were viewed as being superior by collectors and, therefore, more appropriate to their collection. In Leicestershire, whilst a collector of Action Man memorabilia was happy to have his collection displayed at Snibston Discovery Park, near the site of its original production, a collector of pill boxes wanted the collection to be displayed in Leicestershire Museum and Art Gallery rather than the smaller, and less visited,

Table 12.8 *Collectors' opinions on the display of their collection(s) at their People's Show venue*

Response	Frequency	%
Pleased: why? (in descending order of frequency)		69
collection well-displayed and safe	98	
no particular reason given	26	
collector allowed to display collection	9	
people's positive comments	3	
asked opinion on how to display by curator	2	
collection kept on display after close of exhibition	1	
encourages collecting	1	
Pleased, but ...: why? (in descending order of frequency)		18
wanted more of collection on show	7	
not enough space	7	
wanted more information about collection in display	4	
badly displayed in display area	4	
collector could have done better job	2	
not dynamic display	2	
labels provided by collector not displayed logically	2	
not enough care taken in display	2	
felt there were different display possibilities	2	
felt exhibition may not have been worth the effort	2	
collection should have been placed at different site	2	
only collector without photograph in exhibition	1	
Disappointed: why? (in descending order of frequency)		13
wanted clearer display/better lighting	7	
badly placed in display area	5	
collector could have done better job	3	
more space for display than originally told	2	
not enough of collection displayed	2	
shared space with another collection	2	
no particular reason given	1	
not placed in appropriate case	1	
personal reasons	1	
lack of/poor publicity	1	
collection should have been placed at different site	1	
couldn't bring collection to life	1	
needed more explanatory object labels	1	
Total surveyed	201	

Wygston House Museum of Costume. On the application form for Leeds City Museums' People's Show it was stated that 'Collections may be shown at any of the museums, not necessarily those traditionally associated with the subject' (application form). However, two collectors felt that their collections were displayed on inappropriate sites: '[Display was] rather a jumble, [on] a little-visited site' (232), and 'It was shown in a heavy industrial museum with few customers' (206). Where collectors have taken part in order to share their collection with a wider audience, a little-visited site will not make them happy, even if one of the beliefs of host venues is that a People's Show will attract a wider and larger audience.

Labels were of concern to both venues and collectors, and latterly visitors. Walsall had led the way with colourful, commissioned, photographic portraits of collectors, funded by an arts grant, together with labels of quotations of varying lengths from each collector. In 1994, Salisbury and South Wiltshire Museum, Norwich Castle Museum, the Dorman Museum, Walsall Museum and Art Gallery, and Bewdley Museum commissioned photographs for their exhibitions. Salisbury used first-year photography students from Salisbury College; the others commissioned professional photographs, with the help of grant aid. The inclusion of photographs of collectors with their displayed collection is viewed by many as important because of the personalizing effect it has. Personal images of this kind were also used in the various publicity drives.

Whilst 97 per cent of venues used labels for their exhibition, only 59 per cent used photographs. Of this percentage, Bradford had photographs of collectors in a newspaper supplement only, and Bruce Castle Museum only actually had one photograph on display. At Bangor Museum and Art Gallery, photographs were included where provided. In several instances, at least one collector refused to be photographed. At Salisbury, the photography students did not take images of all collectors. At Nuneaton, where two collectors were concerned about photographs because of security, all photographs were excluded 'to be fair'. The organizer commented that 'photos were used of collectors in 1992 – much missed this year'. At Churchill House Museum, as 60 per cent of collectors wanted to remain anonymous, no names or photographs were included on labels. However, the organizer, Eve Finney, later wished that she had included information about each collector's age and sex, which in its own way would have served as a method of personalizing the collections. Whilst many felt, at the time or in retrospect, that photographs were a good idea, there were, inevitably, those who did not, such as this visitor to Walsall's People's Show: 'Fascinating but the accompanying photographs are a bit ... pointless' (visitor book).

Some collectors, who were generally pleased with the display of their collections, were disappointed with the labels. In general, a minimalist approach was taken, with no histories of objects given. Collectors disappointed with this approach said: 'would have benefited from some explanatory notes to go with it' (6) and 'It would have been nice to see how many, the rarest, most valuable, favourite, unusual etc. etc. and maybe sorted them into categories' (184). Stephen J. Sheldon of Margrove Heritage Centre (not part of the 1994 Festival) feels a 'lack of interpretation or context about an object can ... make it meaningless'. The venues were often diverse in the way in which they approached their labels. At Chertsey Museum, the labels were 'very short – would have liked [them] to have been longer'. Many labels had a very strict format, and venues varied the length and style of them depending on the amount of information received from the collector. This was the case for Walsall Museum and Art Gallery. Some labels, whether written by collectors or not, were in the first person, whilst others were in the third person, and some were a mixture.

The role of the People's Show in the life of the museum and of the community

The question of whether the People's Show is significant in the short term only is one which concerns many observers. Many believe it is important to gauge its potential life span as a concept, rather than a phenomenon. Gordon Watson at Wakefield Art Gallery (not part of the People's Show Festival 1994) says that he would 'like to see them [People's Shows] as more developmental rather than one-off displays ... as part of a contemporary collecting project, as part of recording an activity, industry, cultural change etc.' Maria van Helmond of Liverpool Museum of Labour History (not part of the People's Show Festival 1994) is unsure of the future of People's Shows: 'It may not be topical or relevant by the time we would be in a position to participate (1997 or 1998!) but it is a good thing at this point in time.' Walsall Museum and Art Gallery itself is bowing out from People's Shows for the foreseeable future as it feels it (as an institution) should 'move on to something new/different' (Jo Digger, Walsall Museum). However, there are many who 'hope that the concept of People's Shows ... will be ongoing and a regular event in museum exhibition programmes' (Yvonne Cresswell, Manx National Heritage).

As Table 12.9 shows, twenty-nine of the thirty-nine museums surveyed felt that they would like to take part in a People's Show Festival again. Clearly, most museum venues were willing to take the problems associated with mounting a People's Show in their stride as part of the day's work. Nevertheless, a run of difficulties were identified, which are summarized in Table 12.10.

Having established that there is a desire within the museum community to repeat the concept of People's Shows in the future, the

Table 12.9 *Participation by venues in future People's Show Festivals*

Response	Frequency	%
Yes: why? (in descending order of frequency)	29	74
good way of involving the public	11	
more interesting collections in community to see	5	
because People's Show worked/was popular	5	
makes contacts with collectors	3	
quirky show, diverse material	3	
enjoyable experience	2	
to boost visitor figures again	2	
nationwide event	1	
public asking for more	1	
Possibly	3	8
No	3	8
Unknown	4	10
Total surveyed	39	

The questionnaire did not ask about putting on individual People's Shows in the future.

feelings of collectors and visitors involved with the project in 1994 must be examined. Table 12.11 shows how collectors felt about their submission of collection(s) to 1994 People's Show Festival venues. Ninety-seven per cent of the 201 surveyed collectors were glad that they had submitted their collection(s) to a People's Show. The collectors found that their wishes for submitting, such as for the enjoyment and interest of others, simply having their collection(s) on display, meeting other collectors and seeing other collections, were fulfilled. However, 31 per cent of collectors were unhappy with certain aspects of the organization of their People's Show.

When talking of other people's satisfaction and enjoyment in seeing their collections, one collector said that it was 'pleasing to see people enjoy my collection and to reminisce about their memories of them' (281). The following comments from visitors to the People's Shows at Kingston and Walsall show that pleasure *was* derived from the collectors sharing their passions: 'Thank you for the pleasure' (Kingston Museum and Heritage Centre visitor book) and 'Feel privileged to have seen so many people's private possessions, a moving experience and fun' (Walsall Museum and Art Gallery visitor book). The idea of having their collection(s) 'on display' in a museum environment was a thrill to many – 'When your collection is on show it gives you a buzz' (36) – and there is pride in this achievement: 'I can say I've had something in an exhibition' (112).

There is definitely a desire among collectors to meet others of a like

Table 12.10 *Problems encountered by People's Show venues*

Response	Frequency
None given	6
Insufficient display and storage space, small cases	5
Insufficient time budgeted	4
Unknown	4
Insufficient, unsuccessful publicity	3
Collectors unhappy with displays	3
'No problems'	3
Stretched resources, including overtime	3
Low visitor figures	3
Convincing collectors not all collection to be displayed	2
Theft/burglary	2
Wanted more collectors	2
Vulnerability of displays (including open display)	2
Shortage of staff	2
Organization	2
Damage to items in collections by staff	2
Lack of photographs of collectors	1
Keeping tabs on objects and packing	1
Liaison problems with photographer	1
Collectors upset when not selected	1
Collectors slow to collect objects at end of show	1
Insurance	1
Collectors' personalities	1
Gifts to collectors via museum meant more paperwork	1
Need for attention of collectors	1
Total surveyed	39

These responses were given to an open-ended question. Many other museums mentioned these points elsewhere, for example in correspondence, telephone calls, interviews, visits and publications.

frame of mind, and not just those who collect what they do. Whilst Table 12.3 showed that 6 per cent of those collectors surveyed had submitted collections to, in part, meet other collectors, after the event 21 per cent felt that meeting other collectors and seeing other collections had played an important part in their successful participation. Comments such as 'we've made a lot of friends as mad as ourselves' (205) seem to indicate a feeling of isolation among some collectors or, at the very least, a feeling that they need to justify, through the existence of other collectors, what they do. Following the Leicestershire Museum and Art Gallery People's Show 1994, several collectors got together to form the Leicestershire Collectors Club. This group aims to bring together passionate collectors of various items, as

Table 12.11 *Feelings of collectors on the submission of their collections*

Response	Frequency
Pleased: why? (in descending order of frequency)	195
other people's satisfaction/enjoyment	61
collections on display	45
seeing other collections/meeting other collectors	42
satisfaction in being part of large local event	28
personal enjoyment	24
making contacts to expand collection	24
meeting and talking to public	23
sharing	21
teaching and inspiring about collecting/collections	16
forced personal re-evaluation of collection	12
personal pride	11
personal press coverage received	8
no reason given	6
learned about way exhibitions are put on	4
Not pleased	3
Indifferent	3
Total surveyed	201

opposed to, for example, those with like opinions in a stamp collectors' club. This shows that lines of communication are desired, and are opening. People's Shows seem to have a role to play in this move.

To teach and inspire about collecting and collections was one of the aspirations behind museums taking part in the People's Shows, an idea bound up in their wish to throw off a public image of stagnation. Some museums felt a comparison of public and private collecting would be interesting. Collectors too felt this desire to smash barriers. For many it was the achievement of this aspiration which made them feel good about their People's Shows. They felt that it had simply opened more collecting doors: 'I hope other people will be inspired to give collections to museums for similar durations' (16). However, a few collectors came away from their involvement in the People's Show with a new, more positive overall view of their collections. One collector said, 'it opened my eyes to the fact that I *had* a collection' (192), whilst another collector felt that the People's Show made her 'realise and value what before was not "a collection"' (184).

Having established that People's Shows do seem to have had some role to play in the lives of the museums and their communities, particularly collectors, it is interesting to learn to what extent the shows have changed the way in which the public view their local museum. If the surveyed collectors who took part in the People's Show are to be

Table 12.12   *The People's Show as a catalyst for a changing view of museums*

Response	Frequency	%
No: why? (in descending order of frequency)	125	62
no particular reason given	97	
always found museums interesting and enjoyable	23	
just look at work on display and how it is portrayed	1	
People's Show is not a museum exhibition	1	
but hope museum's view of people has changed	1	
only change view if such exhibitions more frequent	1	
not enough support for People's Show shown by public	1	
Yes: why? (in descending order of frequency)	75	37
museums more accessible, up-to-date	42	
realize museum staff's hard work	13	
will see/have seen more of museums since	7	
learned about other aspects of collecting/other collectors	5	
future involvement hoped for	2	
interested in People's Shows, not museums	2	
not happy with museums because of bad experience	2	
museum now thinks about people's wants	1	
museums are places of learning, not stuffy	1	
Indifferent	1	
Total surveyed	201	

used as some sort of measure, then the answer must be: not as much as museums had thought. Table 12.12 shows how, if at all, People's Shows have changed the surveyed collectors' opinion.

It should be noted that collectors are, often, casual, if not frequent, visitors to museums, although this is also dependent on their lifestyle and type of collection. Therefore, it cannot be taken that the surveyed collectors are entirely representative of the general public, but they are a sector of it. A series of visitor surveys are urgently needed in connection with future People's Shows. Of the 62 per cent of surveyed collectors who did not feel that their involvement in a People's Show had changed the way they thought of museums, 78 per cent gave no particular reason. However, popular reasons given included 'I have always enjoyed looking around museums' (239).

Where collectors experienced low visitor figures at their People's Show venue, they voiced the opinion that the effectiveness of the People's Show was limited. Three collectors felt that People's Shows could not affect their view of museums because a People's Show is in no way linked to the proper practices of a museum: 'I didn't view the People's Exhibition as a museum (piece) – just a display of items collected by individuals' (32). (The idea that museums do not display items collected by individuals suggests the question: 'what is a museum display, if not a display of collected items?') However, 37 per cent of the surveyed collectors did think that their involvement in the People's Show had changed their views of museums, most for the better, but some not. These latter individuals had generally had a bad individual experience with their venue, serious or otherwise: 'I didn't realise how careless they could be when transporting the precious exhibits!! – and that's when they were taking care, and being watched by me!!' (230). This view is in stark contrast to the experience of many collectors, who were amazed and delighted with the general hard work and dedication of museum staff: 'you only appreciate what you see, but after seeing them at work with the People's Show, you realise just how much work goes into it, and can appreciate everything that much more' (26). This comment also illustrates one of the strongest reasons for describing a People's Show as an excellent public relations opportunity.

Making museums more accessible to the public, more up to date, was another concern of venues when mounting their People's Shows. Fifty-four per cent wanted to strengthen links within their community and encourage involvement, and 28 per cent wished to democratize museums, whilst 23 per cent wanted to broaden their appeal and bring in new audiences. Many collectors saw this widening of accessibility as being a strength of the People's Show too: 'I believe that museums are for everyone, not just to look at, but to take part in, where possible' (162); 'Anything which encourages people to *discover* museums has got to be worthwhile' (157); 'It also made people aware (including myself!) that the museum actually existed – I never realised this before exhibiting' (245). That last comment about previous non-visitors entering museum doors cannot, however, be sufficiently substantiated.

Two 'success' stories for venues hosting People's Shows in 1994 can be seen at Chertsey Museum and Leicestershire Museum and Art Gallery. In both places, the shows have been instrumental in developing new clubs and societies which can only, one hopes, benefit the museum world and, therefore, society, in the long run. At Chertsey Museum, a collector says that 'as far as Chertsey Museum is concerned the People's Show seems to have made it active rather than passive and to become involved with the community by setting up a "Friends of Chertsey Museum"' (174); whilst in Leicestershire, as already mentioned, the Leicestershire Collectors Club was formed. The state of increasing activity of audiences reflects the changes which museums are making in the late twentieth century to attract visitors as they compete with growing high-tech leisure activities and venues. One collector feels that People's Shows illustrate 'the possibilities for museums to get ordinary people to participate in passing on information that might otherwise lay hidden and eventually get lost' (177). Comments like 'Oh! I had one of those!' (194), overheard by one collector, illustrate the value of a People's Show as a reminiscence tool, just like most other exhibitions. However, in a People's Show the variety and quantity of objects are much more concentrated than in other types of exhibition, and therefore offer a far richer resource. Memories are very important to all people, and as we grow older they often become our greatest hold on our lives. A visitor commented: 'What memories. I enjoyed it very much' (Kingston Museum and Heritage Centre: visitor book).

The events and activities organized by People's Show co-ordinators varied in degree and type from venue to venue. Many venues held 'Meet the Collectors' days and/or practical workshops linked to individual collectors and their collections, such as 'Make a Kite and Fly It' events at Leicestershire Museum and Art Gallery. Specialist talks, both by collectors and by professionals in, for instance, conservation, were also organized. At the Museum of London there were 'Summer Swap Shops', of which most were themed, whilst at Walsall there was a pub tour. At Norwich, where Bonhams sponsored the People's Show, there was a Valuation Day.

With all these activities, there seems to be an important area missing, and that is reminiscence work. This is a great pity, because such work would play on one of the greatest strengths of the People's Show, its historical and cultural wealth, drawn from the general public and their passions rather than an institution and its duty. 'Museums aren't the only ones that have "collections" – maybe people have something to offer too' (211). The role of museums must be to allow people to share their own lives and loves with other parts of the community. Surely, this can only be of benefit to all concerned.

The future of People's Shows does not seem to be bleak in terms of production. As already indicated in Table 12.9, many museums are interested in repeating their experience. Other museums want to 'do' a People's Show too. In 1995, Derby Museum and Art Gallery, Gunnersby Park Museum, the Croydon Clocktower and St Edmundsbury Museums all hosted People's Shows. In November 1996, museums and libraries in West Sussex plan to hold a mini People's Show Festival. Kingston Museum and Heritage Centre, riding on the success of their 1994 show, mounted a themed collectors' show on science fiction. The Herbert Museum and Art Gallery at Coventry also put on a themed People's Show called 'Everything But the Car', solely based on the collections belonging to collectors of car memorabilia. Themed People's Shows seem to be an area which has much potential for progress.

There are certainly collectors who would like to see more projects like the People's Show repeated in their local area: 'We'd do it again. It was hard work but fun and well worth the effort' (219). Walsall completed three People's Show initiatives because of the success which they achieved, and the requests of local collectors and visitors. Museums are often committing themselves to similar future projects, whether in the next few years or later: 'In two years time we shall probably be doing another "People's Show" – so if by then you have another collection you would like to display, please contact the Museum' (Nuneaton Museum and Art Gallery: letter to collectors, 4 August 1994). Barbara Woroncow (of Yorkshire and Humberside Area Museum Council) is very definite in her feelings about the future of People's Shows: 'I very much hope that this initiative continues in future years, as I believe that it is a very valuable way of liaising with the community' (letter). Among the few visitor comments about future People's Shows, the following illustrate that value is perceived and enjoyment found in the experience of the exhibition, which warrants some further exploration: 'People's Show is very interesting. It should take place more often' (Bangor Museum and Art Gallery: visitor book); 'Repeat next year! Bigger!' (Kingston Museum and Heritage Centre: visitor book).

In an information panel for Walsall's 1994 People's Show, it was written

> Now a National Festival! The idea of the 'People's Show' started in Walsall in 1990. Now venues all over Britain have joined us, to create a huge national summer festival. People from all over the country are showing their prized collections in their local museums. Over a thousand collections, containing nearly half a million items, are on display ... What you see at each venue depends entirely on what the local people collect. If you enjoy this 'People's Show', then why not have a day out and visit another one? Please take a leaflet to find out where the other shows are.
>
>   (Walsall Museum and Art Gallery: information panel)

In 1992, fourteen museums had taken part in a smaller national People's Show Festival, but in 1994, over forty venues hosted People's Shows. A collector said, 'To have a show on a national basis was ideal and encouraged people to take part – more so than if it was just local' (53). But how much truth is there in this statement? How successful was the People's Show as a national festival concept?

Only four of the thirty-nine venues gave the fact that the People's Show was a national festival in 1994 as a reason for initially wishing to become a People's Show venue. Opinions of various venues seem to show that the national festival angle only worked as a hard sell to the media. The fact that not all venues used the logo meant that from the start the national element was crumbling, and beyond the leaflet (which was hard for many to understand), and the poster, there was little interaction between venues. Planning meetings were held, but as many venues could not attend, difficulties of networking on such a large and temporary scale inevitably occurred. Amanda Devonshire of Chertsey Museum said, 'I was slightly disappointed that less was done on a national level' (Devonshire, 1994). The scale of the project obviously did make the national identity difficult, especially because of the very local and regional nature of People's Shows. The launch of the festival did not help matters because, as it was held at the Museum of London, it brought more focus on that particular venue, despite its being one of the smaller exhibitions. 'The main aim of the launch is to publicise the Festival and we hope to obtain television coverage as well as press coverage ... The aim of the Launch is to try to secure maximum coverage for all' (Walsall Museum and Art Gallery: letter to participating venues, 17 May 1994). The aim might have been maximum coverage, and this might have been encouraged through the attendance of co-ordinators and collectors from other shows, but from comments received I do not believe that this happened. The national press are based in London, and that is perhaps the fundamental problem with national projects whose profile does not grow high enough.

However, this is not to say that the concept of the People's Show as a national festival is not valid. Several collectors felt that it was an excellent idea, as indicated above, and Neil White of Elmbridge Museum agrees: 'it is a brilliant idea and ... a museum somewhere in the UK should devote a permanent gallery to displaying the collections shown in the nation-wide "People's Show" Festival!' It is perhaps simply necessary to rethink the organization of the format for the national festival, and create greater collective identity amongst participating venues.

Conclusions

The natures of the collector (the private individual) and the museum (the public institution) are very similar, whilst retaining their own 'personality' traits. Collectors collect to satisfy a personal passion and are generally only accountable to themselves, whilst museums are accountable to society (and at their mercy, whether they be public or independent institutions). Both, however, fulfil a single role: the preservation of the past for the future – an aim of the museum but not necessarily of the collector.

The People's Show has, in practice, formed the first stage in an important bridge between the public and private domain, teaching both parties the worth of what collectors do, and the collaboration which is possible. This collaboration is fuelled by the desire of the institution to become more popular and relevant to its current local community, and by the collectors' desire to share their knowledge and passion. Where experiences for either the institution or the collector have not been ideal, the positive aspects have generally outweighed the negative. Whilst many collectors would have desired that things had been done somewhat differently, and museums may have wished for a lighter workload, neither would say that the People's Show should not have taken place at all.

For the future, the importance and the role of the People's Show are twofold. It can contribute in its present form to changing the face of museums where it has not yet been tried (and be repeated where popularity prevails), but it must not be seen as an end in itself. It must not become an exhibition model repeated for its perpetuation alone. Rather, it must be seen as a stepping stone – one which helps one on the way, but must remain just part of the journey.

The People's Show is a high-profile exhibition for a local community. It tells them: look what you are, look what you do. However, like any showcase, it must have more substance if its valuable impact is to continue. It must develop and metamorphose if its relevance is to be felt as society too moves on. Themed exhibitions are one way of continuing the journey, giving way to spotlighting collectors in focus displays. However, the real path forward, on recognizing 'that museums are not the only legitimate place for collections of "things"' (City Museum, Lancaster), is to build on that knowledge. Representatives of Walsall Museum and Art Gallery, City Museum, Lancaster, and Leicestershire Museums Service all feel that the documenting of collections held in the hands of private individuals is one way forward. This would aid the contemporary collecting strategy which must be enacted if today's 'history' is to be preserved for the future. These collectors must be acknowledged as local experts in their own areas: 'Other collectors are now recognised local "experts" in their field and provide advice to us and interested parties in the area' (Dorman Museum). The problem with museums is that they can't collect everything and their curators can't know everything. The impetus brought into being by People's Shows must be acted upon and the 'authority of knowledge' must be extended beyond academic and museum walls: '[It is an] insight into what ordinary people collect ... and how this can exist alongside, and sometimes complement, the collecting done in the field by museums' (Leicestershire Museum and Art Gallery). Collectors must be encouraged to publish their collections, or, at the very least, document them for museum archives, in order that the knowledge is not lost. At the same time, the privacy of the collector must also be observed. However, the differences which occur between the methods of collecting of private and public collectors must be preserved. It is their relative idiosyncrasies which make each so special and important.

The People's Show has been a positive catalyst in several communities, breaking the seemingly unwanted isolation of many collectors. In Leicestershire, Walsall and Newcastle upon Tyne, general collecting groups have been, or are to be, formed. The active rather than passive role of the People's Show, albeit in relation to a small section of a community, can only, in the long run, benefit all involved, and so must be encouraged.

The final word, quite rightly I believe, comes from a collector who took part in the 1994 People's Show Festival:

> To be more people orientated museums must encourage people to visit. Displays must be changed fairly often to encourage return visits. The image of a stuffy boring museum must be replaced by an expectation of something interesting to look at. The People's Shows are a really good thing as hopefully visitors will discover that collecting can be fun, interesting and not necessarily academic. Most of what we collect is historically interesting (some of it only fairly recent history) but I think any collecting can be of interest to others. Some of our serious collecting friends felt that the People's Show was cheap and nasty. We did not agree and did not feel that because some collections were lightweight i.e. like key rings or ducks (of all descriptions!) or sugar bags, they should be disregarded. Children and young people in particular may begin with cheap articles but their interest may change as they get older – look at Robert Opie! (220)

Appendix I

Museum venues

Abbey House Museum, Leeds
Armley Mill Industrial Museum, Leeds
Bangor Museum and Art Gallery
Bewdley Museum
Bruce Castle Museum, London
Callendar House, Falkirk
Cartwright Hall, Bradford (City of Bradford Metropolitan Council)
Castle Museum, Norwich
Ceredigion Museum, Aberystwyth
Chertsey Museum, Surrey
Churchill House Museum, Hereford
City Museum, Lancaster
Clotworthy Art Centre, Antrim, N. Ireland
Dorman Museum, Middlesbrough

Droitwich Heritage Centre
Grosvenor Museum, Chester
The Guildhall, High Wycombe
Harborough Museum, Market Harborough
Harrow Museum and Heritage Centre, London
Hereford and Worcester County Museum
Hexham and Haltwhistle Libraries (Middlemarch Centre for Border History)
Islington Museum and Art Gallery, London
Kingston Museum and Heritage Centre
Leeds City Museum
Leicestershire Museum and Art Gallery (Belgrave Hall, Leicestershire Record Office, Wygston House Museum of Costume, Snibston Discovery Park)
The Moot Hall Museum, Daventry
Museum of London
Museum of Richmond, Surrey
Newarke Houses Museum, Leicester (Melton Carnegie Museum, Melton Mowbray)
Nuneaton Museum and Art Gallery
The People's Gallery, Newcastle Discovery, Newcastle upon Tyne
Powysland Museum, Welshpool
Rhondda Heritage Park, Trehafod, Glamorgan
Salisbury and South Wiltshire Museum
Springburn Museum, Glasgow
Swansea Museum
Thwaite Mills Museum, Leeds
Walsall Museum and Art Gallery
Whitstable Museum and Art Gallery

Questionnaire A

1 How many people worked on the exhibition? (staff, volunteers)
2 What was your budget?
3 Did you gain sponsorship?
4 Were you successful in gaining grant aid?
5 What insurance arrangements were made concerning the entry of collections into your museum?
6 How much gallery space was allocated to the exhibition?
7 What was the period of time from:
   (a) date entry forms first sent out to date of selection?
   (b) date of selection to when collections entered museum?
   (c) date collections entered museum to opening of exhibition?
   (d) Did your exhibition run to schedule?

8   How was your exhibition publicised?
9   How many collectors entered?
10 How many collections were entered?
11 How did you select the collections for the exhibition?
    (a) Were the following considerations when selecting? (age, sex, district)
    (b) Did you interview collectors before selection?
    (c) Who selected the collections?
    (d) How many collectors were selected?
    (e) How many collections were selected?
    (f) Were there any family/joint collectors selected?
12 How did you notify collectors of selection/non-selection?
13 Were interviews conducted?
    (a) By whom?
    (b) How long did they last?
    (c) Was a questionnaire used, or did you use a set of agreed interview questions?
    (d) How was the interview data used?
14 What procedure was followed for entry of collections into museum?
    (a) Was an entry form used?
    (b) Was the collector's signature required on entry?
    (c) Were items in collections counted by museum staff on entry?
    (d) Where were items stored?
    (e) Did you have to collect any of the collections?
15 How was the exhibition designed?
    (a) Who designed the appearance of the exhibition?
    (b) If different from the project leader, how much consultation took place?
    (c) How long did installation take?
16 How was information presented?
    (a) Were introduction panels used?
    (b) Were labels used?
    (c) Were photographs of collectors included in displays?
17 Did you sell exhibition-specific merchandise?
18 Were the following, produced by Walsall Museum and Art Gallery, used by your museum?
    (a) festival logo?
    (b) festival poster?
    (c) festival leaflet?
19 What procedure was followed for exit of collections from museum?
    (a) Was an exit form used?
    (b) Was the collector's signature required on exit?

(c) Were items in collections counted by museum staff on exit?

(d) Did you have to return any of the collections at the end of the exhibition?

20 What were your museum's attendance figures:

(a) during the exhibition?

(b) during comparable period in 1993?

(c) as weekly average for 1993?

21 What problems did you encounter in the course of the exhibition?

22 Did you receive information from Walsall about past People's Shows?

If yes, was it useful to you when you produced your exhibition?

23 Why did your museum take part in the People's Show Festival?

24 Would your museum like to participate again? Why?

25 Ask for photographs of installation of exhibitions.

26 Did you have a comments book for this exhibition?

27 Please provide the names and addresses of ten representative collectors participating in your exhibition whom I may contact. Random selection please.

Appendix II

Questionnaire B

1 How did you hear about the People's Show?

2 Why did you submit your collection to the People's Show?

3 Are you glad that you did? Why?

4 How was your collection displayed?

5 Were you pleased or disappointed with the way it was displayed, and why?

6 Did you visit museums before you took part in the People's Show?

7 Have you been to the museum since your involvement in the People's Show?

8 Has your involvement in the People's Show changed how you think of museums? If so, how?

9 Any other comments?

10 What is your age?

11 What is your gender?

12 What do you collect?

Table 12.13 shows how many of the 201 surveyed collectors were male and how many female. As can be seen, the survey group was fairly well balanced at 48 per cent male, 52 per cent female. This balance was echoed in several of the People's Shows, for example, at Walsall with 44 male and 42 female collectors (not including the class from a local school), at Powysland with 10 male and 10 female collectors, and at Bangor with 14 male and 10 female collectors.

Table 12.13 *Gender of surveyed collectors*

Gender	Frequency	%
Male	96	48
Female	104	52
Unknown	1*	
Total surveyed	201	

* The gender of one responding collector was not determined, though known to be between 25 and 35 years of age.

However, at other People's Shows there were large discrepancies between the number of male and female collectors. For example, at London there were 32 male collectors, but only 17 female collectors, at Bradford 19 male and 8 female collectors, and at Lancaster 19 male and 11 female collectors. This latter trend perhaps represents the historical representation of the recognition of serious collecting, which is generally linked with men rather than women. This is not because women collect less than men, but rather because many of the collections formed by women are of a domestic nature. They are scattered about the house in a decorative rather than any other kind of order, and therefore not always seen as a collection. Men, on the other hand, tend to collect in a more concentrated fashion and will do so as a separate compartment in their lives.

Table 12.14 shows the ages of the 201 surveyed collectors.

Table 12.14 *Age of surveyed collectors*

Age	Frequency	%
Under 11	6	3
11–16	14	7
17–25	7	3
26–40	35	17
41–50	33	16
51 and above	105	52
Unknown	1	
Total surveyed	201	

Percentages are rounded up or down to the nearest whole figure, hence the 2 per cent overall discrepancy in these figures.

Table 12.15 shows the categories of collections and their frequency.

Table 12.15 *The collections and their frequency*

Categorized collections	Frequency*
Domestic life	31
Miscellaneous	27
The natural world	23
Themed collections	18
Transport and travel	12
Packaging	11
Smoking	10
Ceramics	9
Badges/medals/patches	8
Toys and games	7
Fashion	6
Technology	6
Militaria (not badges)	5
Jewellery	4
Bottles	4
Comics	3
Stationery	2
Photography	2
Alcohol	2
Stamps	2
Money	2
Agriculture/farming/hunting	2
The dairy	2
Film	2
Measures	2
Medicine	1

Categorized collections	Frequency*
Football	1
Books	1
Art	1
Glass	1
Theatre/dance	1
Building/joinery	0
Calling-cards, etc.	0
Lighting (not transport)	0
Total surveyed	201

*One questionnaire may produce more than one response, therefore the figure represents the frequency of the response amongst collectors. Seven collectors out of the 201 surveyed said that they collected more than one thing. This is reflected in the above figures.

Appendix III

Lists of collections

Abbey House Museum, Leeds

American comics
Bells
Bottles
Bread forks
BT phonecards
Cat ornaments
Cats
Ceramic advertising plaques
Cigarette packets
Copper jelly moulds
Crocodiles
Crystal Palace memorabilia
Leather bookmarks
Milk bottles
Nail-clippers
Penguins
Plastic carrier-bags
Plates
Scent bottles
Snowstorms
Sugar wrappers
Sweet and tobacco tins
Tank memorabilia

Trade cards
Trade union badges
Vintage televisions

Armley Mill Industrial Museum, Leeds

Camels
Cameras
Card models of railway locomotives
Ceramic jelly moulds
Ceramic teapots
Cruet sets
Indian ephemera
Model aircraft
Model buses
Model vehicles
Military figures
Phonographs and accessories

Bangor Museum and Art Gallery

Badges – Lenin and Soviet Union
Bar towels
Beer cans
Bookmarks
Carnival glass
Crystal bells
Cups, plates and saucers
David Bowie picture discs
Egg-cups
Fire-engines
General badges
Hornby trains
Keys and locks
Magic Roundabout
Metal tins
Miniature shoes
Miniature steam engines
Mugs
Postcards
Snoopies
Special edition and general spirit bottles
Two-gallon petrol cans

Bewdley Museum

Badges
Cats

Clowns
Daleks
Enamel lapel pins
Fruit stickers
Magnets
Matchbooks
Miniature bottles
Pomanders
Rubbers

Bruce Castle Museum, London

Alice Faye memorabilia
Beano comics
Boats, handmade
Cameras
Cigarette-cards
Dolls' houses
Erasers
Hindu sacred wooden sculpture
Medals
Owls
Pelham puppets
Postcards of cats
Stringed-instrument bridges
Teapots

Callendar House, Falkirk

Badges
Beatles memorabilia
Cigarette-cards
Die-cast vehicles
Flat-irons
Ford-Iveco truck models
Golf score-cards
Golly badges
Marilyn Monroe
Postcards
Scottish theatre memorabilia
Scouting memorabilia
Snoopy
Thimbles

Cartwright Hall (City of Bradford Metropolitan Council)

American Western paraphernalia
Brandy balloons

Cigarette-lighters
Clowns
Comic-book annuals
Crested china, Bradford coat of arms
Decorative cast-iron household objects
Egg-cups and egg-timers
Evening bags
Eyebaths
Fats Waller recordings
Handkerchiefs
Key fobs
Model elephants
Model vehicles
Neckties
Pencils
Penguins
Postcards
Robots and space toys
Royal memorabilia
Rubber bands
Toy trains in first half of twentieth century
Unused Mercury phonecards
US presidential buttons
Vintage camera publicity items

Castle Museum, Norwich

Advertising pot lids
African carvings and artefacts
Agricultural items
Antique Norfolk maps
Antique watercolour boxes
Apples
Badges, old and new
Baked-bean tin labels
Bookmarks
Boxes, pots and scent bottles
British studio pottery
Cash registers
Chinese collection
Crested cheese dishes
Curiosities
Dogs
Egg-cups
Egg-timers
Ethnographic curios
Family memorabilia
Film memorabilia

Gordon Baldwin studio ceramics
Home-made wooden boxes, etc.
Ink-wells and writing equipment
International costume dolls
Jugs
Kelims and weavings
L. Davenport pastels and oils
Militaria
Misprinted football programmes
Nelson memorabilia
Old woodworking tools
Orange wrapping papers
Owls
Paintings by Eloise Stannard
Penguins and polar bears
Photographica
Pigs
Postcards
Prams
Royal commemoratives
Rural bygones
78s, Gramophone and recording equipment
Shoes
Soaps
Soft toys
Swimming and life-saving medals
Teapots
Tea-towels
Tortoises
T-shirts
Village history
Vintage motorcycles
Vintage toy boats and engines

Ceredigion Museum, Aberystwyth

Books
Cap badges
China shoes
Chinese mission
Drainpipes
Early plastic
Egg-cups
Fans
Glass bottles
Key-rings
Matchboxes
Pencils

Post Office
Royal Worcester
Seafaring collection
Soap
Tin toys
Treasures from local houses

Chertsey Museum, Surrey

Battleships
Bottle-tops
Brass tea-caddy spoons
British Empire exhibition ephemera
Camels
Circus memorabilia
Decorative handkerchiefs
Egg-cups
Fashion dolls
Frogs
Guinness
London cabs
Paperweights
Perpetual calendars
Postcards
Radios
Rubbers
Russian space stamps
Stone eggs
Stones
Sugar bags
Tea-towels
Trolls
US Air Force
Volkswagens
West Country pottery

Churchill House Museum, Hereford

Bottles
Chamber-pots
Commemorative spoons
Fabergé-style eggs
Hornby Dublo railway
Nursery china
Penguins
Pigs
Theatre programmes

City Museum, Lancaster

American Indian artefacts
Avon moulded scent bottles
Badges
Bird skulls
Bookmarks
Brass blowlamps
Brewery trays
Compliment slips
Dolls
Dragons
Fossils
Glass and stoneware bottles
Glass paperweights
Home music listening
Key-fobs
Lancaster postal history
Matchboxes
Miniature shoes and clogs
Model ambulances
Model railways
Owls
Piggy-banks
Prayer-books
Promotional mugs
Queen pop group memorabilia
Royal Wedding ales
Rubert Bear annuals
Souvenir teaspoons
Sugar casters
Sugar packets
Tea-towels
Witches
Wray village crafts

Clotworthy Art Centre, Antrim, N. Ireland

American police patches
Autographed books
Badges
Bus/rail tickets
Clay pipes
Crested buttons
Cuddly toys
Czechoslovakian and Aden badges
Football memorabilia
Foreign dolls

Fridge magnets
Golly labels
Ink-wells
Key-rings
Manchester United memorabilia
Milk bottles
Money-boxes
Old bottles
Pencil-sharpeners
Plough spanners
Rubert Bear collection
Shells
Slot-machine teddies
Stones, slabs and tree trunks

Dorman Museum, Middlesbrough

Antique books
Autographed photographs
Badges
Belgian dolls
Blown glass fish
Bookmarks
Books
Bottles
British Army cap badges
British plastic tableware
Broadcasting memorabilia
Buttons
Cigar bands
Clay pipes
Coins
Crested china
Cups
Cute cards
Decorative eggs
Dolls
Dolls in national costume
Drinking glasses
Edged weapons
Egg-cups
Elephants
Elliott-Marshall theatre collection
Ennio Morricone soundtracks
Fish
Flying ducks
Frogs
Fruit stickers

Funeral cards
Hat-pins
Hedgehogs
James Bond memorabilia
Kangaroos
Ken Dodd theatre
Key-rings
Kites of the Far East
Ladybirds
Lawn-mowers
Local pictures
Logo bugs
Marbles
Matchboxes and matchbooks
Miniatures, teapots and whimseys
Model horses
Model trucks
Model vehicles
Moscow City Ballet photographs
Nails
1940s autographed photographs
1960s memorabilia
Novelty erasers
Novelty salt and pepper pots
Ornaments
Owls
Pencils
Pigs
Pink glass
Postcards
Postcards and photographs
Primates
Pub water jugs
Regimental badges
Rocks, minerals and fossils
Sewing-machines
Soft toys
Stamps
Sugar bags
Stone bottles
Theatre programmes
Thimbles
Transformers
Treasures of Chinese Imperial dynasties
Victorian cartes-de-visite
Vintage wireless sets
Winnie the Pooh

Droitwich Heritage Centre

Badges
Blue Peter annuals
Boot and shoe ornaments
Fishing reels and tackle
Frog ornaments, etc.
Matchboxes and matchbooks
Matchstick models
Model soldiers
Mugs
Packaging items
Pencils
Penguin ornaments, etc.
Postcards
Razors
Thimbles
Tin clockwork toys

Grosvenor Museum, Chester

Bags and purses
Charles and Di commemorative bottles
Cigarette packets
Cruet sets
Egg-cups
Fretwork toys (made by collector)
Glove stretchers
Handkerchiefs
Irons
Key-rings
Knife-rests
Lawn-mowers
McDonald's novelties
Militaria
Miniature bottles
Models in bottles
Model trains
Money-boxes
Monkees memorabilia
Mugs
Old pennies and halfpennies
Poole pottery
Puzzle jugs
Radios
Star Wars toys
Sugar bags
Thimbles

The Guildhall, High Wycombe

Badges
Bottle-openers
Clothing
Elephants
Key-rings
Lamps
Lancia cars
Letter-openers
Masks
Matchbook covers
Milk bottles
Napkins
Paperweights
Pencils
Pink plates
Postcards
Samurai
Shells
Snow domes
Star Wars
Sugar packets

Harborough Museum, Market Harborough

Australiana
Badges
Bicycle lamps
Bonzo the Dog memorabilia
Bookmarks
Cameras
Candlesticks
Cards
Cars advertising boys' comics and some of their famous characters
Children's museum collection
Crested china
Domestic copperware
Erasers
Gulf War mementoes
Horse-brasses
Ink-wells
Local postcards
Milk bottles
150th anniversary of the Penny Black
Souvenir thimbles
Sugar packets
Textiles
World War memorabilia

Harrow Museum and Heritage Centre, London

Included:
   honey-pots
   Mottoware china
   sugar-cubes
   tea-towels
   theatre programmes

Hereford and Worcester County Museum

Bottle stoppers
Classic cycles
Dairy bygones
Early plastics
Fishing tackle
Fridge magnets
Frogs
Hedgehogs
Model buses
Novelty pens
Oil lamps
Pomanders
Soaps

Hexham Library

Aeroplanes
Antique books
Beermats
Bookmarks
Buttonhooks
Buttons
Cacti
China animals
Enema kits
Giraffes
Glass
Lamps
Noddy
Owls
Radios
Recipe books
Rupert the Bear
Soaps
Teddy-bears
Thomas the Tank Engine
Trunks
Typewriters

Islington Museum and Art Gallery

Arsenal football shirts
Arsenal programmes
Austrian hay forks
Badges
Bee ceramics
Contemporary craft
Dr Who memorabilia
Local history
Merchandising
Milk bottles
Mirror balls
Robertson's gollies
Tourist biros
Tourist plates

Kingston Museum and Heritage Centre

Badges
Banknotes
Bookmarks
Bottles
Brooches
Canals
Candlesticks, miniature
Carrier-bags
Cats
Coins (Roman and crowns)
Coins (Roman) and tokens
Cottages
Dairyama (anything to do with milk)
Foil models (made by collector)
Irons
Knife-rests
Lace
Lamps
Medals
Militaria
Motorbike posters and stickers
Postcards – River Thames
Radios
Rhino models
Shoes, miniature
Snoopy

Leeds City Museum

Amphoras
Beadwork
Bicycles
Bookmarks
Buttonhooks
Buttons
Carnival glass
Castors
Coins
Corkscrews
Darning aids
Delftware
DFE thematic collection
Dolls
Drink pourers
Drinking glasses
Ducks
Egg-cups
Enamelled jewellery
Feeding cups
Goss china
Hat-brushes
Key-rings
Knitting sheaths
Leeds ephemera
Mauchlineware
Miniature furniture
Miniature shoes, ornamental
Money-boxes
Nigerian and North American Indian artefacts
Pigs
Pincushions
Postcards
Scent bottles
Sick-bags
Snails
Sugar-cubes
Swans
Teaspoons
Thimbles
Tin-openers
T-shirts
Tunbridgeware
Victorian and Edwardian photographs
World War I and World War II memorabilia

Leicestershire Museum and Art Gallery (and outreach venues)

Action Man toys
Advertising signs
African sculptures
Animal egg-cups
Badges
Birdcages
Bonzo the Dog
Bookmarks
Bosson heads
British comic annuals
Caddy spoons
Camels
Cans
Carrier-bags
Cats' whiskers
Celtic brooches
Commercial or advertising mugs
Construction equipment models
Contemporary British pictures
Cooking, heating, lighting for paraffin
Cut-out paper dolls
Dart flights
Ducks
Elephants
English clay tobacco pipes
Erasers
Fleas
Fossils
Frogs
Fruit labels
Glass paperweights
Goss-type china ornaments
Guinness memorabilia
Handmade paper kites
Headsquares and handkerchiefs
Indoor games
Insects
Isle of Man stamps
Key-rings
Leicester City FC programmes
Local antique glass, stoneware bottles
Marbles
Matchboxes and matchbox labels
National costume dolls
Needlework boxes and tools
Nineteenth-century lustreware

Owls
Pencil-sharpeners
Picture discs
Pigs
Pillboxes
Postcards
Post office memorabilia
Prehistoric objects
Puppets
Rocks, minerals
Railwayana
Saris and Indian jewellery
Seashells
Shells
Smartie tops
Soaps
Soft toys
Steel pins
Sugar wrappers
Textiles from Guatemala and Peru
Thimbles
Tin-openers
Tins
Toy cars, vans and trucks
Tractors and farm implements
Trolls
Valve radios, 1922–60
Victorian papier mâché
Victorian relief-moulded jugs
Wall vases
West African textiles
Whisky labels
Windmills
Zebras

The Moot Hall Museum, Daventry

Bells
Corkscrews
Cow jugs
Crystals, minerals and gemstones
Cuff-links
Dogs
Elephants
Hats
Key-rings
Matchboxes and matchbooks
McDonald's models

Nigerian bread labels
Poems (mounted)
Postcards
Puppets
Rubbers
Seals
Spanners
Spoons
Sugar-cubes
Teapots
Travel posters

Museum of London

Alexandra Palace postcards
Arsenal Football Club collection
Badges
Bendy toys
Birds
Buttons, cloak-fastenings, cufflinks
Cameras
Cats and dogs
Chewing-gum wrappers
Combs
Computers
Cows
Cruet sets
Domestic gadgets
Egg-cups
Elephants
Fishing tackle
Fruit wrappers
Glass fish
Key-rings
Knitting patterns
Lighters
London stamps
Lonnie Donegan records
Milk bottles
Money (project by local school)
Monopoly boards
Mr Men
Passport photos
Patented items
Penguins
Phonecards
Planet of the Apes collection
Plasters (Band-aid types)

Plastics
Police memorabilia
Post Office van models
Postcards
Pulp novels
Scent bottles
Sherlock Holmes memorabilia
Snack packaging
Snow scenes
Spurs Football Club collection
Streatham memorabilia
Teaspoons
Tennis collection
Winkle Ware pottery
Wiring diagrams
Wool

Museum of Richmond, Surrey

Animals
Archers' thumb rings
African animals, wooden
Badges
Binoculars
Blue-and-white ceramics
Bookmarks
Bottles
Caddy spoons
Candlesticks with snuffers
China teddy-bears
Cigarette packets
Corals and shells from Malaysia and the Philippines
Crossbow bolts
Dice
Dinosaurs
Ducks
Echinoids
Egg-cups
Eggs
1839 tournament at Eglington Castle
Elephants
Fairings
Fans
Fishing reels
Fossils
Goss china
Hippopotami
Jelly moulds

Key-rings
Lead soldiers
Magnets
Matchbooks
'Matchbox' commercial toy cars
Matchboxes
Max Roessler ceramics
Medieval vernacular jewellery
Military, naval commemorative pottery
Milk bottles with advertising slogans
Miniature dolls
Miniature shaving mugs
1940 neckties
1977 Silver Jubilee commemorative miniature spirit bottles
1977 Silver Jubilee postage stamps
1935 Silver Jubilee postage stamps
'Old pottery and porcelain' cigarette-cards
Owls
Paperweights
Pigs
Postage stamps
Postcards
Postcards – Auxiliary Military Hospital
Postcards – God Punish England
Postcards – Firemen of Hampton
Prints of Cumbria
Rabbits
Ribbon plates
Russian ballet
Shells, fossils and crystals
Soaps
Southern Railway platform tickets
Stickers
Sword and dagger scabbard chapes
Teddy-bears
Thimbles
Tins
Welsh costume on nineteenth-century porcelain
Wrestlers

Newarke Houses Museum, Leicester

Bricks
Coins and medals
Home Front World War II memorabilia
Knitting sheaths

Melton Carnegie Museum, Melton Mowbray

Local postcards

Nuneaton Museum and Art Gallery

American comics
Animal brooches
Badges
Cake decorations (mini dolls)
Cameras
Coral and shells
Georgian glass
Handkerchiefs
Local bricks
Locally discovered bottles
Matchbox cars
Model buses
Model witches
Mugs
Porcelain eggs
Postbox models
Post van models
Railchairs
Railwayana
Railway lamps
Shoe buckles
Snowstorm paperweights
Toast racks

The People's Gallery, Newcastle Discovery, Newcastle upon Tyne

Ashtrays
Avon aftershave bottles
Badges
Blue Peter annuals
Budgies
Butlin's badges
Cigarette boxes
Clowns
Commemorative memorabilia
Cream jugs
Crested china
Dinosaurs
Dress clips
Egg-cups
Elephants
Esso football club badges

Hat-pins
Horror memorabilia
Key-rings
Keys
Matchboxes
Milk bottles
Model buses
Mugs
Pens
Pigs
Plastic collectables
Pop cans
Rabbits
Royal memorabilia
Salt and pepper pots
Spoons
Stacking dolls
Tea-towels
Tortoises, terrapins and turtles
Trade union badges

Powysland Museum, Welshpool

Cameras and photographic memorabilia
Cigarette-cards
Coin weights and scales
Comics
Corgi cars
Guinness Book of Records
Hats, bead bags, handkerchiefs and handkerchief holders, pomanders
Miniature bikes
Miniature furniture
Movie posters and comics
Powder compacts
Royal cuttings
Scout and commemorative badges
Shipping memorabilia
Small cups and medicine measures
Spinning wheels
Tea-towels
Wade ceramics
Welsh objects, including postcards

Rhondda Heritage Park, Trehafod, Glamorgan

Collection of collections:
    bottles and crested china
    drinking mugs

    men's ties
    photographs
    postage stamps
    postcards
    Royal commemorative china
    transport models
Crested Welsh china
Elephants
Gerry Anderson puppets
Leather bookmarks
Novelty salt and pepper pots
Peggy Nesbitt dolls
Rhondda Transport bus number-plates
Silver/silver-plated commemorative spoons
Tea-towels

Salisbury and South Wiltshire Museum

Badges
Barge teapots
Bells
Bookmarks
Bookmarks, paper
Books on the royal family
Bottles
Buttons
Carrier-bags
Channel Island milk cans
China face egg-cups
Cigarette-cards and silk cigar cards
Cigarette-lighters
Coffee-cups and saucers
Commemorative china
Corkscrews
Cows
Crested china
Crown cork openers
Cruets
Crystoleums
Destination labels
Dolls
Drills and saw sets
Egg-cups
Elder Dempster shipping lines
Elephants
Ephemera and memorabilia
Frogs
Girl Guide memorabilia

Handkerchiefs
Hands
Hat-pins
Historical costume dolls
HMSO guidebooks
Horseshoes
Hub-caps
Lace
Lemon-squeezers
Lilliput Lane cottages and miniature objects
Matchboxes and Spanish inserts
Metal road signs
Militaria
Miniature china shoes
Miniature kitchenalia
Model buses
Model cars, esp. Volkswagen beetles
Model teddy-bears
Mugs
1950s dresses
Nineteenth-century printing equipment
Noah's Ark ephemera and toys
Novelty egg-cups
Objects of archaeological interest
Orange papers
Paperweights
Photos of LT trams and maps
Photos, postcards of Queen Victoria and descendants
PHQ and OS postcards
Postcards
Rolling-pins
Royal commemorative china
Royal Danish Copenhagen figures
Silver sugar-tongs
'Snaffles' prints
Squirrels
Stamps
Stilton cheese covers
Sugar-cubes and packets
Sugar packets
Sugar papers
Teapots
Thimbles
Things found in the garden
Ties
Tins
Toy soldiers

Wedgwood commemorative mugs

Springburn Museum, Glasgow

Badges
Beermats
Butterflies
Cigarette-cards
Clay pipe heads
Dolls
Horn spoons
Jumbo jet models
Ladybird books
Made objects – man-made, hand-made
Measuring and marking appliances
100 years of costume (from family)
Picture postcards
Regimental badges
Scraps
Shells
Tea-bags from around the world
Whisky miniatures

Swansea Museum

Army metal badges, Welsh regiments
Ballpoint pens, advertising
Bath-oil containers, cartoon characters
Bicycle lamps, early
Carrier-bags
Cats, china
Cats, various media
Ceramic pomanders
Comics, Super Heroes
Cookery books
Crested china cheese dishes
Crested china souvenirs
Dinky models
Drinking glasses
Elephants
Fans
Film posters
First-day covers, stamps
Foreign costume dolls
Foreign dolls
Fruit stickers
German travel literature
Handkerchiefs

Key-rings
Kinder egg toys
Kipper ties
Milk bottles, with adverts
Money-boxes
Mugs
Mugs, commemorative
Owls, various media
Paperweights, souvenir sort
Pillboxes, decorative
Pin-on metal badges
Shirley Temple memorabilia
Stones
Tomato crates
Wood-moulding planes, different shapes and makers

Thwaite Mills Museum, Leeds

Badges
Beer cans
Brewery memorabilia
Corkscrews
Cuckoo clocks
Hat-pins and hair ornaments
Lemon-squeezers
Matchboxes
Pictorial soaps
Pigs
Post Office memorabilia
Railway pocket watches, whistles, carriage keys, badges, buttons
Sugar sachets
Tea-caddies
Tins
Wristwatches

Walsall Museum and Art Gallery

Animals, miniatures
Army cap badges
Art nouveau
Avon bottles
Badges
Banknotes
Baseball caps
Batman items
Beatles memorabilia
Beer bottles, commemorative
Beermats and towels

Bicycles, models and associated items
Bottle-openers and glasses
Bubble-bath figures
Business cards
Buttons
Cameras
Cameras, still and cine
Cards, PG Tips tea
Cars, models
Cats
Ceramic dolls
Chamber-pots
Chocolate mugs
Cigarette-cards in silk
Clint Eastwood
Clowns, smiling faces
Coca-Cola memorabilia
Coins in coffee table
Computers
Cuddly toys
Decorated eggs
Dogs
Dolls
Ducks and geese
Embroidery, Indian states
Erasers
Fire-engines, models
Foreign currency
Glen Miller
Goats
Gramophones and records
Hippos and 'Do not disturb' signs
Horses
Irish collection
Jelly moulds
Key-rings
Kitchen face pots
Maps, Ordnance Survey
Marbles
Matchbox labels
McDonald's toys, etc.
Mice
Militaria
Money-boxes
Monsters
Neckties
Pencils and pens

Pencil-sharpeners
Pennants
Perfume bottles
Pierrot clowns
Pigs
Pinball machines
Postcards
Puppets
Rabbits
Railway signalling equipment
Rocking-horses
Rubbers
Russian items
Shells
Snowstorms
Soaps
Space travel patches, badges and medallions, etc.
Sweet wrappers
Tetley Teafolk collectables
Tigers
Toby jugs
Toys
Toy theatres
Trains, model
Trolls
Wade whimsies
Walking-sticks
Way-bills, transport
Wedgwood and jasperware
Wheel hub-caps

Note

A study of this kind owes a great deal to many people.

First, I would like to thank the 201 collectors who returned my questionnaires for their thoughtful and insightful comments. Without them this survey would have been a very one-sided affair.

Second, I have to thank all the staff who completed my questionnaires on behalf of the thirty-nine venues I contacted which took part in the 1994 People's Show Festival. In particular I would like to thank Jo Digger at Walsall Museum and Art Gallery, Deirdre Figuieredo at Leicestershire Museum and Art Gallery, Rory O'Connell at the Museum of London, Sue Davies at Kettering Museum, Tracey Mardles and Paul Hill at Kingston Museum and Heritage Centre, and Eve Finney at Churchill House Museum and Art Gallery, all of whom allowed me to interview them.

Third, I would like to thank all those whom I contacted in the course of gathering information for this survey, from the directors of Area Museum

Services to the reception staff and volunteers whom I met on my visits to different People's Shows.

Bibliography

Ashworth, S. (1994) Letter to author from Senior Keeper: Social History, Lancaster City Museum, 5 September.

Costigan, J. (1994) Letter to author from Assistant Director (Services), West Midlands Area Museum Service, 14 October.

Devonshire, A. (1994) Letter to author from Curator, Chertsey Museum, 18 November.

Fardell, R.S. (1994) 'From Australiana to world war memorabilia: the People's Show Festival 1994 at Harborough Museum', Museum Studies MA.

Mardles, T. (1995) Letter to author from Public Services Manager, Kingston Museum and Heritage Centre, 1 February.

Read, R. (1994) *Kaleidoscope: Carry on Collecting?* Radio 4, 13 August.

Woroncow, B. (1994) Letter to author from Director, Yorkshire and Humberside Area Museum Council, 30 September.

13

Afterword: acquisition, envy and the museum visitor

JULIAN WALKER

'It's how a museum ought to be', a friend said to me about a little-known local museum, remembering visits to halls of dinosaur bones and curious objects from distant times and places. As museums find their role and their power under scrutiny, the nostalgic charm of the dusty, object-based museum may already be its own most important exhibit. Certainties change; the showing of the products of other people, in styles formerly considered disinterested and rational, are now openly debated in terms of the handling of stolen goods and the portrayal of others in terms over which they have no control. Intellectual debate, previously for the most part the preserve of the well-educated white male, is now carried forward by those who have had the experience of disenfranchisement. Loss of power, more startling to the person experiencing it than lack of power, is now a very real event affecting curatorial authority, resulting from wider general awareness of the possibility of cultural restitution.

Since Picasso's seminal visit to the Trocadero in 1906 artists have drawn inspiration from museums, considering individual pieces and such concepts as continuity, universality, or form and function.[1] The commonplace that the typical artist's studio will contain a shelf holding curiosities of nature and human artifice, a source of study and delight, indicates the shadow of the 'Cabinet of Curiosities' that lies behind the modern museum. A number of contemporary artists working in the areas of race, gender and identity are examining museums as warehouses of cultural identity, both from the point of view of their role as institutions in the post-colonial debate and as indicators of current and historic positions in the changing field of material culture. The comparatively recent phenomenon of artists working in museums should come as no surprise; rather it is a surprise that it should be so recent. For visual artists working with objects, a museum is an

environment in which we may examine how we feel about the things
with which we construct our environment, our boundaries, our view of
our history and ourselves; and given that curatorial discretion both
determines and depends upon the language of object display, we may
also examine how we are told to feel about both ourselves and others.

In this chapter I want to show how, if we can sidestep the authority
of the museum (an act which artists working in museums are being
increasingly empowered to make), the language of collecting can be
seen to lead us into some curious, even contradictory, positions.

It is noteworthy that the interest that some artists are showing in
museums, an interest which is being reciprocated by some museums,
has coincided with an apparent general increase in interest in collecting.
The BBC's *Antiques Roadshow* magazine and 'Collecting' pages in the
Saturday newspapers bear witness to the acceptability of an activity
otherwise seen as obsessive and eccentric, however widespread. After
years of populist vilification, trainspotters are being considered worthy
of media attention. Comments in the *Antiques Roadshow*[2] and its spin-
offs indicate patterns of feelings about objects. Items are variously
described as 'very collectable', 'desirable', 'a beautiful object to look
at', 'very fashionable at the moment', or provoking reactions: 'people
have become wildly excited about ...' or 'Wow, fantastic, look at that
....' Objects may be desired to be in use or not, as appropriate: a clock
– 'I hope you've got it working', or a gun – 'Has this been de-activated?
Have you got a piece of paper to prove it?' There are implications that
objects exert influence over people – 'These have got a great following
now'; that they are offering themselves for our entertainment; or that
where they lead we will follow. And within the broader concept of
usage lies the desire for display: 'You put it in the loft? So it's not even
on exhibition, a magnificent thing like this?' The ambition for the
apparently 'desirable' object is that it should be effectively taken out of
any form of circulation that may result in ownership by another
individual: 'Let's hope that they end up in a museum, ... surely where
they belong', or 'When Major Welsh dies he would like his cards to go
to a museum. Better still ... he would like to open a museum in Bath
devoted to playing cards' (Fewins, 1995). Once past the hurdle of
acquisition by a museum, it has to be hoped that an object is important
enough to remain on permanent display and thus within permanent
public ownership; what better way to avoid such a risk than by
constructing the museum round the object.

Money and obsessive dedication can open this door, but for most
objects the route to preservation follows a pattern going back beyond
the *Wunderkammer*. Krzysztof Pomian (1990) discusses the origin of
the word 'museum' from the classical temples to the muses. Objects
ritually given to temples entered an environment where they would not

be put to utilitarian purposes, where they enjoyed the rights of inviolability and would be displayed for the purpose of being looked at. If they grew to an unmanageable number some items would be housed away from the main temple building, but they could never be disposed of by being returned to circulation. When consecrated objects deteriorated they were broken up, melted down and buried in the vicinity of the temple, but in cases of national emergency Greek city-states borrowed money from their temples (in effect from their gods), which they later had to repay with interest.

The details of the acts have changed but the patterns of behaviour seem familiar. The repayment to posterity with interest has become guilt or embarrassment over the ownership of so many specimens that are as much evidence of nineteenth-century colonial acquisitiveness, control of the view of other cultures, and dominion over nature as they are tribal artefacts, human remains and boxes of butterflies on pins. The act of burying things in the ground of the temple precinct has been replaced by the act of putting things into brown boxes in the museum store. But the pattern of the precious object given into an environment where it will be preserved and displayed and not sold, until pressure of numbers forces its relocation into a place of less prominence, does not seem to have altered. One may even look for a parallel to the loan *in extremis* in the sale of the Mappa Mundi to pay for the upkeep of Hereford Cathedral, a debt repaid in exposure to the media of the moral debate and the frustration of the expectations of a perturbed society.

What we have here is in effect a reading of the life of objects. This may include the making precious of a utilitarian object, from the perception of its active role in the public domain to gradually increasing obscurity to the point where the object is regarded as lost, at which point it may be 'discovered', and then held in a collection whence it aspires to relocation in a museum. Alternatively the object may be perceived as precious or important in the first place, an object of contemplation rather than use, which is somehow 'dishonoured'[3] by contact with the process of exchange and 'saved' by being admitted to a collection. As we have seen from the origin of the museum, once an object is placed within the museum collection it achieves dual status: for the viewer it is an object from the past, while for the curator it is an object for the present and the future. But though the curator may take risks with the present of the object, in terms of display or evidence for a new theory, no risks may be taken with its future. The blame for any physical deterioration of the object is likely to be laid on the curator, so, especially in the current climate of short employment contracts, the long-term future of the object is to be regarded as inviolable.

John Romer's Channel 4 programme *The Rape of Tutankhamun* in

1995 pointed out the apparent destruction by the process of excavation of tombs in the Valley of the Kings, a situation which the Keeper of the Egyptian Antiquities Department of the British Museum appeared to condone or at least accept. Excavation is necessary for documentation, runs the argument, even though exposing the tomb to atmospheric pollution and human activity is likely to destroy the fabric of the structure; opening the tomb at least allows the opportunity to document paintings and preserve objects. The fallibility of the object from the past, subject to deterioration in fashion as well as in substance, is here increased by the need for documentation, the demand of a proprietorial and paternalistic academia. Without rehearsing the debate of 'preserve as found' versus 'removal for optimum conservation purposes', it seems that we are here in the world of the panic-buyer, hoarding against the fear of the failed harvest and the loss of commodity. Many famous and now revered collectors lie within this model, for example Edward Lovett (1852–1933), expert on alpine plants and collector of ephemera, superstitions, toys and inexpensive things; his collections are now in the Horniman Museum, the Science Museum and the Cuming Museum, whose information sheet on him states that he so filled his house with objects that his wife left him. One is forced to ask: 'Who is in control, object or collector?' In the Valley of the Kings the demand of the object for eternal life has pushed archaeology to the edge of rationality, while the Egyptian object, in a kind of parody of Egyptian beliefs, achieves a life after death as drawing, photograph or footnote, like its original owner. In this pattern the archaeologist plays god, simultaneously destroying the object and conferring immortality on the image. When we come to look at the act of documentation we can see that this is more to do with our culture than that of the Egyptian sculptor, designer or architect. Art students in life classes are regularly told that drawing is about looking, that the making of marks in whatever medium is a record of the work done by the eye. Thus the excavation drawing is a record of the act of looking at the uncovered object; it is about now rather than then.

And yet how irrational is this scenario, in which the making of an on-the-spot drawn representation of an Egyptian tomb painting may cost more than a drawing by Rembrandt? Though 'common sense' may lead us to view it as absurd, our incredulity suggests the question, 'Is it in fact wrong to destroy the objects we study?' Yes, obviously, we suppose, because it thus precludes the possibility of their being studied in the future. But we destroy the present every day without thinking that it too has to be preserved for the future. It is perceived as wrong to use things from the past if *using* them *uses them up*. The absence of attachment to contemporary articles, compared to the attitude of reverence for the past and the care to preserve it for the future, would seem to indicate that our attachment is to time rather than objects. We preserve our past to gain immortality in the future; the object preserved for projection into the future becomes a metonym of that future during its existence in the present. Yet the old object is a metonym of the past, our past or that of our culture; and as our culture (whoever 'we' may be) is essentially *a* culture and thus a metaphor for any culture, the object produced in a past culture is both a metonym of and a metaphor for all culture(s), and thus worthy of reverence. Compared with this, reverence for contemporaneous objects is perceived as cultish, childish or odd/collectorish; the collecting of contemporaneous objects is to be discouraged as quirky and an act of surrendering of control to objects; dependence on the material leads to conflict in the desire for independence from the material world. The *use* of the present is contrasted with the *preservation* of the past for the future, assuming some different kind of 'usage' in the future, other than that for which the object was designed. Respect tomorrow, respect for yesterday, but never respect today.

One could also look at this in the framework of the museum (more than one in my recent experience, including a well-known London museum) that requires visitors to leave their bags at the door before entering the museum. I am not talking here about the convenience of the cloakroom, but the mistrust of the visitor. Reasons for this may range from a reasonable fear of sabotage or theft to fear of the possibility of accidental damage, given a large number of visitors and a desire to not put barriers between the object and the viewer. But the desire to bring the visitor close to the object is realized at the cost of removing his or her objects from him or her. The implication in this space and this situation is that the museum's objects are more important than those of the visitor, which is surely the case for the museum. There is no base-line of equality of importance for objects. Pragmatically I must accept that Wellington's uniform is more important than my raincoat, until I lose my raincoat. At this point my coat becomes, through negation, more important in my building of my identity than is my quasi-spiritual contact with a great historical figure through the medium of the sight through a glass case of an article of clothing that was in physical contact with his skin. Anything old provides us with this constructed path to the past, while the contemporary is replaceable (and the replaceable is the contemporary).

The question of the value of the object has become the burden of museums; the collector or owner who has successfully relinquished mental ownership of the object, in return for the immortality and eternal vigilance and expert conservation inherent in the museum, expects or at the very least hopes to see the object put on immediate display in a position of sufficient prominence to be interpreted as gratitude. The reality is, however, that our distant cultural history has left us with a preference for display in a way that is 'neutral' but respectful and precious, rather than preserving as found; and our recent cultural history in questioning and defining the resources to be devoted to this has confronted us with the problem of selecting which items to display and which to store. Thus, with few exceptions, museums have stores occupying as much or more space than their display areas, and these stores are filled with large numbers of remarkably similar boxes containing larger numbers of remarkably similar objects that have been collected in remarkably similar ways. And it is the burden of our collecting society that we have repeated this activity in remarkably similar buildings in most of our major towns and cities.

But, bound up as it is with the individual desire for recognition through a relationship to the material world, this repetitive act appears to be as inevitable as its results are desirable. This we can see in the Victorian cabinets built to house collections of Lepidoptera and other insects; a cabinet made by Thomas Gurney, which I was able to inspect recently, contained twenty drawers, and the drawer that I chose to look at in detail held 221 specimens of the same butterfly. Variety within a species has been a constant source of fascination to naturalists, and as endless as the number of specimens; but as with all fascinations there is an implicit loss of control to the object of fascination. The drive to control the material world is realized in the construction of a way of knowing, and it is that way of knowing that we surrender to rather than the object of knowledge surrendering to us. Where the scientist applies taxonomy, the collector applies grouping into sets; the inevitability of anything notable and out of production becoming a 'collectable', and the apparent infallibility of the 'limited edition' as a marketing ploy, show how we strive with the material world, our desires controlling it and we being controlled by our desires in equal measure.

The secret joy of acquiring by whatever means so many of one thing or type of thing has now become a public embarrassment, consigning the butterfly cabinet to a darkened room for things that are too beautiful to be disposed of. Our perception has changed, but it is unlikely that 4000 dead butterflies will be returned to 'nature' in the way that the museum holding an unnecessary quantity of human remains excavated in the surrounding countryside may intend to return these respectfully to the ground. Rather such an item of display becomes a specimen in itself, an example of a cycle of collecting and display that fed each other to a point where quantity became quality. We may no longer feel it is acceptable to kill and mount vast quantities of animals, and it is this that holds us back from showing these in museums, though some curators have unofficially said to me that things like this make for wonderful educational aids. Our survival instincts will probably keep the human race going long after we have killed off most species of butterfly; consequently we will have an apparently endless supply of human remains while the supply of butterflies will be more restricted. Thus the butterflies' remains become more precious as objects than are human remains. They are precious because we are killing them off, but we have to kill them because that is how we have taught ourselves to display them. The subtext shows us to be caught in a trap of our own making, though like the ensnared animal we do not see the complexity until we are held fast.[4] One wonders how this complexity appears to the butterfly, which presumably is not keen about dying either at the hands of the entomologist in plus-fours or on the windscreen of the small car that takes me round the country to look at interesting museums.

Integral to this kind of specimen is the visual language of the case, the display and the label. The label defines the object, tells us its name and history, though our own recognition and reaction may be based on function rather than form. Just as the incongruous gold plaster frame round the Impressionist landscape tells me how valuable it is, the authority of the mahogany case with well-fitting drawers and beautifully handwritten labels allows the authority of 'old knowledge' to direct my view and tell me that I am looking at a real butterfly, though I know that the butterfly in my garden will not keep still long enough for me to look at it. The label 'Thatching Tool, iron, nineteenth century' does not inform me as much as seeing someone using the thing, and the familiar 'part of a horse's bridle' label does not tell me where this goes on the horse or how the horse is likely to react to having the thing pulled one way or another. This marks a difference between the aesthetic object and the utilitarian object. In a major art gallery I am likely to look at the label before the picture: I am likely to invest more energy in enjoying the piece if I first know that it is a Rembrandt. The recognized name has a greater pull than the unrecognized image.

But the label does more than give us information about the object nearest to it and the object in what is generally thought of as its own time. It tells us about the relationship between our time, the 'now' of looking, and the 'then' of the passing of the information. A nineteenth-century label may feel to us like a specimen of the act of knowing, in a time that can be easily located, while a label from the fifties or sixties looks merely out of date. There is a respect for old knowledge, even though the information may have been reassessed. Old maps are still interesting and somehow complete in themselves, though the coastlines may be non-existent, inaccurate, or even known to be inaccurate at the time. Yet the new label tells us that the latest researches have confirmed the information that is being passed, that the museum is doing its job in

the same 'now' in which we are looking at the object. The old label in
time becomes an adjunct to the object itself, like the catalogue number
drawn on with indian ink, an object worthy of conservation. In many if
not most cases the label of this kind is the only indicator to the public
viewer of the history of the object after its immediate acquisition,
indicating this by its colour, the type of paper or card, and the style of
the text and type or orthography.

But if we take the label away we are left to relate the object to the
wider space of the display case, and then to the building marked by the
title 'museum'. At this point we are put in the position of seeing the object
not in the time or situation of its primary use or life. Rather it becomes
an indication of the 'now' of collection, display and viewing. The
unwritten label that links all items on display reads 'object collected
and deemed suitable for display in a museum'.

Where does this place the visitor to the museum, the observer of the
object from the past looking to preserve its own future? My guess is
that the family that a hundred years ago would have gone to the
museum for delight and instruction now takes in a car-boot fair on the
way to the DIY store and the supermarket. The objects behind glass,
formerly the prize of expert or explorer, can now be bought for 50p,
and the toy I once bought for 10/- would not look out of place in a
museum. The object itself does not change materially, but our
presentation and perception of the object do. The clear and careful
display and the calmness of the well-shown object belie the urgency of
the act of collecting and the clutter of the museum store and the jumble
of changing perceptions of what should be in a catalogue, making the
exhibit simultaneously more desirable and less attainable than the
article in the antique shop. Computer imaging, in threatening the status
of the 'real' object, throws into focus the fact of ownership of that
object, now moving in the direction of redundancy. If we could show
the emotional link between the collector and the museum as an object, I
suspect its label would read 'Envy, Western object based on collecting
and control'.

Notes

1   John Golding (1959) shows that Derain, Matisse and Vlaminck already
    had knowledge of African sculpture before Picasso's exposure to it.
2   Viewing figures for *Antiques Roadshow* indicated an audience of over
    11 million, more than for the most popular BBC2 and Channel 4
    programmes combined, or the number of people doing the National
    Lottery at that time (April 1995). Of course, the 'it could be you' appeal
    applies both to the Lottery and to the 'treasure in the attic' aspect of
    Antiques Roadshow. The connection between lotteries and museums goes

back at least as far as the 1750s, when a lottery funded the purchase of Montagu House for the British Museum.

3   During the process in 1995 of 'saving for the nation' Canova's statue *The Three Graces*, one tabloid newspaper published a photograph of three nude models in the same pose as the statue, with a simultaneous effect of downgrading the 'high art' status of the statue and upgrading the status of soft pornography in tabloid papers.

4   Curiously, the 'crime' of forgery may have helped to save some larger antiquities from being broken up for more convenient sale. A more evolved butterfly would presumably make a fake of itself to lure collectors as well as animal predators away from the 'real' thing.

Bibliography

Fewins, C. (1995) 'The hand of fate builds a house of cards', *The Times*, 4 February.

Golding, J. (1959) *Cubism*, London: Phaidon Press.

Pomian, K. (1990) *Collectors and Curiosities*, Oxford: Oxford University Press.

Index